SYSTEMATIC PROGRAM DESIGN

From Clarity to Efficiency

Yanhong Annie Liu
Stony Brook University, State University of New York

CAMBRIDGE
UNIVERSITY PRESS

CAMBRIDGE UNIVERSITY PRESS
Cambridge, New York, Melbourne, Madrid, Cape Town,
Singapore, São Paulo, Delhi, Mexico City

Cambridge University Press
32 Avenue of the Americas, New York, NY 10013-2473, USA

www.cambridge.org
Information on this title: www.cambridge.org/9781107610798

First published 2013

Printed in the United States of America

A catalog record for this publication is available from the British Library.

Library of Congress Cataloging in Publication Data
Liu, Yanhong Annie, 1965–
Systematic program design : from clarity to efficiency / Yanhong Annie Liu, Stony Brook
University, State University of New York.
pages cm
Includes bibliographical references and index.
ISBN 978-1-107-03660-4 (hardback) – ISBN 978-1-107-61079-8 (paperback)
1. Computer programming. 2. System design. I. Title.
QA76.6.L578 2013
005.1–dc23   2012047527

ISBN 978-1-107-03660-4 Hardback
ISBN 978-1-107-61079-8 Paperback

Systematic Program Design
From Clarity to Efficiency

A systematic program design method can help developers ensure the correctness and performance of programs while minimizing the development cost. This book describes a method that starts with a clear specification of a computation and derives an efficient implementation by step-wise program analysis and transformations. The method applies to problems specified in imperative, database, functional, logic, and object-oriented programming languages with different data, control, and module abstractions.

Designed for courses or self-study, this book includes numerous exercises and examples that require minimal computer science background, making it accessible to novices. Experienced practitioners and researchers will appreciate the detailed examples in a wide range of application areas including hardware design, image processing, access control, query optimization, and program analysis. The last section of the book points out directions for future studies.

Yanhong Annie Liu is a Professor of Computer Science at Stony Brook University. She received her BS from Peking University, MEng from Tsinghua University, and PhD from Cornell University. Her primary research has focused on general and systematic methods for program development, algorithm design, and problem solving. She has published in many top journals and conferences, served more than fifty conference chair or committee roles, and been awarded more than twenty research grants in her areas of expertise. She has taught more than twenty different courses in a wide range of Computer Science areas and presented close to a hundred research talks and invited talks at international conferences, universities, and research institutes. She received a State University of New York Chancellor's Award for Excellence in Scholarship and Creative Activities in 2010.

To all my loving teachers,
especially my parents,
my Scott, Sylvi, and Serene,
and many of my colleagues and students.

Contents

Preface

Design may refer to both the process of creating a plan, a scheme, or generally an organization of elements, for accomplishing a goal, and the result of that process. Wikipedia states that design is usually considered in the context of applied arts, engineering, architecture, and other creative endeavors, and normally requires considering aesthetic, functional, and many other aspects of an object or a process [319]. In the context of this book in the computing world, design refers to the creation of computer programs, including algorithmic steps and data representations, that satisfy given requirements.

Design can be exciting because it is linked to problem solving, creation, accomplishments, and so on. It may also be frustrating because it is also linked to details, restrictions, retries, and the like. In the computing world, the creation of a computer program to accomplish a computation task clearly requires problem solving; the sense of excitement in it is easy to perceive by anyone who ever did it. At the same time, one needs to mind computation details and obey given restrictions in often repeated trials; the sense of frustration in the process is also hard to miss.

Systematic design refers to step-by-step processes to go from problem descriptions to desired results, in contrast to ad hoc techniques. For program design, it refers to step-wise procedures to go from specifications prescribing *what* to compute to implementations realizing *how* to compute. The systematic nature is important for reproducing, automating, and enhancing the creation or development processes. Clarity of the specifications is important for understanding, deploying, and evolving the programs. Efficiency of the implementations is important for their acceptance, usage, and survival.

Overall, a systematic program design method that takes clear specifications into efficient implementations helps ensure the correctness and performance of the programs developed and at the same time minimize the development cost. In terms of human adventure and discovery, it allows us to be free of tedious and error-prone aspects of design, avoid repeatedly reinventing the wheel, and devote ourselves to truly creative endeavors. It is with these motivations in mind that this book was written, to give a unified account of a systematic method that was developed based on significant prior work by many researchers.

The systematic program design method described in this book applies to large classes of problems of many different kinds; it does not yet do the magic of generating efficient implementations from clear specifications for *all* computation problems, if such a magic method will ever exist. For example, the method can derive dynamic programming algorithms from recursive functions, produce appropriate indexing for efficient evaluation of relational database queries, and generate efficient algorithms and implementations from Datalog rules; however, it cannot yet derive a linear-time algorithm for computing strongly connected components of graphs. It is, of course, not the only method for program design.

The method described in this book consists of step-wise analysis and transformations based on the languages and cost models for specifying the problems. The key steps are to (1) make computation proceed iteratively on small input increments to arrive at the desired output, (2) compute values incrementally in each iteration, and (3) represent the values for efficient access on the underlying machine. These steps are called Step Iterate, Step Incrementalize, and Step Implement, respectively. The central step, Step Incrementalize, is the core of the method. You might find it interesting that making computations iterative and incremental is the analogue of integration and differentiation in calculus. Steps Iterate and Incrementalize are essentially algorithm design, and Step Implement is essentially data representation design.

Overview

This book has seven chapters, including an introduction and a conclusion. The five middle chapters cover the design method for problems specified using loop commands, set expressions, recursive functions, logic rules, and objects, respectively. Loops are essential in giving commands to computers, sets provide data abstraction, recursion provides control abstraction, rules provide both data and control abstractions, and objects provide module abstraction.

Chapter 1 motivates the need for a general and systematic design method in computer programming, algorithm design, and problem solving in general; introduces an incrementalization-based method that consists of three steps: Iterate, Incrementalize, and Implement; explains languages, cost models, as well as terminology and notations used throughout the book; and provides historical and bibliographical notes about the method.

Chapter 2 explains the core step of the method, Step Incrementalize, as it is applied to optimizing expensive primitive and array computations in loops. The basic ideas are about maintaining invariants incrementally with respect to loop increment. Because loops are already iterative, and primitives and arrays are easily implemented on machines, there is little to do for Step Iterate and Step Implement. The method is further illustrated on two examples, in hardware design and image processing. Finally, the need for higher-level data and control abstractions is discussed.

Chapter 3 presents Step Incrementalize followed by Step Implement, as they are used to obtain efficient implementations of set expressions. If a set expression involves a fixed-point operation, Step Iterate easily transforms the operation into a loop. We focus on composing incremental maintenance code in Step Incrementalize and designing linked data structures for sets in Step Implement. The method is applied to two additional examples, in access control and query optimization. The chapter ends by discussing the need for control abstraction in the form of recursive functions, which are optimized in Chapter 4.

Chapter 4 studies Step Incrementalize preceded by Step Iterate, as they are applied in optimization of recursive functions. We concentrate on determining minimum increments and transforming recursion to iteration in Step Iterate, and deriving incremental functions and achieving dynamic programming in Step Incrementalize. Step Implement easily selects the use of recursive versus indexed data structures when necessary. Additional examples are described, in combinatorial optimization and in math and puzzles. We end by discussing the need for data abstraction in the form of sets, which are handled in Chapter 3.

Chapter 5 describes Step Incrementalize preceded by Step Iterate and followed by Step Implement, as they are used together to generate efficient implementations from logic rules. Step Iterate transforms fixed-point semantics of rules into loops. Step Incrementalize maintains auxiliary maps extensively for incremental computation over sets and relations. Step Implement designs a combination of linked and indexed data structures for implementing sets and relations. The method gives time and space complexity guarantees for the generated implementation. We present two example applications, in program analysis and trust management. Finally, we discuss the need for module abstraction in building large applications.

Chapter 6 studies incrementalization across module abstraction, as the method is applied to programs that use objects and classes. Object abstraction allows specification and implementation of scaled-up applications. We discuss how it also makes obvious the conflict between clarity and efficiency. We describe a language for specifying incrementalization declaratively, as incrementalization rules, and a framework for applying these rules automatically. We also describe two example applications, in electronic health records and in game programming. At the end, we show how to use incrementalization rules for invariant-driven transformations in general, and we present a powerful language for querying complex object graphs that is easier to use than set expressions, recursive functions, and logic rules for a large class of common queries.

Chapter 7 takes a deeper look at incrementalization, illustrates the ideas on three sorting examples, describes how program design requires both building up and breaking through abstractions, discusses issues with implementations and experiments for the method, and points out limitations of the method and directions for future studies.

How to use this book

This book can be used for both self-study and course study. It is a dense book, but it is intended for both readers with a minimal computer science background and experienced computer science researchers and practitioners. For course study, the book is intended to suit upper-level undergraduate students and beginning graduate students, but selected parts with simpler examples can be taught to lower-level undergraduate students, and full coverage with all examples can be taught to advanced graduate students.

Each of the five middle chapters is relatively independent of the others, except for some of the language constructs introduced in earlier chapters. Nevertheless, studying the materials in order will help one better understand the design method through preview and review of each chapter.

Each of the middle chapters is organized as follows. First, it introduces the problem and a running example and describes the language constructs handled in that chapter. Then, it presents the ideas and steps of the method as applied to the language constructs handled and illustrates them on the running example and other smaller examples. Next, it gives two or more examples to show either additional aspects or certain interesting consequences of the method. Finally, it puts the chapter in the context of the book to motivate the subsequent chapter. Each chapter ends with bibliographic notes.

Exercises are given at the end of each section, to help readers learn the method discussed. Each exercise is given one of two levels of difficulty: purely for practicing or partly for discovery. Exercises of level one are simple examples for programming or for following the method presented in that section. Exercises of level two can lead to discovery of aspects of programming or of the method not discussed in that section. Exercises of level two are indicated with an asterisk (*).

An index at the end of the book lists the terminology and names used in the book. A boldface number following a term denotes the page where the term is defined, and other numbers indicate the pages where the term is used.

Acknowledgments

It is impossible to thank everyone, in an appropriate order, who helped me work on things that contributed to this book, but I will try.

First of all, I would like to thank Anil Nerode. His enlightening comments and encouragement, ever since my years at Cornell University, with his deep insight from mathematics and logic, open mind on hard practical problems, as well as rich experience working with people, are invaluable for the work that led to this book and beyond. All of these, poured on me during the long hours at each of my visits to him, and unfailingly shown through his instant response to each of my email inquiries and visit requests, makes him to me like a master to a disciple seeking some ultimate truth, not to mention that it was while taking his logic class that I met a classmate to be my love in life.

It was with extreme luck that I went to Cornell University for my PhD, took stimulating classes not only from Anil, but also Dexter Kozen, Bard Bloom, Keshav Pingali, Keith Marzullo, and others, and did my dissertation work with Tim Teitelbaum. Tim challenged me to find general principles underlying incremental computation. He provided me with generous advice and knowledge, especially on how to value the importance of research in terms of both principles and practices. Bob Constable showed great enthusiasm for my work and gave excellent suggestions. David Gries gracefully helped polish my dissertation and offered marvelous humor as an outstanding educator.

Since my dissertation work, I have received many helpful comments and great encouragement at the meetings of IFIP WG 2.1—International Federation for Information Processing, Working Group on Algorithmic Languages and Calculi. Bob Paige and Doug Smith, whose papers I had read with great interest before then, were instrumental in discussing their work in detail with me. How I wish that Bob lived to continue his marvelous work. Michel Sintzoff, Cordell Green, Lambert Meertens, Robert Dewar, Richard Bird, Alberto Pettorossi, Peter Pepper, Dave Wile, Martin Feather, Charles Simonyi, Jeremy Gibbons, Rick Hehner, Oege de Moor, Ernie Cohen, Roland Backhouse, and many others showed me a diverse range of other exciting work. Michel's work on designing optimal control systems and games provides, I believe, a direction for studying extensions to our method to handle concurrent systems.

Many colleagues at Stony Brook University and before that at Indiana University were a precious source of support and encouragement. At Stony Brook, Michael Kifer taught me tremendously, not only about deductive and object-oriented database and semantic web, but also other things to strive for excellence in research; David Warren enthusiastically gave stimulating answers to my many questions on tabled logic programming; Leo Bachmair, Tzi-cker Chiueh, Rance Cleaveland, Radu Grosu, Ari Kaufman, Ker-I Ko, C.R. Ramakrishnan, I.V. Ramakrishnan, R. Sekar, Steve Skiena, Scott Smolka, Yuanyuan Yang, Erez Zadok, and others helped and collaborated in many ways. At Indiana, Jon Barwise exemplified an amazing advisor and person as my mentor; Steve Johnson enthusiastically applied incrementalization to hardware design; Randy Bramley, Mike Dunn,

Kent Dybvig, Dan Friedmen, Dennis Gannon, Daniel Leivant, Larry Moss, Paul Purdom, David Wise, and others helped in many ways.

I also benefited greatly from interactions with many other colleagues, including many who visited me or hosted my visits and acquainted me with fascinating works and results: Bob Balzer, Allen Brown, Gord Cormack, Patrick Cousot, Olivier Danvy, John Field, Deepak Goyal, Rick Hehner, Nevin Heintze, Connie Heitmeyer, Fritz Henglein, Daniel Jackson, Neil Jones, Ming Li, Huimin Lin, Zuoquan Lin, David McAllester, Torben Mogensen, Chet Murthy, Bill Pugh, Zongyan Qiu, G. Ramalingam, John Reppy, Tom Reps, Jack Schwartz, Mary Lou Soffa, Sreedhar Vugranam, Thomas Weigert, Reinhard Wilhelm, Andy Yao, Bo Zhang, and others. Neil's work on partial evaluation initially motivated me to do derivation of incremental programs via program transformation. Many other friends in Stony Brook and old friends in Beijing, Ithaca, and Bloomington have helped make life more colorful.

I especially thank colleagues who have given me helpful comments on drafts of the book: Deepak Goyal, David Gries, Rick Hehner, Neil Jones, Ming Li, Alberto Pettorossi, Zongyan Qiu, Jack Schwartz, Michel Sintzoff, Steve Skiena, Scott Stoller, Reinhard Wilhelm, and others who I might have forgotten. Jack Schwartz's comments and encouragement left me with overwhelming shock and sadness upon learning that he passed away soon after we last spoke on the phone. Anil Nerode wrote an enlightening note from which I took the quote for the most important future research direction at the end of the book.

Many graduate and undergraduate students who took my classes helped improve the presentation and the materials: Ning Li, Gustavo Gomez, Leena Unikrishnann, Todd Veldhuizen, Yu Ma, Joshua Goldberg, Tom Rothamel, Gayathri Priyalakshmi, Katia Hristova, Michael Gorbovitski, Chen Wang, Jing Zhang, Tuncay Tekle, Andrew Gaun, Jon Brandvein, Bo Lin, and others. I especially thank Tom for picking the name III for the method out of a combination of choices I had, accepting nothing without being thoroughly convinced, and making excellent contributions to incrementalization of queries in object-oriented programs. Students in my Spring 2008 Advanced Programming Languages class marked up the first draft of this book: Simona Boboila, Ahmad Esmaili, Andrew Gaun, Navid Azimi, Sangwoo Im, George Iordache, Yury Puzis, Anu Singh, Tuncay Tekle, and Kristov Widak.

Scott Stoller deserves special thanks, as a colleague, before that a classmate and then an officemate, and as my husband. He has usually been the first person to hear what I have been working on. He has given me immense help in making my ideas more precise and my writing more succinct, and he has answered countless questions I had while writing this book. He has been a wonderful collaborator and a fabulous consultant. Finally, I thank my parents for designing me, preparing me for both high points and low points in my endeavors, and, perhaps, for unyieldingly persuading me to go to Peking University to study computer science. I thank my two daughters for being so lovely, helping me better understand the need for clear specifications and efficient implementations, and, perhaps, for fighting with my designs from time to time. I especially thank my daughter Sylvi for reading the last draft of this book and giving me excellent suggestions. I thank my daughter Serene for her infinite creativity in keeping herself busy while waiting for me.

Much research that led to this book was supported by the Office of Naval Research under grants N00014-92-J-1973, N00014-99-1-0132, N00014-01-1-0109, N00014-04-1-0722, and N00014-09-1-0651; the National Science Foundation under grants CCR-9711253, CCR-0204280, CCR-0306399, CCR-0311512, CNS-0509230, CCF-0613913, and CCF-0964196; industry grants and gifts; and other sources. Many thanks to my editor at Cambridge University Press, Lauren Cowles, for her wonderful support and advice during the publication process of this first book of mine.

1

Introduction

1.1 From clarity to efficiency: systematic program design

At the center of computer science, there are two major concerns of study: *what* to compute, and *how* to compute efficiently. Problem solving involves going from clear specifications for "what" to efficient implementations for "how". Unfortunately, there is generally a conflict between clarity and efficiency, because clear specifications usually correspond to straightforward implementations, not at all efficient, whereas efficient implementations are usually sophisticated, not at all clear. What is needed is a general and systematic method to go from clear specifications to efficient implementations.

We give example problems from various application domains and discuss the challenges that lead to the need for a general and systematic method. The example problems are for database queries, hardware design, image processing, string processing, graph analysis, security policy frameworks, program analysis and verification, and mining semi-structured data. The challenges are to ensure correctness and efficiency of developed programs and to reduce costs of development and maintenance.

Example problems and application domains

Database queries. Database queries matter to our everyday life, because databases are used in many important day-to-day applications. Consider an example where data about professors, courses, books, and students are stored, and we want to find all professor-course pairs where the professor uses any of his own books as the textbook for the course and any of his own students as the teaching assistant for the course. It is not hard to see that similar queries can be used to detect fraud in financial databases, find matches between providers and suppliers, and identify

rare correlations in data in general. If you care to know, the example query can
be expressed in the dominant database query language, SQL, as follows, where *
denotes everything about the matched data:

```
select * from professor, course
where professor.id = course.instructor
      and exists (select * from book
                   where book.author = professor.name and
                         book.name = course.textbook)
      and exists (select * from student
                   where student.advisor = professor.name and
                         student.teaching = course.id)
```

A straightforward computation would iterate through all professors and, for each
of them, check each course for whether the professor is the course instructor;
further, for each pair of professor and course found, it would check each book
for whether the author is the professor and the book is the course textbook, and
similarly check each student. This can take time proportional to the number of
professors times the number of courses times the sum of the numbers of books
and students. An efficient computation can use sophisticated techniques and take
only time proportional to the size of the data plus the number of answers. For
example, if there are 1,000 each of professors, courses, books, and students, then a
straightforward computation can take time on the order of $1,000 \times 1,000 \times (1,000 +$
$1,000)$, which is 2,000,000,000, whereas an efficient computation takes time on
the order of 4,000 plus the number of answers. How to design such an efficient
computation?

Hardware design. Hardware design requires efficiently implementing complex
operations in computer hardware using operations that already have efficient support in hardware. A good example is the square-root operation. A brute-force way
to compute the square root of a given number is to iterate through a range of possible numbers and find the one whose square equals the given number, where the
square operation uses multiplication, which has standard support in hardware. An
efficient implementation will not use squares or multiplications, but rather a sophisticated combination of additions and *shifts*, that is, doublings and halvings,
because the latter have much more efficient support in hardware. How to design
such efficient implementations?

Image processing. Image processing has a central problem, which is to process
the local neighborhood of every pixel in an image. A simple example is image
blurring. It computes the average of the m-by-m neighborhood of every pixel in
an n-by-n image. A straightforward way to compute the blurred image is to iterate
over each of the n^2 pixels, sum the values of the m^2 pixels in the neighborhood of
the pixel, and divide the sum by m^2. This takes time proportional to $n^2 \times m^2$. A
well-known efficient algorithm computes the blurred image in time proportional
to n^2, by smartly doing only four additions or subtractions in place of summing

over m^2 pixels in the neighborhood of each pixel, regardless of the size m^2 of the neighborhood. How to derive such an efficient algorithm?

String processing. String processing is needed in many applications, from text comparison to biological sequence analysis. A well-known problem is to compute a longest common subsequence of two strings, where a subsequence of a string is just the given string possibly with some elements left out. A straightforward way to compute the solution can be written as a simple recursive function, but takes time proportional to an exponential of the lengths of the two strings in the worst case. An efficient algorithm for this problem tabulates solutions to subproblems appropriately and takes time proportional to the product of the lengths of the two strings in the worst case. How to design such efficient algorithms given recursive functions for straightforward computations?

Graph analysis. Graph analysis underlies analyses of complex interrelated objects. A ubiquitous problem is graph reachability: given a set of edges, each going from one vertex to another, and a set of vertices as sources, compute all vertices reachable from the sources following the edges. Straightforwardly and declaratively, one can state two rules: if a vertex is a source, then it is reachable; if a vertex is reachable, and there is an edge from it to another vertex, then this other vertex is reachable also. An efficient algorithm requires programming a strategy for traversing the graph and a mechanism for recording the visits, so that each edge is visited only once, even if many edges can lead to a same edge and edges can form cycles. How to arrive at such an efficient program from the rules?

Querying complex relationships. Querying about complex relationships, formulated as database queries or graph queries, is essential not only for database and Web applications but also for security policy analysis and enforcement, program analysis and verification, data mining of semi-structured data, and many other applications. In security policy frameworks, complex relationships need to be captured for access control, trust management, and information flow analysis. In program analysis and verification, flow and dependency relations among program segments and values, and transitions among system states, are formulated using many kinds of trees and graphs. For mining semi-structured data, which form trees, segments of trees need to be related along the paths connecting them.

Challenges

The challenges are that, for real-world applications, computer programs need to run correctly and efficiently, be developed quickly, and be easy to maintain, all at low costs. Correctness requires that the developed programs satisfy the problem specifications. Efficiency requires guarantees on fast running times and acceptable space usages for the developed programs. Costs of development and maintenance need to be minimized while achieving desired correctness and efficiency.

Unfortunately, there are trade-offs and thus conflicts among correctness, efficiency, and costs of development and maintenance. The central conflict, as indicated through the example problems just described, is between the clarity and efficiency of computer programs. A straightforward specification of a computation is clear, and thus is not only easier to be sure of correctness but also easier to develop and maintain, but it tends to be extremely inefficient to execute. In contrast, an efficient implementation tends to be sophisticated and not at all clear, and thus is much more difficult to verify for correctness and to develop and maintain.

Of course, there are other challenges besides the trade-offs. In particular, clear specifications, capturing complete requirements of the problems, must be developed, either informally or formally, and efficient implementations, with full details needed for program execution, must be produced at the end, either programmed manually based on informal specifications or generated automatically from formal specifications. We argue here that the ideal way to address all the challenges is through development of clear high-level specifications and automatic generation of efficient low-level implementations from the specifications.

Developing clear specifications. Formal specifications are much harder to develop than informal specifications, but are substantially easier to develop, maintain, and verify than efficient implementations. It would be a significant gain if efficient implementations can be generated automatically by correctness-preserving transformations from formal specifications. How to develop precise and formal specifications? Ideally, we would like to easily and clearly capture informal specifications stated in a natural language in some suitable formal specification language. Practically, we will allow straightforward ways of computations to be specified easily and clearly in high-level programming languages.

Generating efficient implementations. Efficient implementations are much harder to develop than specifications of straightforward computations, but efficient implementations for individual problems are drastically easier to develop than general methods for systematically deriving efficient implementations from specifications. One could perceive many commonalities in solving very different individual problems. What could be a general and systematic method? Such a method should use correctness-preserving transformations starting from specifications. Despite that it must be general, that is, apply to large classes of problems, and be systematic, that is, allow automated support, it must be able to introduce low-level processing strategies and storage mechanisms that are specialized for individual problems.

Overall, we can see that a systematic design method for transforming clear specifications into efficient implementations is central for addressing all the challenges. Clear specifications of straightforward computations, together with correctness-preserving transformations, make correctness verification substantially easier compared with ad hoc implementations written by hand. Exact understanding of the resulting algorithms and implementations derived using a systematic method is key to providing time and space guarantees. Clear specifications of straightforward computations, plus automatic generation of efficient implementations based on a systematic method, minimize development and maintenance costs.

The question is, then: does such a method exist? If yes, how general and systematic is it? In particular, can it solve all the example problems we have discussed, and what other problems can it solve? If it is not yet general and systematic in the absolute sense, that is, solving all problems, how will it grow? It is not hard to see that, for such a method to exist and to grow, to solve increasingly more problems from different application domains, it must be rooted in rigorous scientific principles.

Exercise 1.1 (Problem description) Describe a computation problem that is interesting to you in any way. Can you describe what it is that should be computed without stating how to compute it? That is, describe what is given as input and what is asked as output, including any restrictions on the input and how the output is related to the input, but not how to go from the input to the output.

1.2 Iterate, incrementalize, and implement

This book describes a general and systematic design and optimization method for transforming clear specifications of straightforward computations into efficient implementations of sophisticated algorithms. The method has three steps: Iterate, Incrementalize, and Implement, called *III* for short.

1. *Step Iterate* determines a minimum input increment operation to take repeatedly, iteratively, to arrive at the desired program output.

2. *Step Incrementalize* makes expensive computations incremental in each iteration by using and maintaining appropriate values from the previous iteration.

3. *Step Implement* designs appropriate data structures for efficiently storing and accessing the values maintained for incremental computation.

We describe the essence of each step separately in what follows, especially how they matter in the wide range of different programming paradigms with different programming abstractions. We first introduce these paradigms and abstractions. We then show that the III method applies uniformly, regardless of the programming paradigms used; this starts with Step Incrementalize, the core of the method. We finally discuss why the three steps together form a general and systematic method for design and optimization.

Programming paradigms and abstractions

We consider five main paradigms of programming: imperative programming, database programming, functional programming, logic programming, and object-oriented programming.

1. *Imperative programming* describes computation as commands that update data storage; at the core are *loops and arrays*—commands for linearly repeated operations and consecutive slots for storing data.

2. *Database programming* expresses computation as queries on collections of records in a database; at the core are *set expressions*—expressions for querying sets of data.

3. *Functional programming* treats computation as evaluation of mathematical functions; at the core are *recursive functions*—functions defined recursively using themselves.

4. *Logic programming* specifies computation as inference of new facts from given rules and facts using deductive reasoning; at the core are *logic rules*—rules for logical inference.

5. *Object-oriented programming* describes computation as objects interacting with each other; at the core are *objects and classes*—instances and their categories for encapsulating combinations of data and operations.

Languages for logic programming, database programming, and functional programming are sometimes called *declarative languages*, which are languages that specify more declaratively what to compute, in contrast to how to compute it.

Regardless of the paradigm, programming requires specifying data and control, that is, what computations manipulate and how computations proceed, and organizing the specifications. This is done at different abstraction levels in different paradigms.

1. Loops and arrays explicitly specify how data is represented and how control flows during computations; they are not high-level abstractions for data or control.

2. Set expressions support computations over sets of records used as *high-level data abstraction*. This eliminates the need to explicitly specify data representations.

3. Recursive functions allow computations to follow recursive function definitions used as *high-level control abstraction*. This eliminates the need to explicitly specify control flows.

4. Logic rules let sets of records be represented as predicates, and let predicates be defined using recursive rules; they provide high-level abstractions for both data and control.

5. Objects and classes provide *high-level module abstraction*, which allows modules or components that encapsulate data and control to be composed to form larger modules.

Uses of these language features are not exclusive of each other and could in fact be supported in a single language; in current practice, however, there is not a well-accepted language that supports them all, but many good languages support subsets of them.

Incrementalize

We discuss Step Incrementalize first because it is the core of the III method. Efficient computations on nontrivial input must proceed repeatedly on input increment. Step Incrementalize makes the computation on each incremented input efficient by storing and reusing values computed on the previous input. Whether problems are specified using loops and arrays, set expressions, recursive functions, logic rules, or objects and classes, it is essential to make repeated expensive computations incremental after the values that they depend on are updated.

More precisely, expensive computations include expensive array computations, set query evaluations, recursive function calls, and logical fact deductions. Variables whose values are defined outside a computation and used in the computation are called *parameters* of the computation, and any operation that sets the value of a parameter is called an *update* to the value of the parameter. The values of parameters of expensive computations may be updated slightly in each iteration of the enclosing computation. The goal of *incrementalization* is to incrementally maintain the results of expensive computations as the values of their parameters are updated in each iteration, by storing and using the results from the previous iteration. This often incurs the need to store and use appropriate additional values and maintain them incrementally as well in each iteration; this reflects a trade-off between running time and space usage.

When objects and classes are used to provide module abstraction for large applications, expensive computations and updates to parameter values may be scattered across classes, and thus we must also incrementalize across objects and classes. This allows incrementalization to be used for scaled-up applications.

Iterate

Step Iterate is the first step of the III method, and determines how computations should proceed. Even though it must be decided before incrementalization, it is actually driven by incrementalization: the goal of incrementalization is to maximize reuse, and therefore a critical decision we make is to minimize the increment in each iteration.

When straightforward computations are specified using loops over array computations or over set expressions, the ways of iterating are already specified by the loops, and thus Step Iterate is not necessary. The ways of iterating specified by the given loops often lead to desired efficient computations. However, they do not always do so, and determining appropriate ways of iterating that are different from the specified ways can be very difficult because it requires understanding at a higher level what the given loops compute.

When straightforward computations are specified using general recursive functions or logic rules, which provide high-level control abstraction, the ways of iterating are not specified, and thus Step Iterate is essential. In general, there can be many ways of iterating given a recursive specification. Even with the goal of minimizing the increment, there can be multiple ways that are incomparable with each other. Different ways of iterating may impact both the running time of the resulting computation and the space needed for storing values over the iterations.

Implement

Step Implement is the last step of the III method. It designs appropriate data structures. It first analyzes all data accesses needed by incremental computations and then designs appropriate combinations of indexed and linked structures to make the accesses efficient.

When straightforward computations are specified to process data in arrays and recursive data types, it is easy to map these data representations directly on the underlying machine, as indexed consecutive slots and tree-shaped linked structures, respectively, and thus Step Implement is straightforward. These data representations are sufficient for efficient computations for many applications. However, they are not always sufficient, and determining appropriate data representations that are different from the specified ones can be very difficult because it requires understanding at a higher level what the data representations represent.

When straightforward computations are specified using set expressions or logic rules, which use sets and relations as high-level data abstractions, it is essential to determine how sets and relations can be stored in the underlying hardware machines for efficient access. In general, this can be a sophisticated combination of indexed and linked structures. There are also trade-offs between the times needed for different accesses.

A general and systematic method

The III method is general and systematic for at least three reasons: (1) it is based on languages, (2) it applies to a wide range of programming paradigms, and (3) it is the discrete counterpart of differentiation and integration in calculus for continuous domains.

The method is based on languages, meaning that the method consists of analysis and transformations for problems that are specified using the constructs of languages. This allows the method to apply to large classes of problems specified using the languages, not just some individual problems. It also allows the method to be systematic by formulating the analysis and transformation procedure precisely and completely. We will see that the III method can solve all the example problems discussed earlier and many more that can be specified using the languages we discuss. The higher-level the abstractions used in specifying the problems are, the better the method works. For example, for problems specified using rules in Datalog, the method can generate optimal implementations with time and space guarantees.

The method applies to the wide range of programming paradigms discussed earlier in this section, as summarized in Figure 1.1. The boxes indicate programming paradigms by their essential language features in boldface; the steps in boldface below the line indicate the essential steps for each paradigm. Arrows indicate essential abstractions added to go from one box to another; they do not exclude, for example, loops with sets in the "sets" box and recursion with arrays in the "recursion" box. The gist of this diagram is the following:

- The core step, Step Incrementalize, is essential for all programming paradigms.

- Step Iterate is essential when high-level control abstraction is used.

- Step Implement is essential when high-level data abstraction is used.

- Doing Step Incrementalize across modules is essential when high-level module abstraction is used.

We will see that the driving principles underlying the III method are captured in step-by-step analysis and transformations for problems specified in all of the paradigms. Indeed, the method can be fully automated given simple heuristics for using algebraic laws to help determine minimum increments and reason about equalities involving primitive operations; the method can also be used semiautomatically or manually.

The method is the discrete counterpart of differential and integral calculus for design and optimization in continuous domains for engineering system design, rooted rigorously in mathematics and used critically for sciences like physics. In particular, incrementalization corresponds to differentiation of functions, iteration corresponds to integration, and iterative incremental maintenance corresponds to integration by differentiation. Minimizing iteration increments and maintaining auxiliary values for incrementalization yields the kind of continuity that is needed for differentiation in calculus. The extra concept of implementation is needed because we have to map the resulting computations in the discrete domains onto computer hardware. Indeed, Step Iterate and Step Incrementalize are essentially algorithm design, whereas Step Implement is essentially data structure design.

Overall, the III method unifies many ad hoc optimizations used in the implementations of languages and supports systematic design of algorithms and data

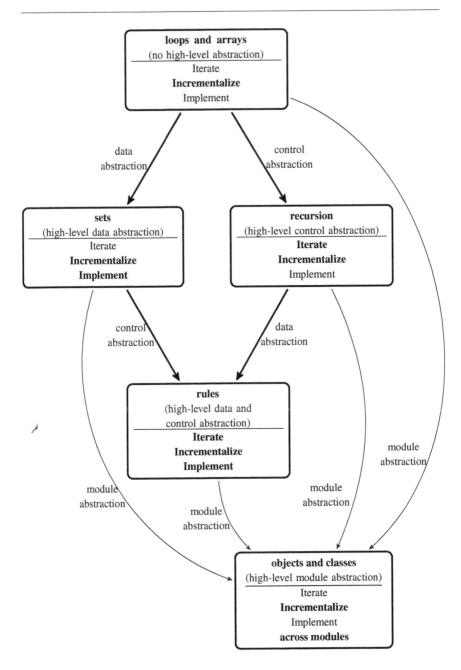

Figure 1.1 III method for different language abstractions.

structures. Compared with mathematics and other sciences, the study of such a systematic method in computer science is still very young and leaves tremendous room for continued extension and growth.

Exercise 1.2 (Solution design) For the problem you described for Exercise 1.1, describe how to compute the solution. Can you describe multiple ways to compute it? In particular, can you think of a straightforward way to compute the solution, and think of expensive computations that you have to do repeatedly in this way? In contrast, can you think of an efficient way to compute the solution, without repeated expensive computations?

1.3 Languages and cost models

We explain the need for languages that support clear specifications of straightforward computations for given problems. We also discuss the cost models we use. We then introduce terminology and notations used throughout the book.

Languages

We need to precisely define the languages used for specifications and implementations, because the method will be presented as analysis and transformations based on the languages. Problem specifications in languages that support more abstractions are generally higher-level and clearer. These specifications are also easier to analyze and potentially easier to transform into efficient designs and implementations.

It is not hard to see that different kinds of problems may best be specified using different kinds of abstractions. For any given problem, we advocate the use of languages that support clear specifications of straightforward computations for that problem. This is in contrast to using a single, high-level, completely declarative language for specifying all problems. While being completely declarative might help reason about the specifications, it is not always the most natural way to express the computations needed and sometimes also poses unnecessary challenges for generating efficient implementations. Clear specifications of straightforward computations are typically the easiest to write and read, and they are also immediately executable, albeit possibly in a completely naive way, and thus transformations to generate efficient implementations may be regarded as powerful optimizations.

Each chapter describes the language constructs, that is, the building blocks of languages, used in that chapter. To simplify the descriptions of the language constructs, we only describe their behavior for cases where no error occurs; in case an error occurs, such as division by zero, the program simply terminates with the error. We discuss at the end, in extensions for future work, that all of the language constructs could be supported in a single high-level programming language.

Cost models

To discuss efficiency, the cost model must be made explicit, which generally means giving the cost of executing each language construct. Note that the cost here is for executing the programs, not developing the programs; reducing the cost of development is a meta-goal achieved through the systematic nature of the design method.

Our primary goal is to reduce significant factors in the running times of the derived programs. In general, this may require the cost model to give the running time of each kind of operation. For efficiency improvement, we focus on significant factors that distinguish between expensive and inexpensive operations. The distinction is to separate operations whose costs differ so significantly that expensive operations are not supported at all on the underlying machine, or are considered much more costly than inexpensive ones, either asymptotically or by an order of magnitude. An *asymptotic improvement* is an improvement by more than any constant factor. An *order-of-magnitude improvement* is an improvement by a notable constant factor, typically a factor of ten. We focus on such distinctions in the cost model, because such significant cost differences must be addressed before finer-grained performance tuning matters.

Our secondary goals are to optimize for smaller constant factors in the running time and to optimize space usage and program size. Our method can consider small constant factors in a similar way as order-of-magnitude constant factors, except that more precise calculations are needed. Our method maintains appropriate auxiliary values, and thus may incur extra space usage, which reflects the well-known trade-off between time and space. The method saves space by maintaining only values useful for achieving the primary goal. Our method does not explicitly calculate code size in the cost model, but rather reduces code size when doing it does not affect the primary goal. These secondary goals are important for many applications; for example, if space usage is too large, it might also increase running time. Clearly, there can be trade-offs among all the goals. We will discuss trade-offs as they come up.

The cost model is not a fixed one for all problems. What is considered expensive depends on the underlying machine, as well as the application. For example, for a machine that implements addition and subtraction but not multiplication and division, the latter two operations may be considered expensive; on most machines, all four are implemented, but square root is not, so it may be that among these only square root is considered expensive; for interactive applications, all five operations may be considered inexpensive, but a query over a set of elements is considered expensive.

Each chapter describes the cost model for the operations used in the language and applications in that chapter. We give costs of primitive operations in the language and use them to analyze the costs of computations; in general, relative costs of two computations may be analyzed more easily and be sufficient for many applications. Our method uses the cost model to identify expensive computations in straightforward implementations, calculate the costs of incremental computations in efficient implementations, and evaluate trade-offs when there are alternative implementations. These tasks are easier for problems specified using higher-level abstractions. For example, we will see that for problems specified using rules in Datalog, we can give precise time and space guarantees for the generated implementations; this is impossible in general for programs that use arbitrary loops.

Terminology and notations

The following terminology is used in the book. It is standard knowledge for upper-level undergraduate students and can be safely skipped by readers with a similar or higher level of knowledge. Individual chapters and sections define additional terminology used in that chapter or section, or afterward. The index at the end of the book includes all the terminology used in the book.

A few basic concepts in discrete mathematics are used extensively in computer science: sets, tuples, relations, functions, and predicates.

- A *set* is a collection of distinct elements. A *tuple* is an ordered collection of components. A *relation* is a set of tuples of the same number of components.

- A *function* maps each input value to a unique output value, where the input value is called an *argument* and the output value is called a *result* or *return value*. A function is equivalent to a binary relation (i.e., a set of tuples of two components each) in which each value can occur in the first component of at most one tuple.

- A *predicate* asserts true or false for a relationship among the components of a tuple. A predicate is equivalent to a relation when it asserts true for and only for tuples in the relation.

We describe some basic terminology used for computer programming languages: program syntax and semantics, identifiers, bindings, data types, and references.

- A *computer program* consists of instructions for a computer to execute; the executions perform operations on data based on the instructions. A *program construct* corresponds to a kind of instruction. The *syntax* of programs and program constructs refers to the characters and their combinations used to form programs; the *semantics* of programs and program constructs refers to their meanings. A *program segment*, or a piece of *code*, is a contiguous segment of a program, formed from one or more program constructs.

- An *identifier*, or a *name*, is a sequence of characters that represents an entity, such as a variable or a function, in a program. A *variable* is an entity that can hold values of some kind, such as the weight of a person or the size of a computer window. A *state* is a snapshot of the values of variables and other configuration information during the execution of a program. When describing transformations, we assume that the identifiers introduced by our method are not already used in the given program; fresh identifiers can always be generated and used for them.

- A *binding* is an association between a variable and a value, where we say that the variable is *bound* to the value. The *scope* of a binding is an enclosing program segment in which the binding holds. Scopes can be nested. A variable that is introduced in an inner scope is a *local variable* in the scope. A variable that is introduced in the outermost scope is a *global variable*. A variable that is used in a program segment but not introduced in the segment is a *free variable* of the segment.

- A *data type* is a kind of data manipulated by a program, such as integers, sets of integers, and so on. A *primitive type* is a data type that is defined in a language as a basic building block, such as the integer type. A *compound type* is a type that is constructed out of primitive types or compound types, such as the type of sets of integers. Operations on data of primitive types are called *primitive operations*. Operations on data of compound types and of non-fixed sizes are called *compound operations*.

- References are a primitive type of data that refer to other data. Generally, a *reference* is a piece of data that allows retrieval of another piece of data. Concretely, it can be thought of as the address information, called a *pointer*, for data stored somewhere in the computer's memory. It is important for efficiently accessing data, because data are stored at addresses in computer memory. Note that we use the term "pointer" for convenience; we do only data access through pointers, not arbitrary operations on pointers. A special value, null, is a reference to no data. References are used to construct many data structures, such as linked lists, described later in this section.

We use a few special notations in programs. We use an increased indentation to indicate an inner scope, instead of using a pair of braces or special keywords. We use double dash (--) to denote the start of a comment that ends at the end of the line. We use aligned double bars (||) in consecutive lines to denote the left boundary of a comment that crosses all the lines involved and whose right boundary is the end of all these lines.

A *compiler* is a computer program that translates programs written in a computer language into another, often lower-level, computer language. *Compile time*, also called *static*, is a property of happenings during program compilation by a

compiler or before program execution in general. *Runtime*, also called *dynamic*, is
a property of happenings during program execution.

A few fundamental *data structures*, that is, ways to represent data of compound
types in computer memory, are used in efficient implementations. Records, linked
lists, and arrays are the most basic; stacks and queues can be implemented easily
using linked lists; hash tables are implemented using arrays, linked lists, and hash
functions.

- A *record* is an aggregate of a constant number of items of possibly different
  types. Each item is stored in a named *field* for efficiently accessing the value
  of the item by name.

- A *linked list* is a data structure for a sequence of nodes, each one represented
  as a record containing arbitrary data fields and one or two reference fields
  pointing to the next and/or previous nodes in the list.

  A *singly linked list* has one link per node, pointing to the next node in the list,
  or to null if it is the last node. It supports efficient access to the data fields
  given a pointer to any node, efficient access to the pointer to the next node,
  efficient insertion of a node after the node pointed to by the given pointer, and
  efficient deletion of the node after the node pointed to by the given pointer.

  A *doubly linked list* has two links per node, one pointing to the next node in
  the list, or to null if it is the last node, and the other pointing to the previous
  node in the list, or to null if it is the first node. It supports efficient access
  to the data fields given a pointer to any node, efficient access to the pointers
  to the previous and next nodes, efficient insertion of a node before or after
  the node pointed to by the given pointer, and efficient deletion of the node
  pointed to by the given pointer.

- A *stack* is a data structure that supports the principle of "Last In, First Out"
  (LIFO) through two efficient operations: a *push* operation adds an element at
  the top of the stack, and a *pop* operation removes the element at the top of the
  stack.

- A *queue* is a data structure that supports the principle of "First In, First Out"
  (FIFO) through two efficient operations: an *enqueue* operation adds an element at the tail end of the queue, and a *dequeue* operation removes the element at the head of the queue.

- An *array* is a data structure for a group of elements of the same type to be
  accessed efficiently by indexing. It occupies a contiguous area of computer
  memory, where each array element takes the same amount of space, so the
  addresses of the elements can be calculated efficiently based on the starting
  address of the array and the indices of the elements.

- A *hash table* is a data structure that associates values called *keys* with values. It supports efficient lookup: given a key (e.g., a person's name), lookup finds the corresponding value (e.g., that person's telephone number). It also supports efficient insertion and deletion of entries. Lookup is implemented by *hashing*, that is, transforming the key using a hash function into a number that is used as an index in an array to locate the desired value; when multiple keys are hashed to the same index, a pointer to a linked list of key-value pairs is stored at the index.

Each operation described for these data structures is efficient in the sense that it takes constant time, defined in the next paragraph. Each operation except hash table operations takes constant time in the worst case. Each hash table operation takes constant time on average, with well-chosen hash functions and hash table loads.

We use the following terminology and notations to analyze running time and space usage of algorithms and programs.

- The *complexity* of an algorithm, or program, is a quantitative measure of the resource usage (such as running time and space usage) of the algorithm, as a function of quantitative measures (such as size) of the input to the algorithm. The notion of *asymptotic complexity* describes the limiting behavior of a complexity function when its argument goes up, ignoring constant factors and smaller-magnitude summands in the function.

- The big O notation is used to denote an *asymptotic upper bound* of a complexity function. For example, the complexity function $2n^2 + 3n + 7$, where n is the problem input size, is $O(n^2)$ in the big O notation; the function $4n + 9$ is also $O(n^2)$, as well as $O(n)$.

- The asymptotic upper bounds $O(n)$, $O(n^2)$, and so on are said to be linear, quadratic, and so on, respectively, in n. For example, if the running time of an algorithm has an asymptotic upper bound $O(n)$ for input size n, we say that the algorithm takes linear time. $O(1)$ is said to be *constant*. $O(n^k)$, for some constant k greater than or equal to 0, is said to be *polynomial*. $O(c^n)$, for some constant c greater than 1, is said to be *exponential*.

- Asymptotic complexity can be used to characterize the worst-case or average-case running time or space usage of algorithms.

- Symmetric to O, Ω is used to denote an *asymptotic lower bound*.

For complexity analysis, we use $\#p$ to denote the size of the value of input parameter p, and we use $time(x)$ to denote the time complexity of executing a program segment x. We use $S \cup T$ and $S \cap T$ to denote the union and intersection, respectively, of two sets S and T.

A *decision problem* is a problem with a yes-or-no answer depending on the values of input parameters. A decision problem is in complexity class P, which stands for *polynomial time*, if it can be solved by a polynomial-time algorithm. A decision problem is in *NP*, which stands for *nondeterministic polynomial time*, if values of parameters that lead to yes-answers have proofs of the yes-answers that can be checked by a polynomial-time algorithm. A decision problem is *NP-complete* if it is in NP and any problem in NP can be translated to this problem in polynomial time. NP-complete problems are so far not known to be computable in polynomial time. A *decidable* problem is a decision problem for which there exists an algorithm that gives a yes-or-no answer for all values of input parameters. An *undecidable* problem is a decision problem for which no algorithm can give a yes-or-no answer for all values of input parameters.

Exercise 1.3 (Programming solutions) For the way or ways to compute the solution that you described for Exercise 1.2, write a program or programs. If you already know one or more programming languages, write in your favorite language. If you know one or more languages that support different programming paradigms, can you write in different paradigms? If you do not yet know a programming language, write the computation steps in the most precise manner you can.

Exercise 1.4 (Cost analysis) For the way or ways to compute the solution that you described for Exercise 1.2, analyze the computation costs. Analyze in terms of the number of different operations required and the amount of space required. Can you describe the costs using the asymptotic complexity notations?

1.4 History of this work

This book is the result of a long sequence of research endeavors and events. The book is about a general and systematic method for designing and developing computer algorithms and programs by transforming clear specifications into efficient implementations. However, I believe that, if I had felt an ambition or mission to create such a method at the beginning, I would have failed miserably.

The work started with my PhD dissertation research at Cornell University. My advisor was Tim Teitelbaum. I started working with him in the summer of 1991. Tim's main research interest had been programming environments [298, 268], to support programming activities based on the syntax and semantics of the programming language, such as by indicating undefined variables or inferring types. Analysis of program syntax and semantics can be expensive. At the same time, the program is being edited repeatedly. For an environment to be responsive, the analysis must be done incrementally with respect to changes to the program.

Almost all of Tim's previous PhD students worked on incremental something. Tom Reps studied incremental attribute evaluation in language-based environments [266], and his dissertation [269] received the 1983 ACM Doctoral Dissertation Award. Susan Horwitz studied incremental computation of relational operations [140], because information about programs can be stored in relational databases [139]. Roger Hoover worked on incremental graph evaluation [136], because program dependencies and flows form graphs. Bill Pugh worked on incremental evaluation of functions by caching [261], which also led him to the invention of skip lists [258]. John Field studied incremental lambda reduction [84], which is a basis of programming language theory.

When it was my turn, I spent a lot of time reading their work and all related work I could find. While it was clear that all these works are different—for example, attribute evaluation and lambda reduction are certainly different—I was most curious about what is fundamentally common among them all. Finally in the spring of 1992, I was able to formulate a simple problem underlying incremental computation: given a program f that takes an input and returns an output, and an operation $\oplus$ that takes an old input and a change to the input and returns a new input, obtain a program f', called an *incremental version* of f under $\oplus$, that takes the old input, the input change, and the old output and returns the new output efficiently. With this, one could see that previous works handled different programs, different input change operations, or different languages for writing programs and input change operations.

Subsequently, my dissertation focused on the development of incrementalization—a general, systematic, transformational method for deriving incremental programs, that is, deriving f' given f and $\oplus$ [216]. Influenced by much new research then, the method was developed for recursive functions and presented following the style of analyses and transformations for partial evaluation [156]. The method uses not only the return value of the previous computation [213], but also intermediate results in the previous computation [212, 210] and auxiliary values not in the previous computation [209, 211]. Additionally, given f and an appropriate $\oplus$, the derived incremental version f' may be used to form a drastically optimized version of f by starting at the base case and repeatedly calling f' after input change $\oplus$. Note that an optimized version computes the result of the original program given an input, whereas an incremental version computes the result after an input change using the result before the change.

Being able to derive drastically optimized programs using incrementalization opened up a close connection with transformational programming and a wide range of new applications. It also quickly became obvious that incrementalization can be used to optimize loops: let f be an expensive computation in the loop body, possibly the entire loop body, let $\oplus$ be the loop increment, derive an incremental version f' of f under $\oplus$, and use f' appropriately in the loop body while removing f. Whereas we developed new optimizations for primitives and arrays in loops [186, 206], Bob Paige developed finite differencing of set expressions in loops twenty years earlier [236]. Paige traced the idea back to Babbage's Difference Engine in the nineteenth century, more than 100 years earlier [243].

These findings also started the longest puzzle I have encountered: now that an incremental version f' can be used to form an optimized version of a program f if an appropriate $\oplus$ is also given, how to find the appropriate $\oplus$ if only f is given? It was not until after my postdoctoral work at Cornell, when I taught algorithm design and analysis to undergraduate and graduate students at Indiana University, that I realized the power of finding $\oplus$: we would be able to derive all dynamic programming algorithms from recursive equations like those in the MIT algorithm textbook [65]. One day, a simple answer to this hard question dawned on me in a blink: incrementalization aims to reuse, so if I have a choice for $\oplus$, a minimum increment would allow maximum reuse!

While this led to a series of advancements in optimizing recursive functions—deriving dynamic programming algorithms [194, 197], transforming recursion to iteration [195, 204], and using indexed and recursive data structures [196, 204]—it also led to another puzzle: the contrast between our method for recursive functions and Paige's method for sets. Having developed the method for recursive functions, I could see that Paige's method exploits the same ideas, but sets are so high-level that he only had to give high-level transformation rules for sets [243], not low-level derivations, and to implement sets using appropriate data structures [239, 42]. Not only do the methods look drastically different, but there are also no common examples. In fact, it is hard to even write recursive functions for the problems that Paige's method handles, such as graph problems, and it is hard to write set expressions for the problems that our method handles, such as dynamic programming problems.

Luckily, in 2000, I moved to Stony Brook University and had the opportunity to learn from several of the best logic programming experts in the world. It turns out that logic rules can be used to easily express problems that can be expressed using either recursive functions or set expressions. Many techniques have been developed for implementing logic programs efficiently, but teaching them led me and my students to a hard problem: the efficiency of the resulting programs can be extremely difficult to predict and can vary dramatically based on the order of rules and hypotheses. So I started developing an incrementalization-based method for implementing logic rules. This led to a method for generating efficient algorithms and implementations from Datalog rules, an important class of logic rules for expressing how new facts can be inferred from existing facts [199, 203]. Building on this result, my PhD student Tuncay Tekle advanced the state of the art for answering Datalog queries on demand [300, 301, 302].

Finally, while relatively small problems can be specified using loops and arrays, set expressions, recursive functions, or logic rules, large applications require the use of language features for building larger programs from components. I started to see that objects and classes provide natural, well-accepted features for building programs from components when I first taught Java in 1997, but it was not until much later that I was able to formulate a method for incrementalization across object abstraction [205]. That work also led to a framework for specifying incrementalization rules declaratively and applying them automatically, leading to a general framework and language for invariant-driven transformations [190]. Additionally, my PhD student Tom Rothamel developed a transformational method for automatically deriving and invoking incremental maintenance code for queries over objects and sets [273, 271]. We have also started developing a powerful language for querying complex object graphs [201, 299].

Bibliographical notes

The ideas of Step Incrementalize underlie much previous research [265], including in particular work by Allen, Cocke, Kennedy, and others on strength reduction [9, 62, 118, 61, 10], by Dijkstra, Gries, and Reynolds on maintaining and strengthening loop invariants [76, 119, 270, 120], by Earley on high-level iterators [78], by Fong and Ullman on inductive variables [88, 86, 87], by Paige, Koenig, and others on finite differencing [235, 236, 285, 243], by Boyle, Moore, Manna, and Waldinger on induction, generalization, and deductive synthesis [37, 220, 221], by Dershowitz on extension techniques [73], by Bird on promotion and accumulation [30, 31], by Broy, Bauer, Partsch, and others on transforming recursive functional programs in CIP [38, 21, 249], by Smith on finite differencing of functional programs in KIDS [287, 288], by many on materialized views and incremental view maintenance in database, e.g., [50, 124, 123], as well as by Liu, Rothamel, and others on incrementalization [213, 186, 210, 211, 206, 205, 273]. Some of the ideas are also shared with other techniques, especially the work pioneered by Michie on memoization and extended by many others on tupling, tabulation, change propagation, and more, e.g., [223, 29, 63, 252, 297, 314, 28, 56, 146, 5, 58]. The most basic idea can be traced back to the method used by the Difference Engine of Charles Babbage in the nineteenth century [102].

The problems addressed by Step Iterate and Step Implement are studied in some of the works just mentioned also, as well as by Liu and Stoller on optimization by incrementalization [195, 196, 197, 203]. The ideas of Step Iterate also underlie the work by many others on transforming recursion to iteration, e.g., [39, 14, 128], by Sharir on formal integration [284], by Goldberg and Paige on stream processing [101], by Cai and Paige on dominated convergence [44], by Waters on transforming series expression [312], and by Wadler, Chin, Hu, and others on deforestation, fusion, and so forth [309, 54, 145]. The ideas of Step Implement also underlie work by Schonberg, Schwartz, and Sharir on selection of data representation for SETL [277], by Paige on real-time simulation [239], by Blaine and Goldberg on data type refinement [32], by Cai, Goyal, and others on type systems for data structure selection [42, 110], by Rothamel and Liu on efficient implementation of tuple pattern based retrieval [272], and by Jung et al. on using recorded execution traces and a machine learning model for selecting best data structures [157].

There have been different languages developed for writing problem specifications. These include algebraic specification languages that are based on set theory and predicate logic, such as Z [293, 150], B [4], and Alloy [151], and generally languages for specifying input and output domains and constraints on the domains. These languages are high-level and completely declarative. Methods have been studied for deriving efficient algorithms from specifications written in these languages, for example, Smith's taxonomy-based method [291, 251]. The ideas of Steps Iterate, Incrementalize, and Implement underlie these methods, either explicitly or implicitly. Specification languages traditionally exclude programming languages, but this book does not make such exclusion, because sets and logic rules are increasingly supported in high-level programming languages. There was also work on wide-spectrum languages that support high-level and low-level constructs in the same language [19].

For background and terminology, there are many excellent textbooks as well as Internet resources on algorithms, databases, and programming languages. The programming language textbook by Scott [281] gives a detailed account of not only programming language constructs, but also their evolution, and moreover their implementation methods. The database textbook by Kifer, Bernstein, and Lewis [166] is a comprehensive explanation of the principles underlying the design and implementation of databases and database applications. The data structure textbook by Aho, Hopcroft, and Ullman [6] is an old but excellent source. Two excellent textbooks on algorithms and algorithm analysis are by Cormen, Leiserson, and Rivest [65] and by Kleinberg and Tardos [171]. There is much work on automatic complexity analysis and other kinds of cost analysis, e.g., [176, 189, 231, 304, 303].

The database query example near the beginning of this chapter was created by Gayathri Priyalakshmi [256]. Other examples can be found in standard textbooks and other literature; references will be given in later chapters when these examples are discussed in more detail.

2

Loops: incrementalize

We first look at computational problems programmed using loops over numbers and arrays. A loop is a command for repeating a sequence of operations. A number is an integer or a real number with an internal representation in a computer. An array is an arrangement of computer memory elements in one or more dimensions. Problems involving arithmetic on numbers were the first problems for which computing devices were built. Problems involving operations on arrays were at the center of many subsequent larger computer applications. Because nontrivial computations involve performing operations iteratively, loops are a most commonly used, most important construct in programming solutions to problems.

Clear and straightforward problem solutions tend to have expensive computations in loops, where the values that these computations depend on are updated slightly in each iteration. To improve efficiency, the results of these computations can be stored and incrementally maintained with respect to updates to the values that they depend on. The transformation of programs to achieve this is called *incrementalization*.

We will use a small example and several variations to explain the basic ideas of incrementalization. We then describe two larger examples: one in hardware design, to show additional loop optimizations enabled by incrementalization, and the other in image processing, to show handling of nested loops and arrays in incrementalization. We discuss the need for higher-level languages at the end.

Example: repeated multiplication

Suppose while doing other things, we need to compute $a \times i$ repeatedly, where a holds some constant value, and i is initialized to 1 and is incremented by 1 as long as it is smaller than or equal to some constant value held in b. Suppose multiplication is much more expensive compared with addition. Can we make the computations of $a \times i$ more efficient?

Why might we need to do this? We might have a grid with b rows and a columns, but whose elements must be stored in a linear fashion in the computer memory in row-major order, that is, by concatenating the rows in order. We might need to do something with the last element of each row. So we must access the $(a \times i)$-th element for each i from 1 to b.

Exercise 2.1 (Index calculation) Suppose you are given a grid with b rows and a columns whose elements are stored in a row-major order. Calculate the position of the element that is at the i-th row and j-th column of the grid.

Exercise 2.2 (Expensive operation) In the operations used in the calculation in the previous exercise, which operation is the most expensive to compute?

2.1 Loops with primitives and arrays

We need to program solutions to problems precisely. For computations involving iteration over numbers and arrays, we use a language that has data types for numbers, Booleans, and arrays, has expressions for operations on data of these types, and has commands for loops, conditionals, sequencing, and assignments.

Language

Numbers include integers and floating-point numbers, two primitive types of data of the language. An *integer* is a positive or negative whole number or zero (0). A *floating-point number* is a string of digits representing a real number in a computer, similar to mathematical notations for representing exact values. Operations on numbers include arithmetic operations addition (+), subtraction (-), multiplication (*), division (/), and exponentiation (^).

Booleans are another primitive type of data. A *Boolean value* is true or false. Operations on Boolean values include conjunction (and), disjunction (or), and negation (not). When there is no confusion, we sometimes write comma (,) in place of and for ease of reading.

Arrays are one of the simplest data types for compound data values. An *array* is a one-dimensional or multidimensional structure whose elements can hold any data of the same type and can be accessed by integer indices in any range in all dimensions. For example, if a is a one-dimensional array, we can access the element at index i using a[i]; if a is a two-dimensional array, we can access the element at row index i and column index j using a[i,j].

An *expression* is a tree of nested operations on data, for evaluation of the operations to produce a value to return. Expressions of the language consist of constants (also called *literals*) of primitive types, variables that can hold data of any type, access of array elements by indices, and recursively arithmetic, Boolean, and comparison operations on subexpressions. Besides using standard notations <, >, and = for comparison, we use >=, <=, and != to denote $\geq$, $\leq$, and $\neq$, respectively. The following examples are all expressions: integer constant 1; variable i; addition i+1; comparison i!=b; conjunction i<=b and b<=j; and array element access a[i+k,j+1].

A *command* is an instruction to perform tasks to have effects of changing the values of variables, and thus changing the state. A command is also called a *statement*. A *variable assignment command*, also called an *assignment command*, is of the form below. It assigns the value of expression *exp* to variable *v*, that is, it makes *v* hold the value of *exp*; *v* can also be an array element, in which case the value of *exp* is assigned to the corresponding element of the array.

$v := exp$

For simplicity, we sometimes abbreviate an assignment command of the form *v := v op exp*, where *op* is any binary operation, as

$v\ op := exp$

A *sequencing command* is of the form below, except that if cmd_1 and cmd_2 are written on the same line, a semicolon (;) is used in between. It simply executes commands cmd_1 and cmd_2 in order.

cmd_1
cmd_2

A *conditional command* is of the form below. It executes commands cmd_1 if Boolean-valued expression *bexp* evaluates to true, and executes cmd_2 if *bexp* evaluates to false. The else branch can be omitted, in which case nothing is done if *bexp* evaluates to false.

```
if bexp:
    cmd₁
else:
    cmd₂
```

There are two kinds of *loop commands*, while loops and for loops. A while *loop* is of the form below; it executes command *cmd* as long as Boolean-valued expression *bexp* evaluates to true.

```
while bexp:
    cmd
```

A for *loop over integers* is of the form below, where *i* is an integer-valued variable, called the *loop variable*, and $iexp_1$ and $iexp_2$ are integer-valued expressions; it executes command *cmd* for each value of *i* ranging from the value of $iexp_1$ up to the value of $iexp_2$. It may use downto instead of to, in which case *i* ranges from the value of $iexp_1$ down to the value of $iexp_2$.

```
for i := iexp₁ to iexp₂:
  cmd
```

We use the following two commands for assigning to variable v a value read from the input and writing to the output the value of expression exp, respectively; we use them only when needed for clarity.

```
v := input()
output(exp)
```

Recall that we use indentation to indicate grouping of commands in the same scope, as opposed to enclosing the group of commands using a pair of braces or special keywords.

For example, the computations described in the repeated multiplication problem on page 22 can be expressed precisely as follows, where i := i+1 can also be written as i +:= 1:

```
i := 1        -- initialize i
while i<=b:    -- iterate as long as i<=b
  ...
  ...a*i...    -- compute multiplication
  ...
  i := i+1     -- increment i by 1
```

For another example, consider the image blurring problem. It computes the average of the m-by-m neighborhood of each pixel in an n-by-n image stored in an array a and stores the result in an array b. The array b is of size n-m+1, to avoid computing averages for boundary pixels that do not have an m-by-m neighborhood. This computation can be expressed precisely as follows, assuming that array indices start at 0:

```
for i := 0 to n-m:           -- iterate through each row
  for j := 0 to n-m:         -- iterate through each column

    b[i,j] := 0              -- initialize sum of neighborhood
    for k := 0 to m-1:       ||
      for l := 0 to m-1:     || sum the m-by-m neighborhood
        b[i,j] +:= a[i+k,j+l] ||
    b[i,j] /:= m*m           -- compute average
```

Cost model

For programs that involve only operations on primitive values like fixed-length numbers, an operation is considered expensive if it is not directly supported on the underlying machine. For operations supported on the underlying machine, the costs can be given based on the underlying machine implementation, and what is considered expensive can be specified based on the application. For example, in the repeated multiplication problem, we specified that * is considered expensive, whereas + is considered inexpensive.

For programs that involve operations on arrays, computations of values aggregated using loops over array elements are considered expensive. The cost of such a computation has a factor that is the number of iterations through the loops. For example, in the image blurring problem, computations of sums over image regions using loops are expensive. For programs that involve operations on compound data types such as arrays, operations on primitive values are usually considered inexpensive and, when asymptotic running time is used, have a constant cost of $O(1)$. For example, integer arithmetic operations for computing array indices are usually considered inexpensive. When constant cost factors are also considered, multiplications are more expensive than additions, and color value operations on pixels are more expensive than gray-scale operations.

Exercise 2.3 (Start index) Write a program for the image blurring problem as discussed except that array indices should start at 1 instead of 0. You may see that, even for straightforward programs, programming with boundary values of indices may be tedious and error-prone.

Exercise 2.4 (Stock averages) Write a straightforward program that computes 50-day stock averages. Assume that the price of a stock is given in an array a with index from 1 to n, where the price of the i-th day is stored in the element at index i. Put the averages of prices of every 50 consecutive days in an array b with index from 50 to n, where the element at index i holds the average of prices of the 50 days ending at the i-th day.

Exercise 2.5 (Integer division) Write a straightforward program that computes the quotient and remainder of the division of two given integers, by using only addition, subtraction, and multiplication in loops.

Exercise 2.6 (Integer square root) Write a straightforward program that computes the integer square root of a given nonnegative integer, by using only addition and multiplication in loops. Because the given integer might not be a square number, the program should compute the smallest integer that is equal or greater than the square root of the given integer.

2.2 Incrementalize: maintain invariants

When an expensive computation is repeatedly performed while the data it depends on are updated a little bit at a time, we want to transform the expensive computation into an inexpensive incremental computation. For example, in the repeated multiplication problem, each next iteration computes a*(i+1), which equals a*i+a; if we store the value of a*i, then each next iteration only needs to add a to it.

While the idea is simple and interesting, the details can be tedious and error-prone. Where in the program to update the stored result of a*i? How to initialize it? Note that if we update before the result is used, then we need to initialize it to 0 before the loop, but if we update after the result is used, then we need to initialize it to a. How to coordinate the updates? What if there are other occurrences of a*i? What additional issues must be addressed?

Maintaining invariants incrementally

The key idea is to store the result of the expensive computation in a variable and maintain an *invariant*—the value of the result variable equals the result of the expensive computation. For example, in the repeated multiplication problem, we store the result of a*i in variable c and maintain an invariant—c = a*i, that is, the value of variable c equals the result of a*i.

To maintain the invariant, whenever the value of a parameter of the computation is updated, the value of the result variable needs to be updated to reestablish the invariant. Instead of performing the expensive computation from scratch, we want to compute the new result incrementally using the old result. For example, to maintain the invariant c = a*i, whenever a or i is updated, the value of c is maintained incrementally:

- at i := 1, we have c = a*i = a*1 = a, so we do c := a.
- at i := i+1, we have a new value of i, i' = i+1, and thus also a new value of c, c' = a*i' = a*(i+1) = a*i+a = c+a, so we do c := c+a;

Note that initialization is taken care of naturally just like for other updates.

Because the invariant holds, whenever the value of the expensive computation is needed, the value of the result variable is used instead, that is, we replace all occurrences of the expensive computation with a retrieval from the result variable. Note that we can do this replacement everywhere the invariant holds. For example, based on the invariant c = a*i, we replace the occurrence of a*i with c.

This transformation improves performance if the cost of maintenance at all updates is smaller than the cost of the repeated expensive computations. For the repeated multiplication problem, the cost of an initial assignment and repeated additions is much smaller than the cost of the same number of repeated multiplications. We obtain the following optimized program:

```
i := 1
c := a        -- new line, for c = a*i = a*1 = a
while i<=b:
   ...
   ...c...     -- a*i is replaced with c
   ...
   i := i+1
   c := c+a    -- new line, for c' = a*i' = a*(i+1) = a*i+a = c+a
```

The replacement of repeated multiplications in loops with additions, as shown in this example, is known as *strength reduction*, one of the oldest and best-known compiler optimizations. It was especially critical for early compilers, when computers were much slower and where array was the main or only data structure in high-level languages such as FORTRAN. For any two-dimensional array, to access any array element, before doing any computation with the element, an expensive multiplication, like above, is needed to calculate the element address. Precisely, for an array x of b rows and a columns stored in row-major order and with indices starting from 0 in both dimensions, calculating the address of an element x[i,j] is performed by adding a*i+j to the address of x[0,0]. Then, most often, this is inside a loop that increments i by 1 in each iteration.

While the basic idea is to maintain invariants incrementally, several important issues need explicit consideration. In the following, we first describe exploiting algebraic properties while taking the cost model into account, maintaining additional values for incremental computation, and applying incrementalization repeatedly. We then show that incrementalization corresponds to differentiation in calculus and describe an additional example, tabulating polynomials. Finally, we discuss additional issues including doing maintenance before or after the update, doing maintenance in an on-demand fashion, and handling nested loops and arrays in general.

Exploiting algebraic properties

Incremental computation exploits algebraic properties of the language constructs. For our language used here, this includes properties of primitives and arrays. For example, in the repeated multiplication problem, with operations multiplication * and addition +, we used distributivity, a*(i+1) = a*i+a*1, and idempotence, a*1 = a.

Algebraic properties may be used in different combinations to produce different ways of incremental computation; one can consider all combinations and choose a best program based on the cost model. While generally there may be many possible combinations, typically only a small number of them—those that yield only inexpensive operations—need to be considered to produce an optimized program.

For example, consider computing x*x as an expensive computation, and incrementing x by 1 as an update. Suppose variable r stores the result of x*x. Because (x+1)*(x+1) = x*x+x+x+1 = x*x+2*x+1, at x := x+1 we could maintain r by doing r := r+x+x+1 or r := r+2*x+1 instead of computing r from scratch. If addition is inexpensive, but doubling is implemented as a multiplication, then only the former reduces cost. If doubling is also inexpensive, because it can be implemented as a shift in hardware, then either way reduces cost; if a more precise cost model is used, then one may determine that the latter is better and compare it more precisely with computing from scratch.

Maintaining additional values

Efficient incremental computation may need additional values beyond just the result of the previous computation. This may include *intermediate results*, that is, values computed in the middle of the original expensive computation, and *auxiliary values*, that is, values not computed in the original computation but useful in computing the new result incrementally.

For an example of intermediate results, consider computing a*x*x as an expensive computation, and incrementing x by 1 as an update. Suppose variable r stores the result of a*x*x. At x := x+1, because a*(x+1)*(x+1) = a*x*x+2*a*x+a, we could maintain r by r := r+2*a*x+a. However, in the maintenance for r, even if both addition and doubling are inexpensive, a*x is still expensive. Note that a*x is an intermediate result of a*x*x, and it can be computed incrementally by adding the value of a exactly as in the repeated multiplication problem. Therefore, to maintain r = a*x*x efficiently, we could store also the value of a*x, say in s, and at x := x+1 do r := r+2*s+a followed by s := s+a.

For an example of auxiliary values, consider computing x*x as an expensive computation, and incrementing x by a constant c as an update. Suppose variable r stores the result of x*x. At x := x+c, because (x+c)*(x+c) = x*x+2*c*x+c*c, we could maintain r by r := r+2*c*x+c*c. Here, even if addition and doubling are inexpensive, both c*x and c*c are expensive. Their values are auxiliary values not computed in the original x*x but useful in computing (x+c)*(x+c). Note that c*x can be maintained incrementally based on c*(x+c) = c*x+c*c, and c*c can be stored and reused without update. Therefore, to maintain r = x*x efficiently, we could store also the values of c*x and c*c, say in s and t, respectively, and at x := x+c do r := r+2*s+t followed by s := s+t.

How to find useful additional values systematically? Useful intermediate results, such as a*x above, can be identified by first maintaining all of them and then eliminating those that are not useful. Useful auxiliary values, such as 2*x*c and c*c above, can be identified among expensive computations that remain in incremental maintenance. Some of the additional values, such as a*x above, can be identified using either of these two methods. When there are alternative ways of using and maintaining additional values, these ways may all be explored and the best result may be selected based on the cost model and the trade-offs considered.

Applying incrementalization repeatedly

Incrementalization may be applied repeatedly to arrive at more efficient incremental computation. This is because, after applying incrementalization, which replaces an expensive computation with incremental maintenance, there may still be expensive computations in the incremental maintenance; incrementalization can be applied again to replace these expensive computations with incremental maintenance, and this process may repeat.

Suppose that doubling is implemented as an efficient shift. In the preceding example for using intermediate results, where we maintain r = a*x*x under x := x+1, the incremental maintenance r := r+2*a*x+a after applying incrementalization once still contains one multiplication, compared with two multiplications in computing r := a*(x+1)*(x+1) from scratch; then, incrementalizing a*x again leads to no use of multiplication at all. In the preceding example for using auxiliary values, where we maintain r = x*x under x := x+c, the incremental maintenance r := r+2*c*x+c*c after applying incrementalization once even contains two multiplications, compared with only one multiplication in computing r := (x+c)*(x+c) from scratch; but then, incrementalizing c*x and c*c again leads to no use of multiplications at all.

In fact, even for computing x*x under x := x+1, which yields incremental maintenance r := r+2*x+1, we could apply incrementalization again to compute 2*x+1 incrementally: let variable r1 store the result of 2*x+1, so the incremental maintenance of r becomes r := r+r1; to maintain r1 = 2*x+1 at x := x+1, because 2*(x+1)+1 = 2*x+2+1 = 2*x+1+2, we can do r1 := r1+2. The table below shows how this computes x*x efficiently for x starting at 0 and going up by 1 each time: initially when x is 0, we have r = x*x = 0 and r1 = 2*x+1 = 1; for each next value of x, r is incremented by r1 from the previous value, and r1 is incremented by 2.

input	x	x:=0	x:=x+1	1	2	3	4	5	6	...
result	r = x*x	r:=0	r:=r+r1	1	4	9	16	25	36	...
auxiliary	r1 = 2*x+1	r1:=1	r1:=r1+2	3	5	7	9	11	13	...

Whether using an extra variable r1 and incrementing by 2 is worthwhile, compared with computing 2*x+1, depends on the cost model of the application.

Similarly, in the preceding examples for using intermediate results and auxiliary values, we could also try to maintain 2*a*x+a and 2*c*x+c*c, respectively.

Relationship with differentiation

If we know a little bit about differential calculus, we can see that incrementalization corresponds to differentiation in calculus, except that incrementalization takes place in discrete domains as opposed to continuous domains.

Specifically, a given specification of a computation, such as a*x or x*x, corresponds to a mathematical function. The *derivative* of a mathematical function describes how the result of the function changes when its input changes. So the incremental maintenance code under a minimum input change corresponds to the derivative of the corresponding mathematical function. For example, we saw that incremental maintenance for a*x under x := x+1 is to increment the result by a; note that a is exactly the derivative of function $a \times x$. For another example, we saw that incremental maintenance for x*x under x := x+1 is to increment the result by 2*x+1; note that $2 \times x$ is exactly the derivative of function x^2, and the extra 1 is because we consider change by 1 in a discrete domain as opposed to infinitesimal change in a continuous domain.

Therefore, just like differentiation is the process of finding the derivative, incrementalization is the process of finding the incremental maintenance code. Clearly, both need to exploit algebraic properties of the operators used in the computation. Fundamentally, for a function to be differentiable, it must be continuous; to make a program incrementalizable, maintaining additional values removes discontinuity. Additionally, in applying incrementalization repeatedly, what we obtain corresponds to higher-order derivatives. We will see even further correspondence between incrementalization and differentiation in Chapter 4, when we see that iterative computation with incrementalized computation in each iteration corresponds to integration by differentiation.

Example: tabulating polynomials

The examples discussed so far in this section actually show the essence of how to tabulate polynomials efficiently in differential calculus, which better shows that incrementalization corresponds to differentiation. Given a polynomial function

$$f(x) = a_n \times x^n + a_{n-1} \times x^{n-1} + \ldots + a_1 \times x + a_0$$

an initial value of x, x_0, and a constant increment, c, the problem is to efficiently compute $f(x)$ for x being x_0, $x_0 + c$, $x_0 + 2c$, and so on. This is important for computing artillery range tables, which was what ENIAC (short for Electronic Numerical Integrator And Computer) was designed and built for during World War II. ENIAC was the first large-scale electronic digital computer capable of being reprogrammed to solve a whole range of computing problems, and it could perform 5,000 additions or subtractions or 385 multiplications per second.

Straightforward computation of the polynomial function requires n additions and $(n^2 + n)/2$ multiplications for each value of x, where $(n^2 + n)/2$ is the sum of $n, n - 1, \ldots, 1$. Even using Horner's rule

$$f(x) = (\ldots (a_n \times x + a_{n-1}) \times x \ldots + a_1) \times x + a_0$$

n additions and n multiplications are required for each x. Using the basic ideas of incrementalization, we can maintain $n + 1$ values, one each for a polynomial of degree n, $n - 1$, $\ldots$, 1, and 0, respectively, and then use each in computing the polynomial of one degree higher after an increment of c by doing an addition. For $x = x_0$, this requires $(n^2 + n)/2$ additions and $(n^2 + n)/2$ multiplications for the n polynomials of different degrees together using Horner's rule, but for each next x, this requires only n additions and no multiplications using incremental computation.

Precisely, we let r store the value of $f(x)$, a polynomial of degree n, and we compute the value r of $f(x + c)$ incrementally based on $f(x + c) = f(x) + r_1$, where we let r_1 store the value of $f(x + c) - f(x)$, a polynomial of degree $n - 1$, which we call $f_1(x)$; we in turn compute the value r_1 of $f_1(x + c)$ incrementally in a similar fashion, and do so repeatedly till r_n for a polynomial of degree 0. This is shown on the left of the following table.

input	x	$x := x_0$	$x := x + c$
result	$r = f(x)$	$r := f(x_0)$	$r := r + r_1$
auxiliary	$r_1 = f_1(x) = f(x + c) - f(x)$	$r_1 := f_1(x_0)$	$r_1 := r_1 + r_2$
auxiliary	$r_2 = f_2(x) = f_1(x + c) - f_1(x)$	$\vdots$	$\vdots$
$\vdots$	$\vdots$	$r_{n-1} := f_{n-1}(x_0)$	$r_{n-1} := r_{n-1} + r_n$
auxiliary	$r_n = f_n(x) = f_{n-1}(x + c) - f_{n-1}(x)$	$r_n := f_n(x_0)$	

Then, after initializing each of $f(x), f_1(x), \ldots, f_n(x)$ for $x = x_0$, we compute $f(x)$ for each next x by adding into r the value of r_1, into r_1 the value of r_2, and so on, ending with adding into r_{n-1} the value of r_n. This is shown on the right of the table above.

For example, the table for computing x*x on page 30 is for a polynomial of degree 2, where the last row for r2 = 2 is omitted.

This method of incremental calculation was originally invented by Henry Briggs, a sixteenth-century English mathematician. It was what the first computing device, the Difference Engine, was designed for, by Charles Babbage, in the nineteenth century. Babbage then worked on the programmable Analytical Engine, although it was never completed. Ada Byron, the daughter of the English poet Lord Byron, and later known as Ada Lovelace, created a program for the Analytical Engine. She is credited with being the first computer programmer, and the programming language Ada was named in her honor.

Maintaining invariants at updates

To maintain an invariant so that it holds everywhere, incremental maintenance must be done simultaneously with an update. For languages where commands must be executed sequentially, this means that incremental maintenance needs to be done immediately before or after the update.

If incremental maintenance at an update does not use the value of the variable updated, then it can be done either before or after the update. For example, we saw that incremental maintenance for c = a*i at i := 1 and i := i+1 are c := a and c := c+a, respectively, which do not use the value of i, and thus can be done either before or after the respective updates; in our resulting program on page 27, we put them after the respective updates.

If incremental maintenance uses the value of the variable before update, it must be done before the update, and symmetrically for after. For example, for r = x*x at update x := x+1, the incremental maintenance r := r+2*x+1 uses the value of x before the update, and thus must be done before the update. Alternatively for this example, incremental maintenance could use the value of x after the update, and be done after the update, as r := r+2*x-1.

Maintaining invariants on demand

The method described above maintains invariants eagerly at all updates, so the maintained value may be used at any point outside the updates and the corresponding maintenance. However, sometimes, multiple updates happen before a maintained result is used, and it may be a worthwhile saving to do incremental maintenance *on demand*, that is, when the result is needed, as opposed to whenever an update occurs. This could be a significant saving when updates are frequent, and when different updates may even cancel each other out.

While it is obvious that generally one can do maintenance just before the result is needed, this requires a mechanism to record and accumulate changes at each update and then do batched incremental maintenance. Such bookkeeping could have a substantial overhead, and when many changes are accumulated, it could be slower than simply computing from scratch when the result is needed and not recording changes at all.

More generally, incremental maintenance can be done at any point after an update and before the result is next needed. A general method for deriving an efficient solution requires a careful trade-off analysis based on not only the cost model but also the pattern of updating the data and using the results. Usually, this issue shows up only when updates can be freely and frequently invoked externally.

Handling loops and arrays in general

Incrementalization enables powerful additional loop optimizations that are difficult or impossible to do otherwise. This will be explained using an example in hardware design in Section 2.4.

Incrementalization also allows nested loops and arrays to be handled systematically. When there are nested loops, we consider them from the inside out, because computations in inner loops are generally more continuous from one iteration to the next. That is, for each loop from innermost to outermost, we identify expensive computations in the loop and transform them into incremental computations under updates to the values of their parameters, including updates to the values of loop variables. When additional values that depend on the values of loop variables need to be stored for efficient incremental computation, we store them in arrays that are indexed by the values of the loop variables. This allows additional values used in different iterations of loops to be accessed easily using the values of the loop variables. This will be illustrated using an example in image processing in Section 2.5.

Exercise 2.7 (Incrementalizing cube) Suppose we want to compute x^3 for x starting at 0 and incrementing by 1 repeatedly. Suppose further that multiplication and exponentiation are considered expensive, and addition is considered inexpensive. How to compute each next value of x^3 efficiently? How many additions need to be performed to compute each next value of x^3? Follow the method discussed:

1. set up the problem of maintaining invariants with respect to changes;

2. use algebraic properties to transform the new computation to use the old result;

3. determine additional values to maintain and maintain them, if needed;

4. apply the incrementalization steps repeatedly, if needed.

Exercise 2.8 (Before or after updates) In the previous exercise, if you did incremental maintenance after each update, how to do it before the update? If you did incremental maintenance before each update, how to do it after the update?

2.3 Iterate and implement: little to do

For loops with arithmetics and Booleans as primitives and with arrays as data structures, there is generally too little to do, or otherwise too much to do, for Step Iterate and Step Implement. This is because loops have basically specified how to iterate, and primitives and arrays have mostly determined how to map the data and operations on the underlying machine.

Iterate

Step Iterate is to determine how to iteratively compute the desired results, but loops already encode ways to iterate. We can basically use the way of iterating specified by the given loops, and therefore there is little to do for Step Iterate. On the other hand, when the given way of iterating does not lead to an efficient program, it can be too difficult in general to determine a different way to iterate.

In general, given a problem, there can be many ways of iteratively computing the solution: we can iterate according to different dimensions of the problem and in different directions in each dimension, and we can also vary the size of the increment in a dimension and a direction. For example, we could process an image in row-major order or column-major order, iterating from left to right or vice versa in each row, and from top to bottom or vice versa in each column, and we could process one pixel, two pixels, or more in each iteration by using an increment of 1, 2, or more, respectively.

Given a particular way of iterating, it is generally very difficult to determine that a different way of iterating could lead to a more efficient program for computing the same result; in fact, it is generally very difficult even to prove that two given ways of iterating compute the same result. The degree of difficulty depends on the computations in the loop and on the different ways of iterating. The difficulty is less for computations that are iteration-independent because of algebraic properties such as commutativity. We will see, in the image blurring example in Section 2.5, that different ways of iterating lead to different efficient programs.

In easier cases where alternative ways of iterating can be determined for efficient computation, the ease is generally because a higher-level specification or certain higher-level properties about what the loops are computing can be obtained by analyzing the loops. Higher-level specifications and properties allow the best ways of iterating to be determined much more easily. Therefore, we advocate the use of higher-level problem specifications that do not specify a way of iterating when it is not necessary, as discussed at the end of this chapter.

Implement

Step Implement is to determine how data and operations in the program are implemented at a lower level on the underlying machine, but primitive and array operations already have direct mappings in hardware.

Arithmetic and Boolean operations are supported directly in machine hardware, leaving little room for choices. An example of a choice is to implement doubling as left shift instead of multiplication, and to implement halving as right shift instead of division, because numbers are represented in binary in hardware, and left and right shifts are much faster. Arrays can be mapped directly onto memory in hardware. Array elements are simply in adjacent memory locations and can be accessed efficiently in hardware once the element addresses have been calculated from the indices.

If we use these straightforward mappings, then there is little to do for Step Implement. If we do not use these mappings, then it can be very difficult in general to design other, better mappings. This is for similar reasons as we discussed for Step Iterate. We will not discuss how to find these other alternatives in general, but instead advocate the use of higher-level data representations in problem specifications when lower-level details are unnecessary.

Exercise 2.9 (Increasing change size*) While minimizing input changes helps incrementalization succeed, increasing the size of changes, when the results after smaller sizes of changes are not needed, helps the incrementalized program compute more efficiently if incrementalization succeeds. How to compute x*x for x starting at 0 and incrementing by 2 repeatedly? How does it compare with incrementing by 1 twice in terms of cost?

2.4 Example: hardware design

We consider the derivation of an efficient binary integer square root algorithm for VLSI (short for Very-Large-Scale Integration) circuit design. It illustrates additional optimizations for initialization, return variable, termination condition, and loop body. These optimizations are readily enabled by incrementalization; even though they do not improve asymptotic running time, they reduce constant time factors, space usage, and program size. Hardware design is an area where these additional optimizations are particularly important.

Non-restoring integer square root

Given a binary integer n of b bits, where $n > 0$, and b is usually 8, 16, 32, and so on, the binary integer square root m of n can be computed using the following non-restoring method, which is exact for perfect squares and off by at most 1 for other integers. The method starts with an initial guess for m to be 2^{b-1}, by setting bit $b - 1$ bit to 1 and the rest to 0, and then iteratively adjusts m by considering bit $b - 2$ to bit 0 in order:

```
n := input()
m := 2^(b-1)              -- initialize m, setting only bit b-1 to 1
for i := b-2 downto 0:    -- for each bit b-2 down to 0
    p := n - m^2          -- subtract given n by square of computed m
    if p > 0:             -- if m is too small
        m := m + 2^i      -- increase m, setting bit i to 1
    else if p < 0:        -- if m is too big
        m := m - 2^i      -- decrease m, setting bit i-1 to 0, bit i to 1
output(m)
```

In hardware, multiplications and exponentiations are much more expensive than additions, subtractions, and shifts, that is, doublings and halvings, so the goal is to replace the former by the latter in repeated computations. Additionally, we show how to reduce the number of inexpensive operations, the number of variables used, and the size of the optimized program.

This example was taken from a case study in formal hardware design. It was conducted by a group of researchers in the Electrical Engineering Department at Cornell University in 1994. They transformed the given specification into a strength-reduced version and further into a hardware implementation. The strength-reduced program was manually discovered and then proved correct using the Nuprl theorem prover at Cornell. The case study was of particular interest in light of the Pentium chip flaw discovered later that year. We will see how incrementalization can systematically derive a strength-reduced program, which helps automate and simplify the VLSI circuit design process. Compared with the strength-reduced version obtained in the case study, our derived program also avoids an unnecessary shift. Many similar programs, such as for various real and integer division and square-root algorithms, can be derived in a similar way using our method.

Iterate

Step Iterate can just use what is already given in the specification, but one additional optimization can often be performed to reduce the size of the optimized program by about half. When incremental computation uses auxiliary values, these values are established at initialization; the code for this establishment is generally similar and thus comparable in size to that for incremental maintenance in the body. Often, this code can be folded into the body, by decrementing the given initial values to zero-like values, so that initialization of the auxiliary values is significantly simplified.

For example, consider the given program, which iterates using i. The initial value of i is b-2, and the increment to i is -1. If we decrement i by increasing its initial value to b-1, we can see that the corresponding m is 0, because using m=0 and i=b-1 in a new first iteration yields m=2^(b-1) and i=b-2 as in the original initialization: in the new first iteration, p=n-m^2=n-0^2=n, and we are given n>0, thus p>0 and the new value of m=m+2^i=0+2^(b-1)=2^(b-1), and the new value of i=i-1=(b-1)-1=b-2. Clearly, m being 0 is much simpler than m being 2^(b-1). We obtain

```
n := input()
m := 0                    -- 2^(b-1) is replaced with 0
for i := b-1 downto 0:    -- b-2 is replaced with b-1
  p := n - m^2
  if p > 0:
    m := m + 2^i
  else if p < 0:
    m := m - 2^i
output(m)
```

For any given for loop, we also separate assignments to i in the initialization and the loop body, because they will be associated with different maintenance code. One could do this by peeling the first iteration of the for loop, but for this example that would undo the transformation just performed, so instead, we transform the for loop into an equivalent while loop:

```
n := input()
m := 0
i := b-1                -- initialization in for-loop
while i >= 0:           -- condition in for-loop
  p := n - m^2
  if p > 0:
    m := m + 2^i
  else if p < 0:
    m := m - 2^i
  i := i-1             -- increment in for-loop
output(m)
```

Incrementalize

The loop updates m in each iteration and returns it at the end; to update m, n-m^2 is tested, and 2^i is added to or subtracted from m. The expensive computations are m ^2 and 2^i. Using the incrementalization method described, we can incrementally compute them with respect to updates to m and i in the loop body.

We can also optimize constant time factors and space usage with a slight generalization of the incrementalization method described; such optimizations matter more significantly in hardware design than in software. The generalization is simply to save and incrementally maintain the results of all needed computations, not just the expensive ones. For example, for the program above, we maintain the values of n-m^2 and 2^i, not m^2 and 2^i. The value of n-m^2 is already in p, so we do not need to maintain an additional value for m^2 and perform a subtraction in each iteration.

Consider maintaining the invariant p=n-m^2. At m := m+2^i and m := m-2^i, we have a new value m' =m+2^i and m' =m-2^i, respectively, denoted together as m' =m±2^i. Note that if the respective operations are first subtraction and then addition, we use ∓ in place of ±. So, we have a new value

```
p' = n - m'^2
   = n - (m±2^i)^2
   = n - m^2 ∓ 2*m*2^i - (2^i)^2
   = p ∓ 2*m*2^i - 2^(2*i)
```

This has expensive computations m*2^i and 2^(2*i). We could maintain the two values -2*m*2^i-2^(2*i) and 2*m*2^i-2^(2*i) as auxiliary values, but it would again require maintaining the value of 2^(2*i). So, we maintain the values of 2*m*2^i and 2^(2*i), which are the least number of values to maintain that include both expensive and non-expensive computations.

So, overall, we maintain the following four invariants

```
p = n-m^2
u = 2^i
v = 2*m*2^i
w = 2^(2*i)
```

as follows:

- At initialization, i=b-1 and m=0, so we have p=n, u=2^(b-1), v=0, and w=2^(2*(b-1)).

- At updates m := m+2^i and m := m-2^i, we have new values p' =p ∓ v - w based on the equations about p' in the previous paragraph and

```
v' = 2*m'*2^i
   = 2*(m±2^i)*2^i
   = 2*m*2^i ± 2*2^(2*i)
   = v ± 2*w
```

- At update i := i-1, we have new values u' =u/2, v' =v/2, and w' =w/4.

Finally, removing `p := n-m^2`, because `p` already holds the value of `n-m^2`, and replacing `2^i` with `u`, we obtain

```
n := input()
m := 0
i := b-1
p := n                  -- p = n-m^2 = n-0^2 = n
u := 2^(b-1)            -- u = 2^i = 2^(b-1)
v := 0                  -- v = 2*m*2^i = 2*0*2^(b-1) = 0
w := 2^(2*(b-1))       -- w = 2^(2*i) = 2^(2*(b-1))
while i >= 0:
                        -- p := n-m^2 is removed, no longer needed here
  if p > 0:
    m := m + u          -- 2^i is replaced with u
    p := p - v - w     -- p' = p - 2*m*2^i - 2^(2*i) = p - v - w
    v := v + 2*w       -- v' = 2*m'*2^i = 2*(m+2^i)*2^i = v + 2*w
  else if p < 0:
    m := m - u          -- 2^i is replaced with u
    p := p + v - w     -- p' = p + 2*m*2^i - 2^(2*i) = p + v - w
    v := v - 2*w       -- v' = 2*m'*2^i = 2*(m-2^i)*2^i = v - 2*w
  i := i-1
  u := u/2             -- u' = 2^i' = 2^(i-1) = 2^i/2 = u/2
  v := v/2             -- v' = 2*m*2^i' = 2*m*2^(i-1) = 2*m*2^i/2 = v/2
  w := w/4             -- w' = 2^(2*i') = 2^(2*(i-1)) = 2^(2*i)/4 = w/4
output(m)
```

The loop body now contains only additions, subtractions, doublings, and halvings; division by 4 is two halvings.

Additional optimizations enabled by incrementalization

Additional optimizations can help reduce constant factors, space usage, and code size, by using the maintained auxiliary values in place of values computed by the original program. In particular, optimizations can be done regarding the values needed at the end of the loop, used in the termination condition, and computed in the loop body.

Eliminate return variable. If the value of the return variable can be retrieved efficiently from the auxiliary values maintained, and if maintaining the auxiliary values does not need the value of the return variable, then the return variable is not needed at all and can be eliminated. In the above program, from the invariant $v = 2*m*2^i$, and $i = -1$ at the end of the loop, we have $v = m$ at the end of the loop, so we can output v instead of m; m is not used to compute anything besides m itself, and thus can be eliminated. Then, u can also be eliminated because it is only used in computing m and itself.

Replace termination condition. If the termination condition using an original variable is equivalent to a condition using only auxiliary values, and if the original variable is not used in computing other values, then the auxiliary values can be used, and the original variable can be eliminated. In the program above, from the invariant w = 2^(2*i), we have that i≥0 is true if and only if w≥1 is true, so we can replace i>=0 with w>=1 as the condition of the while loop and then eliminate i.

Optimize loop body. If there are consecutive incremental updates to a variable without a use of the variable in between, then the updates can be merged. In the above program, v is updated twice if the condition p>0 or p<0 holds, once under the condition, and once afterward, but there is no use of v between the two updates, so we can merge v := v+2*w and v := v/2 into v := v/2+w under p>0, and merge v := v-2*w and v := v/2 into v := v/2-w under p<0.

Note that these optimizations are all enabled by incrementalization, including the explicit use of invariants in incrementalization. They are beyond traditional program optimizations done by compilers. Compiler optimizations can be applied to the resulting program, however. For example, n can be eliminated because it is only used in passing the input to p. We obtain the final optimized program below:

```
p := input()        -- n is replaced with p
                    -- assignments to m, i, p, and u are removed
v := 0
w := 2^(2*(b-1))
while w >= 1:        -- i >= 0 is replaced with w >= 1
  if p > 0:
    p := p - v - w   -- assignment to m is removed
    v := v/2 + w     -- v := v + 2*w and v := v/2 are merged into this
  else if p < 0:
    p := p + v - w   -- assignment to m is removed
    v := v/2 - w     -- v := v - 2*w and v := v/2 are merged into this
  else:
    v := v/2         -- v := v/2 is moved into this branch
  w := w/4           -- assignments to i and u are removed
output(v)
```

Compared with the program before these additional optimizations, the program size is reduced significantly. We also reduced space usage by eliminating four variables (n, m, i, and u) and now using only four variables (p, v, w, and b); this is even fewer than the five variables (n, m, i, b, and p) in the original program, despite the fact that incrementalization needs to maintain auxiliary values. All operations on the eliminated variables are also avoided, improving the running time by a constant factor.

Implement

Clearly, one can implement division by 2 as right shift, division by 4 as two right shifts, and 2^(2*(b-1)) as setting bit 2 × (b − 1) to 1 and the rest to 0. These and addition and subtraction operations can easily be implemented on a hardware chip.

Exercise 2.10 (Incrementalizing integer division) Incrementalize your program for computing integer division for Exercise 2.5. Compare the costs of the programs before and after your incrementalization. Afterward, you will be congratulated for having reinvented the algorithm for the first example in Gries's *The Science of Programming* book.

Exercise 2.11 (Incrementalizing integer square root) Incrementalize your program for computing integer square root for Exercise 2.6. Compare the costs of the programs before and after your incrementalization. Afterward, you will be congratulated for having reinvented the basis of the square root algorithm used in ENIAC.

2.5 Example: image processing

We consider image blurring, a representative problem in image processing. It illustrates the use of arrays, and how to incrementalize expensive array computations in loops.

Image blurring

A digital image is a grid of pixels, each with a value indicating its gray scale or its color. To blur the image, we want each pixel in the blurred image to take the average of the neighborhood pixels in the given image. For example, if the given image is white with a black disk in the middle, then the pixels near the disk boundary will become gray, with those closer to the center being darker and those farther from the center being lighter.

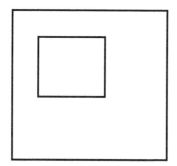

To do the blurring straightforwardly, for each pixel in the blurred image, we sum the values of pixels in its square neighborhood and divide the sum by the number of pixels in that neighborhood. For an n-by-n image, if one uses m-by-m neighborhoods, then blurring straightforwardly considers each of the n^2 pixels in the image, and for each pixel, sums the values of the m^2 pixels in the neighborhood and does a division. The total number of operations is therefore proportional to $n^2 \times m^2$.

It is well known in the image-processing field that there is a faster way of blurring images such that, for each of the n^2 pixels, one needs to do only four operations to obtain the sum, as opposed to summing over m^2 pixels, no matter how large m is. The algorithm is nontrivial, and similar algorithms need to be invented for other image processing operations. How to come up with such an algorithm?

A *straightforward program*

Suppose the n-by-n image is given in an array a, whose indices range from 0 to n-1 in both dimensions, and the resulting image is put in an array b, whose indices range from 0 to n-m in both dimensions, to avoid computing averages for boundary pixels that do not have an m-by-m neighborhood. A straightforward program can simply assign each b[i,j] the sum of the square neighborhood a[i,j],...,a[i,j+m-1], ..., a[i+m-1,j],...,a[i+m-1,j+m-1] and then divide the sum by m*m. We consider the expensive summations, omitting the division at the end:

```
for i := 0 to n-m:
  for j := 0 to n-m:

    b[i,j] := 0
    for k := 0 to m-1:
      for l := 0 to m-1:
        b[i,j] := b[i,j] + a[i+k,j+l]
```

Clearly, this takes $O(m^2)$ additions for each of the $O(n^2)$ pixels, and thus the total time complexity is $O(n^2 \times m^2)$.

Iterate

A particular way of iterating is already specified by the two outer loops given: iterate from row 0 to row n-m and, within each row, iterate from column 0 to column n-m. This also realizes the intuition that one should iteratively consider one pixel at a time and, to minimize the changes and maximize reuse, one should consider adjacent pixels in order.

Incrementalize

Summing the square neighborhood for each pixel in the two inner loops is an expensive computation. We want to compute the sum incrementally with respect to updates by the two outer loops. We do it in two steps, considering first the inner loop over j and then the outer loop over i.

1. Suppose we computed the sum of the square neighborhood for one pixel, then in the inner loop over j, after moving right by one pixel, we can compute the sum of new neighborhood by subtracting a little column on the left and adding a little column on the right, as shown in the following figure. So we could do m additions and m subtractions instead of summing over m^2 pixels.

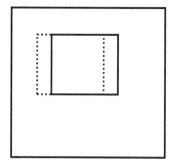

2. We can store the sums of the little columns from Step 1 as auxiliary values, and compute them incrementally. Suppose we computed the sum of a little column, then in the outer loop over i, after moving down by one pixel, we can compute the sum of the new little column by subtracting a pixel on the top and adding a pixel on the bottom, as shown in the following figure. So we can do one addition and one subtraction instead of summing over m pixels.

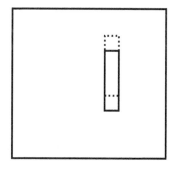

Overall, for each pixel, we do one addition and one subtraction of two pixels to compute the sum of a new little column, and one addition and one subtraction of two little columns to compute the sum of a new square. That is, we only do four operations, no matter how large m is. Of course, this improvement used associativity and commutativity of addition as well as subtraction as the inverse of addition.

The core of the resulting algorithm is as follows. First, for each row i from 0 to n-m and each column j from 0 to n-1, maintain the invariant

$$c[i,j] = \text{sum of the column } a[i,j],\ldots,a[i+m-1,j]$$

and compute c[i,j] incrementally using c[i-1,j]:

$$c[i,j] := c[i-1,j] - a[i-1,j] + a[i+m-1,j]$$

Second, for each row i and each column j from 0 to n-m, maintain the invariant

$$b[i,j] = \text{sum of the square } c[i,j],\ldots,c[i,j+m-1]$$

and compute b[i,j] incrementally using b[i,j-1]:

```
b[i,j] := b[i,j-1] - c[i,j-1] + c[i,j+m-1]
```

While this may sound neat, it is not hard to see that developing a complete, correct program can nevertheless be tedious and error-prone, especially taking care of all the initializations at the boundary. We show how to do it by applying transformations to the straightforward program.

To prepare for incrementalization, we first transform the two inner loops to sum the little columns into c[i,j],...,c[i,j+m-1] before summing them into b[i,j], yielding

```
for i := 0 to n-m:
  for j := 0 to n-m:

    b[i,j] := 0
    for l := 0 to m-1:    -- for each little column in the neighborhood
      c[i,j+l] := 0                       ||
      for k := 0 to m-1:                  || sum the little column
        c[i,j+l] := c[i,j+l] + a[i+k,j+l] ||
      b[i,j] := b[i,j] + c[i,j+l]         -- add sum to b
```

Now, we are ready to incrementalize as shown in the figures earlier, but do it precisely:

1. Consider incrementalizing the loop over j. When j starts with being 0, which is the initialization, the two inner loops are computed from scratch by setting j to be 0. When j is incremented by 1 from 1 to n-m, the two inner loops are incrementalized by computing only the last little column, where l=m-1, and maintaining b incrementally as shown in the core algorithm earlier. This yields

```
for i := 0 to n-m:

  b[i,0] := 0                          ||
  for l := 0 to m-1:                   || two inner loops
    c[i,l] := 0                        || in code above
    for k := 0 to m-1:                 || with j=0
      c[i,l] := c[i,l] + a[i+k,l]      ||
    b[i,0] := b[i,0] + c[i,l]          ||

  for j := 1 to n-m:  -- j starts with 1 instead of 0

    c[i,j+m-1] := 0                              || two inner loops
    for k := 0 to m-1:                           || in code above
      c[i,j+m-1] := c[i,j+m-1] + a[i+k,j+m-1]    || with l=m-1 and
    b[i,j] := b[i,j-1] - c[i,j-1] + c[i,j+m-1]   || b[i,j] incremental
                                                 || under j := j+1
```

2. Consider incrementalizing the loop over i. When i starts with 0, the transformed body above is computed from scratch by setting i to be 0. When i is

incremented by 1 from 1 to n-m, the transformed body above is transformed to compute the little columns c incrementally. This yields the following optimized program:

```
b[0,0] := 0                                      ||
for l := 0 to m-1:                               ||
  c[0,1] := 0                                    ||
  for k := 0 to m-1:                             ||
    c[0,1] := c[0,1] + a[k,1]                    || loop body
  b[0,0] := b[0,0] + c[0,1]                      || in code above
for j := 1 to n-m:                               || with i=0
  c[0,j+m-1] := 0                                ||
  for k := 0 to m-1:                             ||
    c[0,j+m-1] := c[0,j+m-1] + a[k,j+m-1]        ||
  b[0,j] := b[0,j-1] - c[0,j-1] + c[0,j+m-1]     ||

for i := 1 to n-m:   -- i starts with 1 instead of 0

  b[i,0] := 0                                    ||
  for l := 0 to m-1:                             || loop body
    c[i,1] := c[i-1,1] - a[i-1,1] + a[i+m-1,1]   || in code above
    b[i,0] := b[i,0] + c[i,1]                    || with c[i,1]
  for j := 1 to n-m:                             || and c[i,j+m-1]
    c[i,j+m-1] := c[i-1,j+m-1] - a[i-1,j+m-1]    || incremental
                            + a[i+m-1,j+m-1]     || under i := i+1
    b[i,j] := b[i,j-1] - c[i,j-1] + c[i,j+m-1]   ||
```

The optimized program does four addition and subtraction operations for each pixel and takes $O(n^2)$ time. It requires maintaining $O(n^2)$ sums of little columns in c, but note that only $O(n)$ of them are needed at any time, because only the n sums for the preceding row are needed to compute the n sums for the next row. To achieve this space optimization, we simply remove the first dimension of c, that is, replace each instance of c[x,y] with c[y], because program analysis can determine that the only use of a value of a previous row, c[i-1,j+m-1], in computing c[i,j+m-1], can be safely done by using c[j+m-1] in computing its new value directly.

Following a systematic method, we have arrived at a nontrivial algorithm that is complete and precise and that has a high level of correctness assurance. Not only do we not have to reinvent the wheel, we also do not have the headache of writing a lot of tedious and error-prone code for initializations, some of which also require incrementalization by themselves, and together many times longer than the code for the core algorithm.

Implement

This needs no work, because additions, subtractions, and array operations have direct implementations on the underlying machine.

A different way to iterate and to maintain additional values

If the optimized program we have obtained is not difficult enough for you, there is an even less obvious optimized program. It can be obtained by following the same optimization method, except to incrementalize with respect to the outer loop first, yielding a more drastic space reduction to only two auxiliary sums. In fact, we could be given a program as before but with the two outer loops interchanged to start with. How does our method do on it?

So consider the same program except with the two outer loops interchanged, prepared for incrementalization by storing sums of little columns as before:

```
for j := 0 to n-m:  -- iterate over j instead of i
  for i := 0 to n-m:  -- iterate over i instead of j

  b[i,j] := 0
  for l := 0 to m-1:
    c[i,j+1] := 0
    for k := 0 to m-1:
      c[i,j+1] := c[i,j+1] + a[i+k,j+1]
    b[i,j] := b[i,j] + c[i,j+1]
```

1. Incrementalizing the inner loop over i yields

```
for j := 0 to n-m:

  b[0,j] := 0                                    ||
  for l := 0 to m-1:                             || two inner loops
    c[0,j+1] := 0                                || in code above
    for k := 0 to m-1:                           || with i=0
      c[0,j+1] := c[0,j+1] + a[k,j+1]            ||
    b[0,j] := b[0,j] + c[0,j+1]                  ||

  for i := 1 to n-m:  -- i starts with 1 instead of 0

    b[i,j] := 0                                  || two inner loops
    for l := 0 to m-1:                           || in code above
      c[i,j+1] := c[i-1,j+1] - a[i-1,j+1]        || with c[i,j+1]
                            + a[i+m-1,j+1]       || incremental
      b[i,j] := b[i,j] + c[i,j+1]                || under i := i+1
```

2. Incrementalizing the outer loop over j yields

```
b[0,0] := 0                                      ||
for l := 0 to m-1:                               ||
  c[0,1] := 0                                    ||
  for k := 0 to m-1:                             ||
    c[0,1] := c[0,1] + a[k,1]                    || loop body
  b[0,0] := b[0,0] + c[0,1]                      || in code above
for i := 1 to n-m:                               || with j=0
  b[i,0] := 0                                    ||
  for l := 0 to m-1:                             ||
    c[i,1] := c[i-1,1] - a[i-1,1] + a[i+m-1,1]   ||
    b[i,0] := b[i,0] + c[i,1]                    ||
```

2.5 *Example: image processing*   47

```
for j := 1 to n-m:  -- j starts with 1 instead of 0

  c[0,j+m-1] := 0                             ||
  for k := 0 to m-1:                          || loop body
    c[0,j+m-1] := c[0,j+m-1] + a[k,j+m-1]     || in code above
  b[0,j] := b[0,j-1] - c[0,j-1] + c[0,j+m-1]  || with l=m-1 and
  for i := 1 to n-m:                          || b[i,j]
    c[i,j+m-1] := c[i-1,j+m-1] - a[i-1,j+m-1] || incremental
                             + a[i+m-1,j+m-1] || under j := j+1
    b[i,j] := b[i,j-1] - c[i,j-1] + c[i,j+m-1] ||
```

As can be expected, this program is exactly the same as the one above, except for different order of iterating, which simply interchanged the initialization of $b[i,0]$ for i from 1 to n-m and $c[0,j+m-1]$ for j from 1 to n-m. However, this interchange allows something different to be done, as follows.

We see that, in the body of the main loop over j, $c[0,j+m-1]$ is initialized by the loop over k, and each next $c[i,j+m-1]$ is incrementally computed in the body of the inner loop over i and used in computing $b[i,j]$ on the last line. We can see that the other value, $c[i,j-1]$, used in computing $b[i,j]$ can be initialized and incrementally computed similarly. That is, we can use just two auxiliary variables, say $c1$ and $c2$, in place of $c[i,j-1]$ and $c[i,j+m-1]$, respectively, and two additional operations for incrementally computing $c1$ in the body of the inner loop over i. Thus, the main loop over j does not need the array c at all. Then, in the initialization for $j = 0$, we can also eliminate array c, compute $b[0,0]$ by directly adding $a[k,1]$ to it, and compute each next $b[i,0]$ incrementally by starting with $b[i-1,0]$ and directly subtracting $a[i-1,1]$ and adding $a[i+m-1,1]$ for 1 from 0 to m-1. This yields

```
b[0,0] := 0                    ||
for l := 0 to m-1:             || as code above but
  for k := 0 to m-1:           || directly add to b[0,0]
    b[0,0] := b[0,0] + a[k,1]  ||
for i := 1 to n-m:
  b[i,0] := b[i-1,0]                          || as code above but
  for l := 0 to m-1:                          || directly update b[i,0]
    b[i,0] := b[i,0] - a[i-1,1] + a[i+m-1,1]  || starting with b[i-1,0]

for j := 1 to n-m:
                               || as code above but
  c1 := 0                      || compute c[0,j-1] in c1,
  c2 := 0                      || replace c[0,j+m-1] by c2,
  for k := 0 to m-1:           ||
    c1 := c1 + a[k,j-1]        ||
    c2 := c2 + a[k,j+m-1]      ||
  b[0,j] := b[0,j-1] - c1 + c2 || use c1 and c2 instead
  for i := 1 to n-m:
    c1 := c1 - a[i-1,j-1] + a[i+m-1,j-1]     || compute c[i,j-1] in c1,
    c2 := c2 - a[i-1,j+m-1] + a[i+m-1,j+m-1] || repl c[0,j+m-1] by c2,
    b[i,j] := b[i,j-1] - c1 + c2             || use c1 and c2 instead
```

The result is, for each new pixel in a new column, we incrementally compute the
little column to the left of the current square, and the rightmost little column of the
current square, and use them to incrementally compute the sum of the square. This
is a total of six operations for each pixel, but it only uses two additional variables
instead of an array of size $O(n^2)$ or $O(n)$.

A different way to exploit algebraic properties

There is yet another nontrivial alternative for incremental maintenance, if one exploits algebraic properties further. It does six operations for each pixel without
using any additional variables, but uses the sums of the squares one pixel to the
left, one pixel above, and one pixel to the left and above diagonally, and the values
of the four corner pixels:

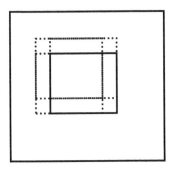

```
b[i,j] = b[i,j-1] − left lower column
              + right lower column
       = b[i,j-1] − (left upper column − left upper corner
                              + left lower corner)
              + (right upper column − right upper corner
                              + right lower corner)
       = b[i,j-1] − left upper column + right upper column
              + left upper corner − left lower corner
              − right upper corner + right lower corner
       = b[i,j-1] + b[i-1,j] − b[i-1,j-1]
              + a[i-1,j-1] − a[i+m-1,j-1]
              − a[i-1,j+m-1] + a[i+m-1,j+m-1]
```

The first two equalities are as we had used previously, exploiting commutativity,
associativity, and inverse, but the third equality exploits these properties more
exhaustively. The fourth equality uses a variation of what we used previously:

```
           − left upper column + right upper column = b[i-1,j] − b[i-1,j-1]
```

A trade-off for this more sophisticated use of available values, derived less systematically, is that it is less obvious how to initialize at the left and top boundaries
of the image.

In general, algebraic properties might not be exploited exhaustively when increasingly larger amount of effort is required. However, when such exploitation yields improvements, the results can be put in a library and reused for later applications without having to be rediscovered repeatedly.

Exercise 2.12 (Incrementalizing stock averages) Incrementalize your program for computing 50-day stock averages for Exercise 2.4. Compare the costs of the programs before and after incrementalization.

Exercise 2.13 (Three-dimensional blurring*) How to do blurring for a three-dimensional image? You may see that all the ideas we discussed apply, but it is extremely tedious to program and analyze by hand.

Exercise 2.14 (Image blurring with no additional space*) For the image blurring problem, can we do four operations per pixel, but use no additional space for the array c and keep the same algorithms otherwise?

2.6 Need for higher-level abstraction

Use of loops and arrays inevitably encodes decisions about *how* to iterate and *how* to represent data, which are generally lower-level than specifications that focus on *what* data is given and *what* result is to be computed. As a result, higher-level properties useful for deriving efficient computations could be lost or difficult to recover in lower-level specifications. Even in cases where loops with primitives and arrays give closer to high-level problem descriptions, such as for problems in image processing, whether a fixed iteration order or array representation is necessary cannot in general be determined from the uses of loops and arrays.

For example, to process every pixel in an image, a nested loop encodes either a row-major or a column-major order of traversing the pixels, and to sum the values of a set of pixels in an image, a loop encodes a fixed order of considering the pixels, but these orders may or may not be desired for a particular application. These orderings also make it harder to see what is computed, even if arrays and loops capture image processing relatively straightforwardly. In higher-level specifications, aggregate expressions may be used to indicate the property that an order does not matter.

Using aggregate expressions

We may use the following *array construction* expression for the construction of an array. It first evaluates integer-valued expressions $iexp_1$ and $iexp_2$ to, say, i_1 and i_2, respectively, and then constructs and returns an array with elements indexed by integers from i_1 to i_2 and where the elements have the values of exp, evaluated with variable i bound to each integer from i_1 to i_2.

array(*exp*: *i* in *iexp₁* .. *iexp₂*)

Similarly, we can use the following aggregate expression for high-level aggregate computations, such as count, sum, min, and average, over a set of values. It first evaluates $iexp_1$ and $iexp_2$ to, say, i_1 and i_2, and then computes the aggregate value, as specified by operator op, of the values of exp for integer variable i ranging over integers from i_1 to i_2.

op{*exp*: *i* in *iexp₁* .. *iexp₂*}

We allow the forms of these expressions to be extended to multiple dimensions by adding more index variables and their ranges, separated by commas.

For the image blurring example, we may use the following higher-level specification for computing the blurred image of a into b:

```
b := array(sum{a[i+k,j+l]: k in 0..m-1, l in 0..m-1}
          : i in 0..n-m, j in 0..n-m)
```

In fact, the analysis and transformations for implementing the incrementalization method we have discussed build such a specification in the first place. Writing this specification explicitly makes it completely clear that the order of iterating through the pixels in the images and the order of summing the square neighborhood do not matter. Besides being clear and saving the analysis needed, this specification is also more succinct.

Higher-level data abstraction and control abstraction

Representing data using sets is higher-level than using arrays, because sets abstract away predetermined orders of representing the elements and fixed indices for accessing the elements. This makes it easy to specify what to compute on the elements in general. Arrays are simply binary relations, that is, sets of index-element pairs. Of course, while arrays map easily to computer memory, more sophisticated methods are needed to implement sets.

Expressing control using recursion is higher-level than using loops, because recursion abstracts away linearly repeated execution of straight-line code. This makes it easy to specify what to compute, by expressing solutions to a problem as combinations of solutions to recursively occurring subproblems. Linear execution of loops can be viewed as a trivial case of recursion. Of course, while loops may be easily executed on a computer efficiently, recursion requires more sophisticated implementation methods for efficient execution, especially when subproblems overlap.

Exercise 2.15 (Stock averages using aggregate expressions) Write a program for computing the 50-day stock averages in Exercise 2.4 using aggregate expressions.

Bibliographical notes

Loops and arrays are the hallmarks of commonly used high-level programming languages, including, starting from the oldest, FORTRAN, ALGOL, BASIC, Pascal, and C, to the most modern, Ada, C++, Python, and Java.

The Science of Programming by Gries [119] is an excellent book on programming with loops and arrays. It has many simple examples that exploit more algebraic properties than the examples in this chapter. It uses the incrementalized integer division program as the first example. Strengthening loop invariants is discussed specially by Gries [120]. Other work related to optimizing loops includes compiler optimizations for APL [315, 122, 91], optimization using invariants by Katz [159], and transforming series expressions by Waters [312].

Standard references for strength reduction are Cocke and Kennedy [61] and Allen et al. [10], but I learned from David Gries that it was invented earlier by Friedrich Bauer's group at Technical University of Munich working on an Algol 60 compiler [116] and was described in Gries's early compiler textbook [118]. Gries's *The Science of Programming* says that it was used as early as the late 1950s and calls it "taking an assertion out of a loop" [119, p. 241]. Goldstine [102] describes the Difference Engine and Analytical Engine by Charles Babbage and the ENIAC computer built during World War II. How ENIAC computed square root is described in Van der Spiegel et al. [72].

Systematic derivation of strength-reduced operations in loops, with application to the hardware design example, is briefly discussed in Liu et al. [209, 211]. A more comprehensive description of the transformations, plus the additional optimizations enabled, all applied to the hardware design example, are given in Liu [186]. Systematic incrementalization of aggregate array computations and the image processing example are discussed in Liu et al. [193, 206]. The method and applications to examples have been made simpler in this chapter. The method was later extended to handle to a more general class of problems [98].

The case study in formal hardware design that led to our example was described in O'Leary et al. [233]. It was brought to my attention by Bob Constable, who led the development of the Nuprl theorem prover [64] that was used in the case study. Soon after that case study, the Intel Pentium chip flaw was discovered [99]. As a result, Intel hired a large group of PhDs to significantly increase its hardware verification effort. Johnson et al. [155] later applied the method in Liu [186] to hardware design more generally.

The image processing example was given to me by Richard Szeliski then from DEC Cambridge Research Lab during his visit to Cornell University in 1995. Ramin Zabih at Cornell had developed a similar algorithm as an important part of his dissertation work [331, 330] at Stanford University. They both pointed out that dynamic programming underlies solutions to similar problems [316, 126, 313]. The alternative way of iterating that uses only two additional variables was discovered by Ning Li in 2000 after she implemented the method and tried that way. The alternative way of incremental maintenance that uses no additional variables was discovered by Jing Zhang during a lecture of mine at Tsinghua University in 2004.

3

Sets: incrementalize and implement

Most computer applications must handle collections of data. A set is a collection of distinct elements. Operations on sets, such as union and difference of the elements of two sets, are higher-level than operations on arrays, which are assignment and access of elements at indexed positions. The largest class of computer applications that involve collections is database applications, which typically handle large collections of data and provide many kinds of queries and other functionalities. Because of their higher-level nature, sets and set operations can be used to express problem solutions more clearly and easily, and have been used increasingly in programming languages, though typically only in applications that are not performance critical.

Problem solutions programmed using high-level set operations typically have performance problems, because high-level set operations typically involve many elements and are often repeatedly performed as sets are updated. To improve performance of applications programmed using sets, expensive high-level operations on sets must be transformed into efficient incremental operations, and sets must be implemented using data structures that support efficient incremental operations. These correspond to Steps Incrementalize and Implement, respectively. Step Iterate just determines a simple way of iteration that adds one element at a time to a set.

Because graph problems are typically specified using sets, we first describe the method using the graph reachability problem as an example, showing how efficient graph algorithms can be derived systematically. We then discuss two additional examples: access control, to show how to derive rules used for incrementalizing set expressions using appropriate result maps and auxiliary maps, and query optimization, to show how to derive optimal implementations of join queries using straightforward iterations and appropriate auxiliary maps. At the end, we discuss the need for higher-level control abstraction, which complements high-level data abstraction provided by sets.

Example: graph reachability

Given a graph with a set e of edges and a set s of source vertices, we want to find the set r of vertices reachable from the vertices in s following the edges in e.

A straightforward way to do this is to start at the source vertices and follow the edges to new vertices until no more new vertices can be reached. This can be specified as

```
r := s                        -- start with letting r be s
while exists x in e[r] - r:    -- while there is a new reachable vertex x
    r add x                   -- add x to r
```

where e[r] here is the set of vertices reachable from vertices in r following any one edge in e, and e[r]-r is the set of vertices in e[r] but not in r, and thus is the set of vertices newly reachable following any one edge. Note that there is no confusion between e[r] and array element access because r is a set whereas the index of an array element is an integer. The precise definitions of set operations are given in the first section of this chapter. We can write a clear and succinct specification as above because sets and set operations allow us to ignore how the graph is represented and how to visit a node and follow an edge in the graph.

While this specification is easy to write, there are three problems with it. First, how does one have any confidence that this is a good specification, at least in the sense that its execution terminates instead of looping infinitely? Second, even if this is a good specification, computing e[r] and computing e[r]-r are both expensive, meaning non-constant time, because they require iterations over sets, if they are computed from scratch every time r is updated. Third, even if only incremental set operations are performed, these operations cannot be implemented directly and efficiently on existing computer architectures, which support only operations with given memory addresses.

Solutions to these problems correspond exactly to Steps Iterate, Incrementalize, and Implement, respectively, as explained in detail in this chapter. The basic idea is to start with a fixed-point specification; then Step Iterate transforms the fixed-point specification into a while loop; Step Incrementalize transforms expensive set operations in the while loop into incremental operations; and Step Implement transforms incremental set operations into operations on appropriate linked and indexed data structures.

Exercise 3.1 (Graph reachability in other ways*) For the graph reachability problem, think of different ways to compute the set of reachable vertices. The program discussed computes them by considering a new reachable vertex at a time.

Are there other ways to compute in each iteration? What are some advantages and disadvantages of different ways to compute?

3.1 Set expressions—data abstraction

We use a language that has sets, tuples, and maps as data types for describing collections of data, and operations on these data types. All operations described here are expressions involving sets, except the commands for element addition and removal and the for loop over sets. Use of these high-level data types and operations not only helps represent data at a high level but also helps significantly reduce the use of loops, so the specifications are more declarative: showing more clearly what is computed, rather than how it is computed.

Language

A *set* is a collection of distinct elements. Elements in a set are not ordered, and they can be sets themselves. We use {} to enclose elements in a set. For example, a set containing numbers 1, 3, and 5 is denoted {1,3,5}, and it is the same set as {3,5,1}. Operations involving sets include expressions for empty set, range set, size, union, difference, intersection, cross product, subset test, and membership test, commands for element addition and removal, and element retrieval, as listed below. Some of these are shorthands of others for convenience.

- {}, empty set, denotes the set that contains no element.

- i..j, range set, returns the set that contains integers ranging from i to j.

- #s, size of set s, returns the number of elements in s.

- s + T, union of sets s and T, returns the set of all elements that are in either s or T.

- s - T, difference of sets s and T, returns the set of all elements that are in s but not in T.

- s & T, intersection of sets s and T, returns the set of all elements that are in both s and T.

- s * T, cross product of sets s and T, returns the set of all pairs whose first component is from s and second component is from T.

- s subset T, subset test, returns true if all elements in set s are also in set T, and false otherwise.

- x in s, membership test, returns true if x is an element of set s, and false otherwise.

- x not in s, also membership test, is equivalent to not(x in s).

- S `add` x, element addition, is a command that adds x to set S, that is, S := S + {x}.

- S `del` x, element deletion, is a command that deletes x from set S, that is, S := S - {x}.

- `exists` x `in` S, existential element retrieval, returns `true` if S is not empty, and `false` otherwise, and binds x to any element in S if S is not empty.

Elements of a set are often tuples. A *tuple* is an ordered collection of elements also called *components*. Elements in a tuple are ordered by their index positions. We use [] to enclose elements in a tuple. For example, a tuple with elements 1, 4, and 2 in order is denoted [1,4,2], and it is a different tuple from [2,1,4].

Tuples in a set often have two elements. A *map* is a set of 2-tuples, that is, pairs. If [x,y] is a pair in a map M, we say that M maps x to y. Operations on maps include domain, range, and image:

- `dom(M)`, domain of map M, is the set of elements that are in the first component of the pairs in M.

- `ran(M)`, range of map M, is the set of elements that are in the second component of the pairs in M.

- `M{x}`, image of x under map M, is the set of elements in `ran(M)` that M maps x to.

The maps we refer to are also called *multi-maps*, because there may be multiple pairs with the same first component, that is, each element in the domain may be mapped to multiple elements in the range. For example, map {[4,1],[3,7],[4,9]} maps 4 to 1 and 9; the image of 4 under the map is {1,9}; the domain of the map is {3,4}; and the range of the map is {1,7,9}.

The most powerful kind of set expression is set comprehension, which can express all operations above that return a set, except for the range set operation i..j. A *set comprehension* is a set-valued expression of the form below. Each variable v_1 through v_k enumerates elements in the value of set-valued expression $sexp_1$ through $sexp_k$, respectively, and for each combination of values of v_1 through v_k, if Boolean-valued expression $bexp$ evaluates to `true`, then the value of expression exp is an element of the resulting set.

$$\{exp: v_1 \text{ in } sexp_1, \ldots, v_k \text{ in } sexp_k \mid bexp\}$$

We read the expression as "the set of exp where v_1 is from $sexp_1$, ..., and v_k is from $sexp_k$ such that $bexp$". We abbreviate $\{v: v \text{ in } sexp \mid bexp\}$ as $\{v \text{ in } sexp \mid bexp\}$, and we omit $\mid bexp$ when $bexp$ is true. For example, the following set comprehension returns the set of pairs of elements from two respective sets where the element from the first set plus 1 is greater than or equal to the element from the second set; the return value is {[5,6],[2,3],[5,3]}.

$$\{[x,y]: x \text{ in } \{1,5,2\}, y \text{ in } \{9,3,6\} \mid x+1>=y\}$$

An *aggregate expression*, generalizing the definition in Section 2.6, is of the form below or, in general, *op* followed by any set-valued expression *sexp*. It evaluates the set-valued expression to a set, say s, and then computes the aggregate value, as specified by operator *op*, such as sum, average, min, and max, of values in s. In general, *op* can also be any binary operation that has an identity and is commutative and associative over the elements in s. We overload min and max to be binary operations too.

$$op\{exp:\ v_1\ \text{in}\ sexp_1,\ \ldots,\ v_k\ \text{in}\ sexp_k\ |\ bexp\}$$

An *existentially quantified expression* is of the form below, generalizing existential element retrieval described above. It returns true if and only if there exists a combination of values of variables v_1 through v_k, taken from the set values of expressions $sexp_1$ through $sexp_k$, respectively, such that Boolean-valued expression *bexp* evaluates to true; when it returns true, the variables v_1 through v_k are bound to such a combination of values.

$$\text{exists}\ v_1\ \text{in}\ sexp_1,\ \ldots,\ v_k\ \text{in}\ sexp_k\ |\ bexp$$

A *universally quantified expression* is the same except that exists is replaced with all. It returns true if and only if for all combinations of values of v_1 through v_k, taken from elements in the set values of expressions $sexp_1$ through $sexp_k$, respectively, Boolean-valued expression *bexp* evaluates to true. We omit | *bexp* when *bexp* is true.

A for *loop over sets* is of the form below. Each variable v_1 through v_k enumerates elements in the value of set-valued expression $sexp_1$ through $sexp_k$, respectively, and for each combination of values of v_1 through v_k, if the value of Boolean-valued expression *bexp* is true, then execute command *cmd*.

$$\text{for}\ v_1\ \text{in}\ sexp_1,\ \ldots,\ v_k\ \text{in}\ sexp_k\ |\ bexp:$$
$$cmd$$

We read the entire command as "for each v_1 in $sexp_1$, ..., and v_k in $sexp_k$ such that *bexp*, do *cmd*". Again, we omit | *bexp* when *bexp* is true.

In the clause "v_1 in $sexp_1$, ..., v_k in $sexp_k$ | *bexp*" in all of set comprehensions, aggregate expressions, quantified expressions, and for loops, a tuple pattern *tpat*$_i$ may occur in place of variable v_i. A *tuple pattern* is a tuple expression where each component is one of three kinds: an expression whose variables are all bound in the enclosing scope; a fresh variable that is not yet bound, called a *pattern variable*; or recursively a tuple pattern. A tuple value t *matches* a tuple pattern *tpat* if they have the same number of components and, recursively, the same number of components for components or subcomponents of *tpat* that are recursively tuple patterns; the value of each component or subcomponent expression in *tpat* equals the corresponding component or subcomponent value in t; and variable components and subcomponents of *tpat* that are the same variable correspond to the component and subcomponent values of t that are the same.

When tuple patterns are used, each tuple value $[v_1, \ldots, v_k]$, formed by a combination of elements v_1 through v_k from the set values of expressions $sexp_1$ through $sexp_k$, respectively, is matched against the tuple pattern $[x_1, \ldots, x_k]$. If the match succeeds, then pattern variables in $[x_1, \ldots, x_k]$ are instantiated with the corresponding values in $[v_1, \ldots, v_k]$, and subsequently used in checking Boolean-valued expression *bexp* and the remaining computations in the set comprehension, aggregate expression, quantified expression, or for loop.

For example, the following set comprehension returns a set of elements x where x is the second component of a pair in the given set whose first component equals 3 and where x is greater than 4; the return value is {6}.

```
{x: [3,x] in {[3,6],[1,5],[3,2] | x>4}
```

Cost model

Operations on sets that require iterating through one or more sets are considered expensive. Set size, union, difference, intersection, cross product, subset test, comprehension, quantified expressions, and for loops are such operations. Operations that involve a single element and a single set, if implemented naively, are also expensive, but they can be implemented with efficient data structures, as discussed in Step Implement in Section 3.4, in worst-case or average-case $O(1)$ time. Membership test, element addition and deletion, and element retrieval are such operations. Domain, range, and image operations of maps are also expensive if implemented naively, but with efficient data structures, a reference to the resulting sets can be returned in $O(1)$ time.

The time complexity of a set comprehension can be analyzed precisely as the following, where s1 through sk are the set values of expressions $sexp_1$ through $sexp_k$, respectively:

$$O(time(sexp_1) + \ldots + time(sexp_k) + \#\text{s1} \times \ldots \times \#\text{sk} \times (time(bexp) + time(exp)))$$

The time complexity of a quantified expression is the same except without the summand *time(exp)*. The time complexity of a for loop over sets is the same except that *time(exp)* is replaced with *time(cmd)*.

Exercise 3.2 (Set operations*) Write definitions of the following set operations using set comprehensions: union, difference, intersection, and cross product. The definition of the union operation needs more creativity.

Exercise 3.3 (Map operations*) Write definitions of the following map operations using set comprehensions: domain, range, and image. The definition of the image operation needs more care.

Exercise 3.4 (Image union*) Given a map M and a subset S of the domain of M, write a definition of M[S], the union of the image sets M{x} for all x in S, called *image union*, using set comprehension or other set operations already defined. Can you write multiple definitions? Note that this is different from array element access a[i], despite that a corresponds to a single-valued map (i.e., a map where each element in the domain is mapped to only one element in the range), because i is an element, not a subset, of the domain of this map; in particular, i is an integer, not a set.

Exercise 3.5 (Inverse map) Write a set comprehension that returns the inverse of a given map. That is, if y is in the image of x under the given map, then x is in the image of y under the inverse of the given map, and vice versa. You may see that this is extremely easy because our maps are multi-maps. If our maps were single valued, that is, each element in the domain may be mapped to only one element in the range, then an image set must be kept explicitly as a set, making it much messier to compute the inverse.

3.2 Iterate: compute fixed points

We can specify the solution to a problem as a *fixed point* of a function, that is, a value such that applying the function to the value returns the same value. Starting with fixed-point specifications has at least two advantages. First, fixed-point theorems may ensure that a fixed point exists and can be computed in a finite number of iterations, in contrast to using an ad hoc loop that might not terminate. Second, fixed-point theorems may allow a simplified initialization before iterations, which can reduce the size of the optimized program by about half.

For the graph reachability problem, we regard a set of vertices as a value, and consider functions that take a set of vertices and return a set of vertices. The set of reachable vertices can be specified as the least fixed point of a function, where the fixed point includes the set of source vertices, and the function takes a set r of vertices and returns the union of r and the set of all successors of vertices in r. We write this precisely as follows, where e[r] is the image union of map e over set r, {y: x in r, y in e{x}}, and min r: is read as "the minimum r such that":

```
min r: s subset r, r + e[r] = r
```

Writing fixed-point specifications can be difficult in general, because they already imply iterative computations but do not express those directly. We will see in Chapter 5 that it is much easier and more natural to write specifications using logic rules, which can then be automatically translated into a fixed-point specification.

Transforming into a loop

Step Iterate transforms a fixed-point specification into a while loop. This is based on fixed-point theorems in set theory, which state when a fixed point exists and how to compute it iteratively in a finite number of iterations. The latter means that execution of the loop always terminates, as desired. More refined theorems could even state how many iterations are needed.

A well-known theorem states that the fixed point above can be computed by starting with r being the set s of source vertices and repeatedly updating r with the result of computing $f(r) = $ r+e[r], that is, adding vertices in r+e[r] into r, until r does not grow any more—a fixed point of function f is reached. This would lead to the following loop:

```
r := s
while r + e[r] != r:
  r +:= e[r]
```

However, this loop requires that each iteration considers all vertices in e[r] that are not in r, and thus it is difficult to ensure that no computations are repeated.

Adding one element at a time

Another, less well-known but important theorem states that each iteration only needs to consider any one element in e[r] that is not in r. This realizes our general method of taking a minimum increment for iteration. It yields exactly the while loop in our original straightforward specification, copied below:

```
r := s
while exists x in e[r] - r:
  r add x
```

Now, we can transform this loop to compute each iteration efficiently, by incrementally maintaining values that are affected by adding only one vertex, as will be discussed in Step Incrementalize. The transformed program will be asymptotically faster than computing the loop straightforwardly.

Simplifying initialization

Besides termination, theorems about equivalence of fixed-point specifications can be used to give an additional benefit—a significant decrease in the size of the final code. Specifically, the least fixed point above is equivalent to the least fixed point of the function that takes a set r of vertices and returns the union of the set s of source vertices, the set r, and the set e[r] of all successors of vertices in r:

```
min r: s + r + e[r] = r
```

This is then transformed into the following loop, where r is initialized to the empty set, and the while clause contains a union with s:

```
r := {}
while exists x in s + e[r] - r:
  r add x
```

We will see in Step Incrementalize that this does not affect the size of the incrementalized loop body much, but reduces the initialization code from being the same size as the loop body to almost nothing.

Exercise 3.6 (**Least of fixed points***) In the fixed-point specification of the graph reachability problem, why must the *least* fixed point be taken?

Exercise 3.7 (**Number of iterations***) In the program for the graph reachability problem, what is a good upper bound for the total number of iterations executed by the `while` loop?

Exercise 3.8 (**Using power set operation***) Write a specification of the graph reachability problem using `pow(S)`, the set of all subsets of `S`, called *power set*, but not using fixed points or loops.

3.3 Incrementalize: compose incremental maintenance

Step Incrementalize transforms expensive set operations into incremental set operations, drastically reducing the running time. It considers all expensive operations from the inside out, and transforms the program to store and incrementally compute the result of each expensive operation with respect to all updates to the values of the parameters of the operation. The transformation replaces an expensive operation with a retrieval from its stored result, and inserts code that incrementally maintains the result at each update to the value of a parameter.

Setting up invariants

First, we identify all expensive operations in an inside-out order. We consider our original straightforward specification, copied below:

```
r := s
while exists x in e[r] - r:
    r add x
```

The expensive operations are the image union and set difference operations in `e[r]-r`, in an inside-out order. We store the results of these two operations in `t` and `w`, respectively, that is, we maintain two invariants

$$t = e[r]$$
$$w = t - r$$

where `t`, for "to-set"—the set of vertices reached to following single edges, is the union of the successors of vertices in `r`; and `w`, for "work-set"—the set of elements to be worked on, is the set of vertices in `e[r]` but not `r`.

Maintaining invariants by composition

Then, we transform the program to incrementally maintain the invariants, in an inside-out order, at all updates to their parameter values. We use this ordering because it follows dependencies among the variables used in the invariants: when the result of an expensive operation is used in computing the result of another expensive operation, the result of the first operation is maintained first, which then triggers maintenance of the result of the second operation. While maintenance code corresponds to derivatives in differential calculus, applying the transformations following the chain of dependencies in an inside-out order corresponds to the chain rule in calculus. Because w depends on t, we incrementally maintain t and w, in that order.

Recall from Chapter 2 that, to maintain an invariant $v = exp$, we replace all occurrences of expression exp with variable v, and insert code to incrementally maintain the value of exp in v at each update to a variable used in computing exp.

We first maintain t = e[r] incrementally with respect to update r add x. This replaces e[r] with t, and inserts the code that incrementally computes the new value of t, that is, the value of e[r+{x}], using the old value of t, that is, the value of e[r]. The maintenance code retrieves each successor y of x, from e{x}, and, if y is not already in t, adds y to t. We obtain

```
while exists x in t - r:    -- e[r] is replaced with t
  for y in e{x}:            || incrementally
    if y not in t:          || maintain t
      t add y               || under r add x
  r add x
```

We then maintain w = t-r incrementally with respect to updates t add y and r add x. This replaces t-r with w, and inserts code for incrementally maintaining w, that is, the value of t-r, at each of the two updates: at t add y, if y is not in r, add y to w; at r add x, if x is in t, delete x from w. This yields

```
while exists x in w:    -- t - r is replaced with w
  for y in e{x}:
    if y not in t:
      if y not in r:   || incrementally maintain w
        w add y        || under t add y
      t add y
    if x in t:         || incrementally maintain w
      w del x          || under r add x
  r add x
```

In the maintenance code, we have consistently used explicit membership tests before element additions and deletions to make the additions and deletions *strict operations*, that is, operations with real effect. This makes real changes explicit. It avoids unnecessary propagation of updates, and allows each addition and deletion to be done in constant time. Furthermore, it makes membership test basically the only kind of operation that requires data structure support for efficient implementation, as will be discussed in Step Implement.

In the transformations above, we have used code that incrementally maintain the value of an expensive computation with respect to an update, but we have not said how to obtain such code. With the access control example in Section 3.5, we will describe a systematic method for deriving such maintenance code for many expensive set expressions. We do not yet know how to derive such maintenance code for all expensive computations, but a library of rules, called incrementalization rules, including rules developed in ad hoc fashions, can be built and reused. In general, multiple rules might apply to an expensive computation, with trade-offs. The cost and frequencies of all the expensive and incremental computations should be considered explicitly and used to choose the rules that give the best trade-offs.

Adding initialization

Next, consider initialization of t and w at r := s. This can be done by first replacing r := s with a for loop that adds elements of s to r one at a time:

```
r := {}
for x in s:
  r add x
```

and then setting t and w to {} at r := {}, based on t = e[r] and w = t-r, and incrementally maintaining t and w under r add x as in the body of the while loop.

The final incrementalized code is simply the initialization code followed by the incrementalized body:

```
w := {}              -- w = t - r = {} - {} = {}
t := {}              -- t = e[r] = e[{}] = {}
r := {}
for x in s:
  for y in e{x}:     ||
    if y not in t:   ||
      if y not in r: ||
        w add y      || same as the body
        t add y      || of the while loop
  if x in t:         ||
    w del x          ||
  r add x            ||
while exists x in w:
  for y in e{x}:
    if y not in t:
      if y not in r:
        w add y
        t add y
  if x in t:
    w del x
  r add x
```

Using simplified initialization

Note that the initialization code above repeats the loop body and makes the code twice as long, but if we apply Step Incrementalize to the version of the loop at the end of Section 3.2 that initializes r to {} and does a union with s in the `while` clause, we can eliminate the repetition in the initialization, reducing the code size by about half. The only difference in the loop body is that we incrementally compute w = s+t-r instead of w = t-r, which just adds a test of membership in s for each of the two updates in the loop body. The new initialization simply sets t to {} and w to s at r := {}, based on t = e[r] and w = s+t-r, respectively. This yields

```
w := s                          -- w = s + t - r = s + {} - {} = s
t := {}                         -- t = e[r] = e[{}] = {}
r := {}
while exists x in w:
  for y in e{x}:
    if y not in t:
      if y not in r and y not in s:  -- added: and y not in s
        w add y
      t add y
    if x in t or x in s:        -- added: or x in s
      w del x
    r add x
```

In both this version and the one before, the outer loop iterates $O(V)$ times, where V is the number of vertices, because the algorithm starts with vertices in s and every vertex is added to work-set w at most once; the inner loop iterates through each outgoing edge of the vertex considered by the outer loop, and thus the body of the inner loop is executed $O(\#e)$ times. We will see in Step Implement in Section 3.4 that every other operation in the algorithms takes $O(1)$ time, and thus the total time complexity is $O(\#e)$.

Discussion: pros and cons of composition

The derivation above achieves incremental maintenance of invariant w = e[r]-r under update r add x by decomposing the invariant into two simpler invariants and composing incremental maintenance of simpler invariants t = e[r] and w = t-r under update r add x. For the version with simplified initialization, the derivation achieves incremental maintenance of w = s+e[r]-r by composing incremental maintenance of t = e[r] and w = s+t-r. Even though we did not do so, the last invariant, w = s+t-r could indeed be decomposed further into a union u = s+t and a difference w = u-r.

The advantage of composition is that only incremental maintenance of a set of basic invariants is needed to incrementalize any invariant built from the basic ones, as shown in this section. The disadvantage is that the composed incremental maintenance might not be the best possible, as shown next; while additional optimizations could make it better, this may be difficult for some problems while easy for others.

For example, we may incrementally maintain the invariant `w = s+e[r]-r` under update `r add x` directly as follows:

```
for y in e{x}:
   if y not in r and y not in w:
      w add y
w del x
```

and obtain the following incrementalized program from the initial `while` loop with simplified initialization:

```
w := s
r := {}
while exists x in w:            -- s + e[r] - r is replaced with w
   for y in e{x}:               ||
      if y not in r and y not in w: || incrementally maintain w
         w add y                || under r add x directly
      w del x                   ||
      r add x                   ||
```

How to derive the incremental maintenance used here is a separate issue for study. The resulting program is clearly simpler and more efficient than the program derived before this that uses simplified initialization.

In the program derived before this that uses simplified initialization, conditions involving `t` can be removed or replaced, based on the invariant `w = s+t-r`; afterward the intermediate variable `t` and the code `t add y` become *dead*, that is, no longer needed, and thus can be eliminated:

- The condition for `w del x`, `x in t` or `x in s`, is true, and thus can be eliminated. This is because: `x` is from `w` and `w = s+t-r`, so if `x` is in `w`, then `x` must be in `t` or `s`.

- The conditions for `w add y`, `y not in t` and `y not in r` and `y not in s`, equal `y not in w` and `y not in r`. The is because: `w = s+t-r`, so `y not in t` and `y not in s` equal `y not in w`.

Eliminating dead intermediate results: an example. As an example where unnecessary intermediate results can be easily removed, consider maintaining

$$n = \#\{x \text{ in } s + t \mid x > 95\}$$

under update `s add x`. We can maintain the following three simpler invariants, in order, under update `s add x`:

$$u = s + t$$
$$g = \{x \text{ in } u \mid x > 95\}$$
$$n = \#g$$

First, inserting incremental maintenance of `u` under `s add x` yields

```
if x not in t:  || incrementally maintain u
  u add x       || under s add x
s add x
```

Then, inserting incremental maintenance of g under u add x yields

```
if x not in t:
  if x>95:      || incrementally maintain g
    g add x     || under u add x
  u add x
s add x
```

Finally, inserting incremental maintenance of n under g add x yields

```
if x not in t:
  if x>95:
    n +:= 1    -- incrementally maintain n under g add x
    g add x
  u add x
s add x
```

Because g and u are not used anywhere else, they are dead and can be eliminated, yielding

```
if x not in t:
  if x>95:
    n +:= 1
s add x
```

Although the examples on sets so far exploit only intermediate results, we will see in the examples on access control in Section 3.5 and on query optimization in Section 3.6 that auxiliary values, in the form of maps, are essential for efficient incremental computations.

Exercise 3.9 (Incrementalizing set union and difference) Write incremental maintenance code for S+T and S-T under element addition and deletion to S and T, assuming that the addition and deletion are strict operations.

Exercise 3.10 (Composition) For each of the two invariants U=R-S-T and V= R-(S+T), derive incremental maintenance code under update s add x, by composing the incremental maintenance code from the previous exercise. What is the difference between the two resulting codes, and what are the consequences?

Exercise 3.11 (Composition under a different update) Do the same as in the previous exercise, except to consider update R add x instead of s add x.

3.4 Implement: design linked data structures

Step Implement transforms operations on sets into operations on appropriate linked lists, records, and arrays or hash tables based on how sets and set elements are accessed, so that each operation can be performed in constant time. The idea is to design sophisticated linked structures, whenever possible, so that each operation can be performed in *worst-case* constant time and with at most a small constant factor of space overhead. When linked structures alone are not sufficient, arrays may be used, but with a larger space overhead, or hash tables may be used, but with average-case instead of worst-case time complexities.

Associative access and other low-level set operations

We use a special concept, *associative access*, to refer to membership test (x in s and x not in s) and image operation (e{x}); such an operation requires the ability to locate an element (x) in a set (the set s or the domain of e). Consider the incrementalized program that is transformed from the original straightforward specification. We copy it here and comment it with the kinds of operations on each line, where access means associative access:

```
w := {}                 -- initialize w
t := {}                 -- initialize t
r := {}                 -- initialize r
for x in s:             -- retrieve x from s
    ...                 -- same as the body of the while loop below
while exists x in w:    -- retrieve x from w
    for y in e{x}:      -- access   x in domain of e
                        -- retrieve y from range of e
        if y not in t:  -- access   y in t
            if y not in r: -- access   y in r
                w add y    -- add      y to w
                t add y    -- add      y to t
        if x in t:      -- access   x in t
            w del x     -- delete   x from w
        r add x         -- add      x to r
```

Recall that all additions and deletions are strict operations. Additionally, the deletion of x from w happens after x is located in w; this is easy to see here because x is retrieved from w, but otherwise a test of x in w can be inserted before the deletion to locate x in w.

Using simple data structures

Now, consider using a linked list for each set, including the domain set and image sets of each map, and let each element in a domain set linked list contain a pointer to the element's image set linked list. In other words, represent a set as a linked list, and represent a map as a linked list of linked lists. Then, if associative access can be done in worst-case constant time, so can all other low-level operations:

- set initialization (s := {}) and emptiness test (s={}),
- element addition (s add x) and deletion (s del x),
- element retrieval (in while exists x in S and for x in S), and

- domain operation (dom(M)).

To see this, note that adding or deleting an element to or from a set can be done in constant time after doing an associative access of the element in the set, retrieving an element from a set only needs to locate any element or any next element in the set, and a domain operation simply returns a pointer to the set.

An associative access would take linear time if a linked list is naively traversed to locate an element, but there are several solutions to this problem. A classical solution is to use hash tables instead of linked lists, but this gives average-case, not worst-case, constant time for each operation, and it has the overhead of hashing-related computations for each operation. Another solution is to use arrays, but this gives worst-case constant-time operations only when the sets do not change dynamically, and it may use asymptotically more space than necessary and may have bad memory performance when the arrays are large.

Designing sophisticated linked data structures

We describe a better solution, called *based representation*, for a general class of set-based programs. It is a powerful method for designing linked structures that support associative access in worst-case constant time and with little space overhead. The basic observation is that an access, x in s, in a program, is not isolated—the element x must be retrieved from some set w before the access, as in

```
...
... -- retrieve x from W
...
... -- access x in S
...
```

That is, we want to locate x in s after it has been located in w. The idea is to use a set B, called a *base*, to store values for both w and s, so that a retrieval of a value from w also locates this value in s.

- Base B is a set of records (this set is only conceptual), with a K field storing the key (i.e., value).

- Set s is represented using an s field of B: records of B whose keys are in s are connected by a linked list whose links are stored in the s field; records of B whose keys are not in s store a special value, null, indicating undefinedness in the s field. If set s is never retrieved from, then the s field can be a bit indicating whether the key is in s.

- Set w is represented as a separate linked list of pointers to records of B whose keys are in w.

Thus, an element of s is represented as *a field in* the record, and s is said to be *strongly based* on B; an element of w is represented as *a pointer to* the record, and w is said to be *weakly based* on B.

This representation allows an arbitrary number of weakly based sets, but only a constant number of strongly based sets, because there can be any number of pointers to a record, but only a constant number of fields in a record. So this representation applies if and only if there is a constant number of strongly based sets. Essentially, base B provides a kind of indexing to elements of s starting from elements of w.

For the graph reachability program, consider the kinds of operations on each line. We need to design data structures for sets s, w, t, r, and map e. First, consider the body of the while loop:

- after x is retrieved from w, it is accessed in the domain of e, and in t, so all elements of w, the domain of e, and t are in a base;

- after y is retrieved from the range of e, it is accessed in t, and in r, so the range of e, t, and r are in a base.

Because t is common to both groups of sets, elements of all of these sets are in one base, yielding the data structure in Figure 3.1:

- the key of the records is the id of the elements, that is, vertices;

- there is a field in the record for each set with element access: the domain of e (a pointer to the image set), t (a bit), and r (a bit); and

- there is a linked list of pointers to the records for each set with element retrieval: w and the image sets of e.

Then, consider the for loop before the while loop. Everything is the same as for the while loop except that x is retrieved from s instead of w, so we simply need to represent s as another linked list of pointers to the records.

For the incrementalized program with simplified initialization, that is, with r initialized to {} and a union with s done in the while clause, the linked list for s is replaced with an additional field, a bit, for testing membership in s.

The space complexity is $O(V)$, where V is the number of vertices, because of the additional space used for the fields and linked lists for dom(e), r, t, s, and w, which are all for vertices. This is, in general, much smaller than the space for input, which is $O(\#e)$.

Discussion: adjacency-list versus adjacency-matrix representations and depth-first versus breadth-first search

The data structures we have derived are in fact exactly the *adjacency-list representation* for graphs, which uses a linked list of linked lists for edges. It is preferred over the *adjacency-matrix representation* for graphs, which uses an array of arrays for edges, and can take asymptotically more space than the adjacency-list representation when the graphs are *sparse*, that is, when there are few edges going in or out of most vertices.

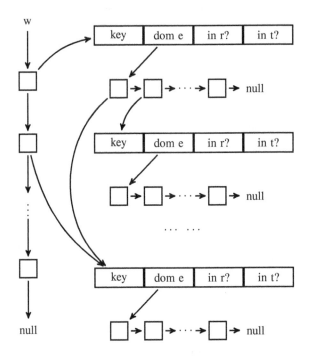

Figure 3.1 Resulting data structure for the graph reachability example.

While element additions and deletions can now be implemented efficiently, there is in fact a choice for whether to add and delete elements at the head or tail of a linked list. For example, for work-set w in the graph reachability problem, if additions and deletions are at the same end, then the linked list is a stack, and the resulting algorithm is exactly doing a *depth-first search (DFS)*, which traverses a graph by going deep first; if additions are at one end, and deletions are at the other end, then the linked list is a queue, and the resulting algorithm is exactly doing a *breadth-first search (BFS)*, which traverses a graph by going wide first.

Compare the method described here with the materials taught in the algorithms and data structures literature. There, before any graph algorithm is discussed, there are separate descriptions and comparisons of the adjacency-list and adjacency-matrix representations and of the DFS and BFS strategies. Then, for each algorithm, a graph representation and a search strategy are picked before the algorithm is presented. Here, the method described automatically derives the preferred data structures. Also, the freedom, or nondeterminism, created at a high level by picking any element in e[r]-r in each iteration allows the search strategy used to be a low-level choice that can be determined at the end.

These choices for search strategies and for data structures also help show that, for implementing set expressions, Step Incrementalize and Step Implement are essential and more sophisticated, while Step Iterate is straightforward.

Exercise 3.12 (Data structure design) Suppose that the resulting code for maintaining the invariant for U in Exercise 3.10 is in a loop `for x in U`. Design data structure for sets R, S, T, and U in the resulting code. You may assume that all other operations in the loop do not involve these sets.

Exercise 3.13 (Using doubly linked lists*) When are doubly linked lists needed in based representations?

Exercise 3.14 (Number of strongly based sets*) When is there an unbounded number of strongly based sets? What data structures should we use in that case?

3.5 Example: access control

We consider the core component in role-based access control (RBAC), as defined in an American National Standards Institute (ANSI) standard, and show how to systematically derive rules for incrementally maintaining the results of many expensive set expressions, including all expensive set expressions in RBAC, with respect to updates to their parameter values. *RBAC* is a framework for controlling user access to resources based on roles. Efficient implementations require making many complex queries incremental with respect to many possible updates, and therefore a systematic method for deriving the needed rules is extremely beneficial.

Core RBAC queries and updates

The ANSI standard for core RBAC defines core functionalities on permissions, users, sessions, roles, and a number of relations among these sets, while the rest of the standard adds a hierarchical relation over roles, in hierarchical RBAC, and restricts the number of roles of a user and of a session, in constrained RBAC. Precisely, core RBAC has essentially five sets: OBJS for objects, OPS for operations, USERS for users, ROLES for roles, and SESSIONS for sessions, and the following four relations, specified with associated constraints. An operation-object pair is called a permission.

```
PR subset (OPS * OBJS) * ROLES  -- assignment of permissions to roles
UR subset USERS * ROLES         -- assignment of users to roles
SU subset SESSIONS * USERS      -- sessions with session users
SR subset SESSIONS * ROLES      -- sessions with active roles
```

Core RBAC functionalities involve 16 kinds of queries of 9 different forms and 19 kinds of updates in 12 functions.

We use the expensive query in function CheckAccess, called the CheckAccess query, as an example, because it is the most important and most frequently used query; the method applies to all other queries as well. The CheckAccess *query* takes a session, an operation, and an object, and returns the set of roles that are active in the session and are assigned the operation-object pair as a permission:

```
{r: r in ROLES | [session,r] in SR, [[operation,object],r] in PR}
```

The CheckAccess function grants access if this set is not empty.

We need to determine updates to the values of the parameters of the query. A parameter of a query is a variable defined outside the query and used in the query. For the CheckAccess query, the parameters are ROLES, SR, PR, session, operation, and object. An update to the value of a parameter is any operation that sets the value of the parameter. For the CheckAccess query, parameters ROLES, SR, and PR are set by addition and deletion of an element, and initialization to {}, while parameters session, operation, and object are set by calls to the CheckAccess function.

Deriving incrementalization rules

For each kind of expensive query, we need to determine how to incrementally maintain the query result with respect to each kind of update to the value of a parameter of the query; this is captured by an *incrementalization rule*. Deriving such rules boils down to systematically addressing three main issues.

First, to handle parameters that can be set to any value, we maintain a *result map* that maps the values of those parameters to the results of the query. For the CheckAccess query, we maintain a map, called MapSP2R, that maps any given session and permission, that is, operation-object pair, to the desired set of roles. Then, the CheckAccess query can be replaced with a fast retrieval

```
MapSP2R{[session,operation,object]}
```

which locates the result set in constant time. The CheckAccess function can then test the emptiness of the result set in constant time, and thus is overall constant time and optimal.

Second, to handle other parameter value updates, we derive code for incrementally maintaining the result of the query at each kind of update. For the CheckAccess query, MapSP2R must be incrementally maintained when ROLES, SR, and PR are updated by element addition and deletion in 9 other functions.

The derivation starts with generic code for maintaining the result set, obtained from the query by iterating over both the sets enumerated and the sets tested for membership. For example, the generic code for the CheckAccess query is the following; the additional membership test on the second line ensures that addition to the result map is a strict operation:

```
for r in ROLES: for [s,r] in SR: for [[op,o],r] in PR:
    if r not in MapSP2R{[s,op,o]}: MapSP2R{[s,op,o]} add r
```

A variable that becomes bound in an outer loop is used as a filter for the values enumerated in an inner loop. For example, in the nested for loops in the generic code above, the variable r becomes bound in the outermost loop, so for each value of r, among tuples enumerated in the two inner loops, only those whose second component equals the value of r are considered.

To quickly retrieve values of unbound components of tuples given values of bound components, *auxiliary maps* are maintained to map values of bound components to values of unbound components. These maps serve essentially as indices. For the CheckAccess query, the generic form above shows the need to find all s's and all [op,o]'s that match each r in SR and PR, respectively. So, we maintain two auxiliary maps:

- SRMapR2S maps each role in ran(SR) to its corresponding set of sessions in SR.

- PRMapR2P maps each role in ran(PR) to its corresponding set of permissions in PR.

That is, SRMapR2S and PRMapR2P are the inverse maps of SR and PR, respectively.

Together, the result map and two auxiliary maps yield the following three invariants to be maintained at updates to ROLES, SR, and PR:

```
MapSP2R{[s,op,o]}  =  {r: r in ROLES | [s,r] in SR, [[op,o],r] in PR}
SRMapR2S           =  {[r,s]: [s,r] in SR}
PRMapR2P           =  {[r,[op,o]]: [[op,o],r] in PR}
```

Now, to obtain the specific maintenance code at each addition and deletion of an element, we start with the generic code, and do four things:

1. eliminate the loop over the set being modified, because in incremental maintenance, only the element being added or deleted needs to be considered for this loop;

2. replace each loop whose loop variables are all bound with a test on the loop variables, because bound variables are filters of the values;

3. use auxiliary maps in loops that have both bound and unbound loop variables to iterate over only the values of the unbound variables; and

4. update an auxiliary map when its corresponding set of tuples is updated.

For the CheckAccess query at element additions to ROLES, SR, and PR, we obtain the maintenance code below, shown as a set of **at**-*update*-**do**-*maintenance* clauses, where each *update* and *maintenance* is followed by its time complexity. The maintenance code can be inserted either before or after the corresponding update.

```
at ROLES add r                                                      O(1)
do for s in SRMapR2S{r}: for [op,o] in PRMapR2P{r}:                 O(s/r × p/r)
     if r not in MapSP2R{[s,op,o]}: MapSP2R{[s,op,o]} add r

at SR add [s,r]                                                     O(1)
do if r in ROLES: for [op,o] in PRMapR2P{r}:                        O(p/r)
     if r not in MapSP2R{[s,op,o]}: MapSP2R{[s,op,o]} add r
   SRMapR2S{r} add s

at PR add [[op,o],r]                                                O(1)
do if r in ROLES: for s in SRMapR2S{r}:                             O(s/r)
     if r not in MapSP2R{[s,op,o]}: MapSP2R{[s,op,o]} add r
   PRMapR2P{r} add [op,o]
```

For example, at addition of an element [s,r] to SR, the loop over ROLES becomes a test because r is bound, the loop over SR is eliminated because [s,r] is being added to SR, the auxiliary map for PR is used to iterate over only unbound variables [op,o] for the bound r, and the auxiliary map for SR is maintained. At addition of an element to PR, the maintenance code is similar. At addition of an element to ROLES, the maintenance code is simpler.

The complexity analysis assumes that Step Implement realizes each operation that involves a single element in $O(1)$ time. We use s/r to denote the maximum number of sessions per role, and p/r to denote the maximum number of permissions per role; note that in the maintenance code, r is looked up in dom(SRMapR2S) and dom(PRMapR2P), which both equal ROLES, s is from ran(SRMapR2S), which equals SESSIONS, and [op,o] is from ran(PRMapR2P), which equals OPS * OBJS, that is, the set of permissions.

Deletion is symmetric and has the same cost, that is, is exactly the same except that if r not in is replaced with if r in and add is replaced with del.

Third and finally, the result map and auxiliary maps are initialized: the map for the query result is set to empty when any of the sets being iterated over is set to empty, and an auxiliary map is set to empty when the corresponding set of tuples is set to empty. The cost is always $O(1)$.

```
at ROLES := {}                                                     O(1)
do MapSP2R := {}                                                   O(1)

at SR := {}                                                        O(1)
do MapSP2R := {}                                                   O(1)
   SRMapR2S := {}

at PR := {}                                                        O(1)
do MapSP2R := {}                                                   O(1)
   PRMapR2P := {}
```

Putting all these clauses together with the query and query result retrieval, we obtain a complete incrementalization rule, of the following form, where each of the *query*, *result*, *update*'s, and *maintenance*'s is followed by its time complexity.

$$\textbf{inv } result = query$$
$$(\textbf{at } update$$
$$\textbf{do } maintenance)+$$

The clause **inv** *result* = *query* indicates that *result* = *query* is an invariant. The plus sign (+) after the right parenthesis indicates that there may be one or more **at**-*update*-**do**-*maintenance* clauses.

For the CheckAccess query, the derived incrementalization rule is the following invariant followed by **at**-*update*-**do**-*maintenance* clauses derived above for element addition and deletion and initialization.

```
inv MapSP2R{[s,op,o]}                                    O(1)
    = {r: r in ROLES | [s,r] in SR, [[op,o],r] in PR}    O(#ROLES)
```

The space complexity is for storing the result map MapSP2R and auxiliary maps SRMapR2S and PRMapR2P. The result map MapSP2R supports constant-time lookup of the resulting roles given a session, an operation, and an object, and its space complexity is bounded by $O(\#\text{SESSIONS} \times \#\text{OPS} \times \#\text{OBJS} \times \#\text{ROLES})$. The auxiliary maps SRMapR2S and PRMapR2P are inverses of SR and PR, respectively, and take space $O(\#\text{SR})$ and $O(\#\text{PR})$, respectively.

Additional issues

We consider three additional issues: simplification of maintenance code, join order, and copying of query results.

Two kinds of simplifications can be made to the maintenance code in core RBAC to improve the analyzed running time asymptotically, although they do not improve the actual running times asymptotically. First, the maintenance code under updates ROLES add r and ROLES del r can be eliminated, and its time complexity can be tightened to $O(1)$, because in RBAC the range of SR must be a subset of ROLES, and thus SRMapR2S must map the role being added or removed to the empty image set; this optimization cannot be done without the subset constraint. Second, in the maintenance code under updates SR add [s,r] and SR del [s,r], the condition if r in ROLES can be removed, again because the range of SR must be a subset of ROLES, and thus the r in a pair being added to or removed from SR must be in ROLES.

Other queries in core RBAC are of four simpler kinds and four other kinds similar to the CheckAccess query. The simpler kinds of queries each needs to store, use, and maintain just one auxiliary map. For some of the other kinds of queries, different order of sets and relations being iterated may lead to different time complexities, because of differences in the order of binding the variables. This is essentially the well-known join order problem. The number of possible orders is, in the worst case, exponential in the number of sets being iterated, but it is typically a small constant, so we can simply consider all of them, and choose the one with the best complexity based on the sizes of the sets.

All queries in core RBAC are independent of each other, so rules for incrementalizing them can be applied in any order. There is an additional detail when applying individual rules: although a query result can be located in constant time, if it is iterated over, then a copy of it needs to be made for the iteration if the query result may be incrementally updated at updates to the values of the query parameters during the iteration. Note that this copying does not increase the overall asymptotic running time, because the cost of copying is amortized over the subsequent iteration.

Exercise 3.15 (RBAC review functions) In core RBAC, review functions `AssignedRoles` and `SessionRoles` are both queries of the following form:

    {r: r in R | [t,r] in TR}

Derive incremental maintenance code under element addition to R and TR.

Exercise 3.16 (RBAC advanced review functions) In core RBAC, advanced review functions `UserPermissions` and `SessionPermissions` are both queries of the following form:

    {[op,obj]: r in R, op in OPS, obj in OBJS
        | [t,r] in TR, [[op,obj],r] in PR}

Derive incremental maintenance code under element addition to R, TR, and PR.

3.6 Example: query optimization

We show how to derive optimal algorithms for computing general join queries. A join query computes results by relating elements of two sets of tuples. Join queries are at the core of relational calculus queries as used in SQL, the dominant database query language. The derivation illustrates how to iterate in a straightforward manner and how to discover auxiliary maps for efficient incremental computation.

Join queries

Join queries are of the following canonical form, where f and g are functions, for example, for selecting particular components of x and y, respectively.

$$r \;=\; \{[x,y]: x \text{ in } s, y \text{ in } t \mid f(x) = g(y)\}$$

An example of this query in SQL is the following, which selects all professor and course pairs where the professor is the instructor of the course:

```
select *
from professor, course
where professor.name = course.instructor
```

Clearly, if computed straightforwardly, such join queries have a running time of $O(\#s \times \#t)$. In the worst case, all pairs of elements in s and t could satisfy the equality condition and be returned, which indeed takes $\Omega(\#s \times \#t)$ time. However, it is easy to see that in practice, there may be much fewer pairs that satisfy the condition. For the professor-course example, each professor is likely the instructor of a few courses, not all the courses. Can we compute the result more efficiently? In particular, can we compute the query result in optimal time, that is, $O(\#s + \#t + \#r)$ time, where r is the query result? This is considered optimal because the query must at least read the input s and t and write the result r.

Join queries are the most extensively used expensive queries in relational databases, and optimizations for them have been extensively studied. An algorithm that achieves the optimal time complexity has indeed been given previously, as shown below. It maintains inverse maps of f and g and computes the cross product of all combinations of results from the two inverses.

```
finverse = {[f(x),x]: x in s}
ginverse = {[g(y),y]: y in t | g(y) in dom(finverse)}
r = {[x,y]: z in dom(ginverse), x in finverse{z}, y in ginverse{z}}
```

Expanded into loops, the algorithm is

```
finverse := {}              || expanded
for x in s:                 || computation
  finverse add [f(x),x]     || of finverse
ginverse := {}              ||
for y in t:                 || expanded
  if g(y) in dom(finverse): || computation
    ginverse add [g(y),y]   || of ginverse
r := {}                     ||
for z in dom(ginverse):     || expanded
  for x in finverse{z}:     || computation
    for y in ginverse{z}:   || of r
      r add [x,y]           ||
```

The first two loops iterate through s and t, respectively. The nested loops at the end add a new pair to r every time, because f and g being functions determines that, for different values of z, values of x must be different and values of y must be different. Assume that each operation that involves a single element takes constant time, as discussed earlier for Step Implement. The time complexity of the algorithm is thus $O(\#s + \#t + \#r)$, that is, input size plus output size, which is optimal.

Can our systematic method derive this algorithm? No. Instead, our method can derive a better algorithm—an algorithm that not only has the same optimal asymptotic time complexity, but also has a smaller constant factor, uses half or less of the space, is simpler and shorter, and, above all, is systematically derived so we have higher confidence that it is correct.

Iterate

It is clear that a minimum increment for iteration is to consider either one element at a time for s or one element at a time for t. We simply choose the former, and use a loop to iterate over s, that is, we are to compute

$$r = \{[x,y]: x \text{ in } s1, y \text{ in } t \mid f(x) = g(y)\}$$

incrementally as each element of s is added to s1 starting from s1 = {}:

```
s1 := {}
for x in s:
  s1 add x
```

We obtain the following, after eliminating dead code for computing s1:

```
r := {}                                 -- maintain r under s1 = {}
for x in s:
  r +:= {[x,y]: y in t | f(x) = g(y)}   -- maintain r under s1 add x
```

Incrementalize

We compute the expensive expression {[x,y]: y in t | f(x) = g(y)} in the loop incrementally with respect to a given x in each iteration. Given x, the value of f(x) becomes given. So we need to find y's in t such that g(y) equals some given value. This leads us to maintain an auxiliary map that maps such a value of g(y) to y for y in t. In general, an *auxiliary map* is used to map from known values to the desired values. We call the map here ginverse, because it corresponds to the inverse of g:

$$\text{ginverse} = \{[g(y),y]: y \text{ in } t\}$$

Now, the set of y's in t such that g(y) equals a given value f(x) is just the set of y's in ginverse{f(x)}. We obtain the following algorithm:

```
ginverse := {[g(y),y]: y in t}          -- compute ginverse
r := {}
for x in s:
  r +:= {[x,y]: y in ginverse{f(x)}}   -- use ginverse
```

Expanded into loops, the resulting algorithm is

```
ginverse := {}              || expanded
for y in t:                 || computation
  ginverse add [g(y),y]     || of ginverse
r := {}
for x in s:
  for y in ginverse{f(x)}:  || expanded
    r add [x,y]             || additions to r
```

The first two loops iterate through t and s, respectively. The loop nested in the second loop adds a new pair to r every time, because each x considered by the outer loop is different, and for each x, each y considered by the inner loop is different.

Implement

To compare our derived algorithm with the previous optimal algorithm, it is sufficient to assume that sets are implemented using hash tables for both algorithms.

Analysis and comparison

Compared with the previous optimal algorithm, our derived algorithm has the same optimal asymptotic time complexity and is significantly better in at least four other aspects.

- Our algorithm has an asymptotic running time of $O(\#s + \#t + \#r)$, that is, input size plus output size, because the three loops in the algorithm iterate $O(\#t)$, $O(\#s)$, and $O(\#r)$ times, respectively. Therefore, it achieves the same optimal asymptotic running time as the previous algorithm, and its complexity analysis is easier.

- Our algorithm has a smaller constant factor, because it has fewer operations on each element in the sets, in a total of 3 loops instead of 5, and has no other conditional tests. Thus, it has better absolute running time.

- The auxiliary space used by our algorithm is $O(\#t)$, for storing ginverse, but can be made $O(\#s)$ if s is smaller than t, by simply iterating over t instead of s in Step Iterate. Thus, the auxiliary space is $O(\min(\#s, \#t))$, and is no more than half of the $O(\#s + \#t)$ auxiliary space used by the previous algorithm for storing both finverse and ginverse.

- Our algorithm is much shorter and simpler, being about half of the size of the given optimal algorithm. Thus it takes less code space, and is also much easier to understand.

- Above all, our algorithm is obtained by following a systematic method, not using ad hoc techniques. This gives higher assurance of the correctness of the algorithm.

Exercise 3.17 (Existential selection query*) Derive an efficient algorithm for selection queries with existential quantification, that is, queries of the form

```
{x: x in s | (exists y in t | g(y) = f(x))}
```

Exercise 3.18 (Existential join query*) Derive an efficient algorithm for join queries with existential quantification, that is, queries of the form

```
{[x,y]: x in s, y in t | f(x) = g(y) and
                    exists z in u | h1(z)=f1(x) and h2(z)=g1(y)}
```

You may notice that this is essentially the first example problem near the beginning of Chapter 1.

3.7 Need for control abstraction

While sets provide high-level data abstraction, and set expressions allow clearer, more declarative specifications, programs written using loops and set expressions are still straight-line code, lacking functions and procedures that provide control abstraction, especially recursive functions that allow certain more powerful queries.

For example, the Fibonacci function, defined below, for $n \geq 0$, cannot be written straightforwardly using loops and set expressions:

$$fib(n) = \begin{cases} 0 & \text{if } n = 0 \\ 1 & \text{if } n = 1 \\ fib(n-1) + fib(n-2) & \text{otherwise} \end{cases}$$

but it can be specified directly using a simple recursive function definition:

```
def fib(n) where n>=0:
  if n=0 then 0
  else if n=1 then 1
  else fib(n-1) + fib(n-2)
```

Problem specifications using recursive functions, as well as methods for deriving efficient implementation for them, will be discussed in the next chapter.

Exercise 3.19 (Fibonacci using loops*) Write a definition of the Fibonacci function using loops.

Exercise 3.20 (Fibonacci using set operations*) Write a definition of the Fibonacci function using set operations without loops.

Bibliographical notes

Sets and operations on sets are supported in many languages, including the pioneer set-based programming language SETL [280, 292], functional programming language Miranda and Haskell, object-oriented programming languages Smalltalk and Python, logic programming language Prolog, database and XML query languages SQL and Xquery, and specification languages Z [293, 150] and OCL [234].

Incremental computation of set expressions has been studied both in databases and in very high-level programming languages at least as early as the 1970s [78, 88, 86, 87]. In database research, there has been special effort on database view maintenance, e.g., [50, 124, 123]. In programming languages, there has been a variety of related research, e.g., [285, 139, 329], but the work by Paige et al. stands out. In particular, Steps Iterate, Incrementalize, and Implement for set computations correspond to Paige et al.'s dominated convergence [40, 44], finite differencing [236, 243], and real-time simulation [239, 42, 110], respectively, except that Paige et al. use high-level rules without giving methods for deriving them.

Paige et al.'s method was used and extended to derive new or improved algorithms for solving a wide range of problems, including database integrity control and query and transaction optimization [237], partition refinement [245, 244], attribute closure [242], relational calculus subset [43, 112], multi-pattern tree pattern matching [48], ready simulation [33], DFA minimization [160], transforming regular expressions to DFA [51], copy elimination [113], model checking mu-calculus [110], constraint solving [191], regular path queries [215, 192], implementing Datalog [203], program pointer analysis [111], and implementing RBAC [214].

Paige also built a system, APTS, to automatically transform specifications that use fixed points and high-level set expressions into efficient implementations in C [241]; the system was successfully experimented with on eight different problems including the graph reachability problem in this chapter [46]. Additionally, Paige et al. studied methods for reading input in transformed programs [240, 246], detecting duplicates in language processing [47], and implementing languages with predictable time complexities [43, 45].

The idea of using a minimum increment for incrementalization was first described for optimizing recursive functions [194, 197]. For optimizing set expressions, this naturally yields the increment of adding one element at a time; the general idea was not yearned for because one could simply use a fixed high-level transformation rule to handle one element at a time [44]. The method for deriving incrementalization rules for set expressions is discussed in Liu et al. [214] and used there to generate efficient implementations of core RBAC. It is extended by Rothamel and Liu [273, 271] to more general queries over objects and sets. Gorbovitski et al. [103] study composition of incrementalization rules. The based representation [239, 42] was augmented with extensive use of arrays when linked lists are not sufficient [191, 203].

The access control example is taken from Liu et al. [214], where all queries in the core component of the ANSI standard for RBAC can be incrementalized. The ANSI standard for RBAC [13] uses the specification language Z [293, 150]. It was simplified by removing unnecessarily maintained invariants and other unnecessary complications [202]. It was also made executable by expressing the operations directly using set queries and updates in Python, before efficient implementations with complexity guarantees are generated [214]. The simplification and implementation effort also uncovered other anomalies [202].

The original optimal algorithm for join queries and other relational calculus operations was designed by Willard, first in his dissertation [320], further developed six and twelve years later [321, 322], and part of which further developed eighteen years later [323]. The design was simplified and formulated as formal transformations first by Cai and Paige [43] and further by Goyal and Paige ten years later [112]. Priyalakshmi [256] implemented the transformations described

in Goyal and Paige [112]. The systematic derivation and improved algorithm for
join queries in this chapter are briefly discussed in Liu et al. [205].

Graph search strategies and representations are discussed in standard algorithm
textbooks [65, 171]. Hopcroft and Tarjan [137] advocated the use of adjacency-list
representation over adjacency-matrix representation for sparse graphs. Optimizing
join orders is a well-known problem in database systems, for which many different
methods have been studied, e.g., [295].

4

Recursion: iterate and incrementalize

Many combinatorics and optimization problems can be solved straightforwardly by combining solutions to subproblems, where the subproblems may overlap in complicated manners. Such ways of solving the problems can be easily specified using recursive functions—functions whose definitions involve calls to the functions themselves, called recursive calls. The recursive calls are used for solving subproblems. Applications include many kinds of data analysis and decision-making problems, such as the great many kinds of analysis and manipulations needed on sequences, be they sequences in biological computing, document processing, financial analysis, or sensor data analysis.

Straightforward evaluation of recursive functions may be inefficient, and may in fact be extremely inefficient when they are used to solve overlapping subproblems, because subproblems may share subsubproblems, and common subsubproblems may be solved repeatedly. An efficient algorithm solves every subsubproblem just once, saves the result appropriately, and reuses the result when the subsubproblem is encountered again. Such algorithms are called *dynamic programming* algorithms. To arrive at such efficient algorithms, we must determine how efficient computations should proceed, and how computed results should be saved and reused. These correspond to Steps Iterate and Incrementalize. Step Implement just determines a straightforward way of storing the saved results in appropriate data structures.

We first describe the method with illustrations on the longest common subsequence problem, a well-known problem in sequence processing. We then discuss additional examples in combinatorial optimization and in math and puzzles: the 0-1 knapsack problem illustrates the use of maps and indexed data structures, as opposed to nested tuples and linked data structures for the longest common subsequence problem; the factorial, Ackermann function, Fibonacci number, and Tower of Hanoi examples demonstrate that our systematic method for iteration leads to successful optimizations where ad hoc methods may fail or lead to worse solutions. We discuss, at the end, the need for higher-level data abstraction, which complements high-level control abstraction provided by recursive functions.

Example: longest common subsequence

A subsequence of a given sequence is just the given sequence possibly with some elements left out. Given two sequences $x_1, x_2, \ldots, x_n$ and $y_1, y_2, \ldots, y_m$, we want to compute the length of a *longest common subsequence* (*LCS*) of the two sequences. This can be computed as $lcs(n, m)$, where $lcs(i, j)$ computes the length of an LCS of $x_1, \ldots, x_i$ and $y_1, \ldots, y_j$ and is defined recursively as, for $i, j \geq 0$,

$$
lcs(i, j) = \begin{cases} 0 & \text{if } i = 0 \text{ or } j = 0 \\ lcs(i - 1, j - 1) + 1 & \text{if } i \neq 0 \text{ and } j \neq 0 \text{ and } x_i = y_j \\ \max(lcs(i, j - 1), lcs(i - 1, j)) & \text{otherwise} \end{cases}
$$

If $i = 0$ or $j = 0$, that is, if either sequence is empty, then the resulting length is 0. If both sequences are not empty and $x_i = y_j$, then every LCS must end with this common element, and the resulting length is 1 plus the length of an LCS of $x_1, \ldots, x_{i-1}$ and $y_1, \ldots, y_{j-1}$. Otherwise, that is, if both sequences are not empty and $x_i \neq y_j$, then an LCS either does not end with y_j or does not end with x_i, so the resulting length is the maximum of the length of an LCS for $x_1, \ldots, x_i$ and $y_1, \ldots, y_{j-1}$ and the length of an LCS for $x_1, \ldots, x_{i-1}$ and $y_1, \ldots, y_j$.

If executed directly, such straightforward programs may solve common subproblems repeatedly and take exponential time. For example, $lcs(i, j)$ may call $lcs(i, j - 1)$ and $lcs(i - 1, j)$, where the former may call $lcs(i, j - 2)$ and $lcs(i - 1, j - 1)$, and the latter may call $lcs(i - 1, j - 1)$ and $lcs(i - 2, j)$, so $lcs(i - 1, j - 1)$ is called repeatedly; the overall computation may blow up exponentially and take $O(2^{i+j})$ time. We transform such programs into efficient dynamic programming algorithms that cache and reuse appropriate values and avoid repeatedly solving common subproblems. For example, we will derive an optimized program for $lcs(i, j)$ that takes $O(i \times j)$ time and $O(\min(i, j))$ space.

Exercise 4.1 (Longest common subsequence in other ways*) For the longest common subsequence problem, think of different ways to compute the answer. The recursive function defined has actually limited the answer search space significantly. Are there other, brute-force ways to compute the answer? What are the costs of them?

4.1 Recursive functions—control abstraction

Recursive functions such as the one described for the LCS problem can be expressed straightforwardly in a language that supports function definitions that may use primitive functions, data constructions and accesses, conditions, variable bindings, and recursive function calls.

Language

A *function definition* is of the following form, where f is the name of a function, v_1 through v_k are names of variables, called *parameters*, Boolean-valued expression *bexp* constrains the values of v_1 through v_k, and expression *exp* defines the value of f using the values of v_1 through v_k and possibly using f and other functions.

> def $f(v_1, \ldots, v_k)$ where *bexp*: *exp*

To reduce clutter, we omit where *bexp* when it is irrelevant to the point under discussion. Expression *exp* may be of the kinds described in the following.

First, as before, an expression can be a constant, a variable, or recursively an arithmetic, Boolean, or comparison operation on subexpressions. It can also be any *primitive function*, that is, function on primitive types that is built in the language, applied to subexpressions.

An expression may also be a construction or access of a data structure using a constructor, tester, or selector; data structures constructed in recursive functions may be recursive, yielding recursive data structures. Specifically, a *constructor application* is of the form below, where c is the name of a constructor. It evaluates argument expressions exp_1 through exp_k and then returns a structured data that is indicated with constructor c and whose components are values of exp_1 through exp_k. For example, pair(1+2,4) is a constructor application, and it evaluates to pair(3,4). When there is no argument, $c()$ is abbreviated as c. That is, a constructor with no argument is equivalent to a constant.

> $c(exp_1, \ldots, exp_k)$

A *tester application* is of the form below, where c is a constructor. It evaluates the argument expression *exp* and then, if the value of *exp* is a structured data that is indicated with constructor c, returns true, and otherwise, returns false.

> $c?(exp)$

A *selector application* is of the form below, where c is the name of a constructor, and i is an integer. It evaluates the argument expression *exp* and then, if the value of *exp* is a structured data that is indicated with constructor c and has at least i components, returns the i-th component.

> $c.i(exp)$

For convenience, we use [] to denote a tuple constructed by our method, and use 1st, 2nd, 3rd, and so on to select the corresponding component of the tuple.

An expression may also be an array construction or array element access. An *array construction* expression is as introduced in Section 2.6 and is of the form below. It first evaluates integer-valued expressions $iexp_1$ and $iexp_2$ to, say, i_1 and i_2, respectively, and then constructs and returns an array with elements indexed by integers from i_1 to i_2 and where the elements have the values of exp, evaluated with variable i bound to each integer from i_1 to i_2.

array(exp: i in $iexp_1$..$iexp_2$)

An *array element access* expression is of the form below, where $aexp$ is an array-valued expression, not just an array variable as in Section 2.1. It evaluates the array-valued expression $aexp$ and integer-valued expression $iexp$ to, say, a and i, respectively, and then returns the element of array a at index i.

$aexp[iexp]$

An expression may be a *conditional expression* of the form below. It first evaluates $bexp$ and then, if the value of $bexp$ is true, evaluates exp_1 and returns the value, and otherwise, evaluates exp_2 and returns the value.

if $bexp$ then exp_1 else exp_2

An expression may also be a *binding expression* of the form below. It first evaluates exp and then returns the value of exp_1 evaluated with variable v bound to the value of exp.

let v := exp in exp_1

In general, we allow any command to be between let and in, and any binding introduced in the command to be used in exp_1.

Finally, an expression may be a *function application*, also called a *function call*, of the form below, where f is defined by def $f(v_1,\ldots,v_k)$ where $bexp$: exp. It first evaluates argument expressions exp_1 through exp_k to, say, v_1 through v_k, respectively, and then returns the value of exp evaluated with v_1 through v_k bound to v_1 through v_k, respectively, if the value of $bexp$ with these bindings is true.

$f(exp_1,\ldots,exp_k)$

Note that the definition of a function may contain a call to the function itself, or to another function whose definition contains a call back to the first function; this cyclic call relation may also involve more than two functions. A *recursive function* is a function whose definition involves a call to itself, directly or indirectly through a chain of calls to other functions. Implementation of function calls and returns uses a stack, to push argument values when a function is called, and pop with a return value when the function returns.

In general, to easily express iterative versions of the optimized programs, we also allow function definitions of the form

def $f(v_1, \ldots, v_n)$ where *bexp*: *cmd*

where *cmd* is a command in which every flow of control ends with a return *command* of the form

return *exp*

Note that iteration can be expressed using *tail recursion*, which is a recursion that performs no computation after the recursive call returns and thus may be implemented by copying the argument values and then jumping to the body of the called function without pushing on the stack, eliminating the need for stack space. While specifications of some programming languages require this implementation for tail calls, other languages consider this a compiler optimization. We use loops for iteration because they are more straightforward and more common.

For convenience, we allow global variables to be implicit parameters to functions; these variables are always bound to the same values from the input because functions do not update global variables.

For the longest common subsequence problem, the recursive function can be written in our language as follows, where the arrays x and y, for the two given sequences, are implicit parameters to the function:

```
def lcs(i,j) where i>=0, j>=0:
  if i=0 or j=0 then 0
  else if x[i]=y[j] then lcs(i-1,j-1)+1
  else max(lcs(i,j-1), lcs(i-1,j))
```

Cost model

We use an asymptotic model for measuring time complexity. We assume that primitive functions take constant time. Thus, only function applications that involve recursive functions could be asymptotically expensive. So we consider only values of function applications as candidates for caching and reuse in incremental computation. The cost of a recursive function in terms of running time is bounded by the number of times it recurses multiplied by the maximum time of a single call to the function excluding recursive calls to the function. The cost in terms of space is bounded by the sum of the stack space and the space for constructed data, where the former is proportional to the maximum depth of recursive calls, and the latter is proportional to the maximum size of construct data that is reachable from the stack.

Exercise 4.2 (Edit distance*) The *edit distance* between two strings is the minimum number of edits needed to transform one string into another, where the allowed edit operations are insertion, deletion, or substitution of a single character. Write a straightforward recursive function definition that computes the edit distance. Give an upper bound for its time complexity if computed straightforwardly.

Exercise 4.3 (Binomial coefficient) The *binomial coefficient* $bin(n, k)$, for $0 \leq k \leq n$, is the number of k-element subsets of an n-element set and can be computed by the following straightforward recursive function definition:

```
def bin(n,k) where k>=0, k<=n:
  if k=0 or k=n then 1
  else bin(n-1,k-1) + bin(n-1,k)
```

Give an upper bound for its time complexity if computed straightforwardly.

4.2 Iterate: determine minimum increments, transform recursion into iteration

The core of Step Iterate for recursive functions is to determine an appropriate increment to perform repeated incremental computation. We will see here that it is extremely easy to determine such an increment, but it is deceiving to think that it is indeed that simple. The method was actually the most difficult to discover. Indeed, if one took any recursive function and so easily knew how to compute it iteratively, one would have solved the well-known hard problem of transforming recursion to iteration, but too easily to believe. So we must motivate and justify the deceivingly simple and easy solution.

Determining appropriate increment

The problem is to determine how computations should proceed. We know that efficient computation proceeds by processing data in an incremental fashion. The critical question is: what is the appropriate input increment for a recursively defined function?

For example, the famous Fibonacci function is defined as follows, as seen in Section 3.7:

```
def fib(n) where n>=0:
  if n=0 then 0
  else if n=1 then 1
  else fib(n-1) + fib(n-2)
```

An efficient way to compute fib(n) is to compute fib(i) for $i = 0, 1, 2, \ldots, n$, that is, at the increment of 1. Why is the increment of 1 used? Why not 2, or 3, or some parameter k, or -1?

For another example, the well-known *binomial coefficient* function is defined as follows, as seen in Exercise 4.3:

```
def bin(n,k) where k>=0, k<=n:
  if k=0 or k=n then 1
  else bin(n-1,k-1) + bin(n-1,k)
```

An efficient way to compute bin(n,k) is to compute bin(i,k) for i = k, k+1, ...,
n, that is, at the increment of 1 for the first argument, and for each i, compute
bin(i,k) by computing bin(i,j) for j = 0, 1, ..., k, that is, at the increment of 1 for
the second argument. Why is it appropriate to consider the increment of 1 to the
first argument first? Why not the second argument first, or both arguments at the
same time, or an increment of 2 or more?

In general, a computation may proceed incrementally in multiple ways, depending on the operations involved. There is no general method for identifying all
possible increments or the best ones. However, we have found an extremely easy
method that can systematically determine a general class of them: simply let the
increment be a minimum change from arguments of recursive calls to parameters
of the defining function. The rationale is that minimizing change allows maximiz-
ing reuse in incremental computation, the essence of our overall approach.

Precisely, to determine how a recursive function f can be computed incrementally, we proceed in three steps:

1. We identify all possible recursive calls to f. For example, in the definition of
   fib(n), recursive calls to fib are fib(n-1) and fib(n-2); in the definition of
   bin(n,k), recursive calls to bin are bin(n-1,k-1) and bin(n-1,k); in the definition of lcs(i,j), recursive calls to lcs are lcs(i-1,j-1), lcs(i,j-1), and
   lcs(i-1,j).

2. Among arguments of recursive calls to f, we identify one that corresponds to
   a minimum change from the parameters of f. The amount of change is measured using a partial order: a change involving fewer parameters is smaller; a
   difference in one parameter with smaller magnitude is smaller; other differences are incomparable. For example, for fib(n), the minimum one is n-1; for
   bin(n,k), it is [n-1,k]; for lcs(i,j), it can be either [i,j-1] or [i-1,j]. This
   gives a *decrement operation*.

3. We take the opposite of a decrement to yield a corresponding increment operation. We use $next(x)$ to denote the resulting increment operation on x.
   For example, for fib(n), the opposite of the minimum decrement is n+1, that
   is, $next(n) = $n+1; for bin(n,k), it is [n+1,k], that is, $next(n,k) = $[n+1,k]; for
   lcs(i,j), it is [i,j+1] or [i+1,j], that is, $next(i,j) = $[i,j+1] or $next(i,j) = $
   [i+1,j].

When multiple minimum increments exist for a function, such as for lcs, any of
them may be used. We call such an increment a *minimum increment*. For example,
for lcs, we will use $next(i,j) = $[i+1,j]; everything will be symmetric if we use
the other one.

This method for determining increment operations provides an answer to the questions about fib and bin posed earlier in this section. Determining input increments in general is theoretically hard, because these increments correspond to well-founded orderings in domain theory and steps for induction in proof theory. Yet, the above method is simple and powerful, albeit a heuristic. It has been used easily and successfully on all the problems we encountered in standard algorithm textbooks and in the program optimization literature.

Forming optimized program

After determining a minimum increment operation *next* for a function f, we can form an optimized program that performs repeated incremental computation at the increment of *next*. Incremental computation may require caching, using, and incrementally maintaining additional values, as will be discussed in Step Incrementalize in Section 4.3, but regardless of how those are done, we can form an optimize program as follows.

- Let fExt be a function that extends f to compute and return appropriate additional values for incremental computation, and let *orig* be a function that projects out the value of $f(x)$ from the value of fExt(x). We have

$$f(x) = orig(f\text{Ext}(x)).$$

- Let fExt' be a function that incrementally maintains the appropriate values after an increment by *next*, that is, fExt' computes fExt$(next(x))$ efficiently using x and the result rExt of fExt(x). We have

$$\text{if rExt} = f\text{Ext}(x), \text{ then } f\text{Ext'}(x,\text{rExt}) = f\text{Ext}(next(x)).$$

- Let fExt0 be a function that is fExt specialized for the base-case condition $base\_cond$ and initial argument $init\_arg$. We have

$$\text{if } base\_cond(x) \text{ or } x = init\_arg, \text{ then } f\text{Ext0}(x) = f\text{Ext}(x).$$

The *base-case condition* is the condition on the argument under which the function is not called recursively. The *initial argument* is the first argument always encountered that satisfies a condition in the function when applying the decrement operation one or more times to any input not satisfying the base-case condition.

With these three functions, whose definitions will be derived in Step Incrementalize in Section 4.3, we form an optimized program fExtOpt, of fExt, that calls fExt0 under the base-case condition and calls fExt' repeatedly at each increment by *next*. The definition of fExtOpt can be either recursive or iterative, as described below. The construction of fExtOpt succeeds if the needed functions fExt0 and fExt' can be constructed and, for the iterative version, the needed initial argument can also be constructed.

- The recursive definition of fExt0pt is as follows, where $prev(x)$ is the decrement operation that reverses the increment operation $next(x)$; fExtOpt computes the base-case result using fExt0 and computes other results by recursively calling itself and then computing incrementally using the incremental version fExt':

```
def fExtOpt(x):
    if base_cond(x) then fExt0(x)          -- base case
    else let rExt := fExtOpt(prev(x)) in   -- recursion
        fExt'(prev(x),rExt)                -- incremental computation
```

- The iterative definition of fExtOpt is as follows, where x_1 is a local variable; fExtOpt returns the base-case result using fExt0 if the base-case condition holds, and otherwise starts at $init\_arg$ and its result using fExt0 and iteratively takes an increment $next$ and calls fExt' until the input x is reached:

```
def fExtOpt(x):
    if base_cond(x): return fExt0(x)              -- base case
    x₁ := init_arg; rExt := fExt0(x₁)             -- initialization
    while x₁ != x:                                -- iteration
        x₁ := next(x₁); rExt := fExt'(prev(x₁),rExt) -- incremental comp
    return rExt
```

Note that when x is a tuple of parameters, assignments to x_1 need to update only the values of the parameters that are incremented.

In the base case, to simplify code, any part of the base-case condition that is satisfied by the initial argument can be removed, because an input satisfying that part of the base-case condition will cause the while loop to be skipped and the corresponding base-case result to be returned anyway.

In the while loop, the loop body can instead be the following; the displayed form above has the same form of call to fExt' as in the recursive definition, for familiarity.

```
rExt := fExt'(x₁,rExt);  x₁ := next(x₁)
```

Finally, we define an optimized program $f$opt, of f, that retrieves the value of $f(x)$ from the value of fExtOpt(x):

```
def fOpt(x): orig(fExtOpt(x))
```

In general, fExt' might still contain repeated recursive calls to common subproblems; it can then be optimized by applying the III method again.

The time and space complexities of an optimized program that uses an incremental program are usually easy to analyze. For time complexity, computations that proceed in an incremental fashion usually contribute linear factors independently. For space complexity, the size of the cached values contributes directly to the space consumption.

- The time complexity of fExtOpt is the number of repetitions multiplied by the time complexity of the incremental version fExt'. The time complexity of fExt0 is smaller. Retrieval using *orig* takes constant time.

- The space complexity of fExtOpt is the size of the data structures used and built by fExt', plus, for the recursive version, the depth of the recursion to account for the size of the stack.

The iterative version eliminates not only the stack space but also the overhead of allocating and deallocating the stack.

For the LCS example, Step Incrementalize in Section 4.3 will construct lcsExt and its incremental version lcsExt' to return a tuple where the value of lcs is in the first component, and construct a function lcsExt0(i,j) for the base-case condition i=0 or j=0. We will have *orig*(lcsExtOpt(i,j)) = 1st(lcsExtOpt(i,j)) and lcsExt0(i,j) = [0], which can be simply expanded. So we form the following recursive optimized program:

```
def lcsOpt(i,j): 1st(lcsExtOpt(i,j))

def lcsExtOpt(i,j):
  if i=0 or j=0 then [0]                    -- base case
  else let rExt := lcsExtOpt(i-1,j) in      -- recursion
       lcsExt'(i-1,j,rExt)                  -- incremental computation
```

and the following iterative optimized program:

```
def lcsOpt(i,j): 1st(lcsExtOpt(i,j))

def lcsExtOpt(i,j):
  if j=0: return [0]                              -- base case, i=0 is removed
  i1 := 0; rExt := [0]                            -- initialization
  while i1 != i:                                  -- iteration
    i1 := i1+1; rExt := lcsExt'(i1-1,j,rExt)      -- incremental computation
  return rExt
```

In the base case of the iterative optimized program, condition i=0 is removed because an input satisfying i = 0 will cause the while loop to be skipped and the corresponding base-case result to be returned anyway.

Both versions of lcsExtOpt call lcsExt' a total of i times. Both use an auxiliary array rExt of size j, as used and built by lcsExt'; the recursive version also uses a stack space of size $O(i)$. We will see in Step Incrementalize in Section 4.3 that lcsExt'(i,j,rExt) takes $O(j)$ time and uses and builds a structure of size $O(j)$. So the total time complexity of the optimized program is $O(i \times j)$, and the space complexity is $O(i + j)$ for the recursive version and $O(j)$ for the iterative version.

If we use *next*(i,j) = [i,j+1] instead of *next*(i,j) = [i+1,j], then the result is exactly symmetric. In particular, the total time complexity of the optimized program is still $O(i \times j)$, and the space complexity is still $O(i + j)$ for the recursive version but is $O(i)$ instead of $O(j)$ for the iterative version. So depending on which one of i and j is smaller, we may choose to increment over the other one in an iterative optimized program to lead to the smaller space usage of $O(\min(i,j))$.

Note that both the iterative and recursive versions need only linear space by reusing space after computation on each increment. This significantly improves over the $O(i \times j)$ space that is often used but not needed.

Relationship with integration by differentiation

We have seen in Chapter 2 that incrementalization corresponds to differentiation in calculus, and in Chapter 3 that incrementalizing subcomputations following the chain of dependencies corresponds to using the chain rule in differentiation. Further correspondence between incrementalization and differentiation becomes clear when we consider minimizing input increment by Step Iterate in order to succeed in incrementalization by Step Incrementalize. Minimizing input increment helps increase continuity. More importantly, the overall optimized program computes iteratively after each input increment and uses the incrementalized computation in each iteration. This iterative computation with incrementalized computation in each iteration corresponds exactly to integration by differentiation in calculus.

Exercise 4.4 (Minimum increment for edit distance) Determine a minimum increment for your recursive function definition for computing edit distance for Exercise 4.2.

Exercise 4.5 (Another minimum increment for binomial coefficient*) For the binomial coefficient problem, what is another possible increment even if our simple method for finding a minimum increment does not find it?

4.3 Incrementalize: derive incremental functions, achieve dynamic programming

Given a function f and an input increment function *next*, Step Incrementalize constructs two functions, fExt and fExt', where fExt extends f to compute appropriate additional values, if needed, for efficient incremental computation on incremented input, and fExt' incrementally maintains the values computed by fExt under the input increment. This step also constructs fExt0 to compute the results of fExt for the base-case condition and initial argument.

Determining appropriate values to maintain

First, we determine additional values that need to be computed and cached for f for efficient computation on repeatedly incremented input:

> We identify, in the computation of f on the incremented input $next(x)$, all possible subcomputations, that is, function calls, whose values are needed but are not already in the return value of f on the un-incremented input x.

These are the additional values that should be computed together with f, if not already computed as intermediate results in f, and be stored together with the return value of f. This allows their values to be used in the computation on the incremented input, and in the maintenance of these values on the incremented input.

For the LCS example, the computation of lcs on the incremented input [i+1,j], after expanding the definition of lcs, on page 87, and simplifying i+1-1 to i, is

```
lcs(i+1,j) = if i+1=0 or j=0 then 0
             else if x[i+1]=y[j] then lcs(i,j-1)+1
             else max(lcs(i+1,j-1), lcs(i,j))
```

This computation needs the values of three function calls: lcs(i,j-1) in the second branch, and lcs(i+1,j-1) and lcs(i,j) in the third branch.

- The value of lcs(i,j) is just the return value of lcs on un-incremented input.

- The value of lcs(i,j-1) is computed as an intermediate value in the third branch of lcs(i,j), but it may be needed in incremental computation regardless of whether x[i]=y[j] holds in lcs(i,j).

- The value of lcs(i+1,j-1) can be, recursively, computed incrementally using the value of lcs(i,j-1), just as we compute the value of lcs(i+1,j) incrementally using the value of lcs(i,j).

Therefore, we need to extend lcs(i,j) to compute and return also the value of lcs(i,j-1) regardless of whether x[i]=y[j] holds, as required by the second item above, and extend recursively for lcs(i,j-1), as required by the third item above.

Next, we extend f to fExt that computes and returns the determined additional values together with the original return value of f. There are two cases:

1. Often, the number of possible additional values is a constant for each call to f. This is often the case because there is a constant number of function call expressions in the expanded computation of $f(next(x))$, such as three in lcs(i+1,j), and in each such expression, the arguments of the function call are often uniquely determined by the value of x.

   In this case, we create a tuple for the return value of fExt, where the original value of f is put in the first component of the tuple, and each additional value to be cached is put in an additional component. When additional values are cached recursively for recursive calls, such as for lcs(i,j-1) in lcs(i,j), the tuples constructed during executions are nested recursively, forming tree-like structures. Every use of an original value retrieves the value from the first component.

2. Other times, the number of possible additional values is not a constant for each call to f. This happens when an argument of a function call in the ex-

panded $f(next(x))$ may have a range of possible values because it depends on global variables whose values are independent of the value of x. For example, if x[i] was in an argument of a call in the expanded lcs(i+1,j), then the argument may have a range of possible values because it would depend on the global variable x whose value is independent of the value of i.

In this case, we first determine the range of possible values of the argument, by simplifying the expression for the argument under the constraints obtained from the function definition. We then extend f to fExt, which computes and caches all possibly needed values, including the original value of f, in a map, mapping each possible value to the result of the function. The value of f is easily retrieved from the map.

For the LCS example, the additional values to cache are for lcs(i,j-1) in lcs(i,j) recursively, so we return a pair where the original return value is in the first component, and the recursively cached additional values is in the second component:

```
def lcsExt(i,j) where i>=0, j>=0:
    if i=0 or j=0 then [0]                       -- return [0] instead of 0
    else let v := lcsExt(i,j-1) in               -- bind additional value
        if x[i]=y[j] then [lcs(i-1,j-1)+1, v]  || return pair of orig value
        else [max(1st(v),lcs(i-1,j)), v]       || and additional value
```

The original return value of lcs(i,j) can be retrieved from the value of lcsExt(i,j), as 1st(lcsExt(i,j)).

Note that, among the additional values identified for caching, those that are not computed as intermediate results in f are auxiliary values. Computing auxiliary values together with f incurs extra computations not in the computation of f. Thus, in general, explicit time and space analysis is needed to determine whether it is worthwhile. However, because these values are needed in the computation on the incremented input, the rationale is that the cost could be amortized, and saving and using them to make computations incremental could yield overall large speedup.

Using and maintaining cached values

Let fExt be the program that extends f to compute and return appropriate additional values for caching. Let $orig$ be the function that projects out the value of $f(x)$ from the value of fExt(x).

We now transform the extended program fExt on the incremented input $next(x)$, to use and maintain the cached result rExt of fExt on the un-incremented input x. This has three steps and yields an incremental extended program fExt'$(x,$rExt$)$.

1. Introduce function fExt'$(x,$rExt$)$ to compute fExt$(next(x))$, by setting up

$$f\text{Ext}'(x,\text{rExt}) = f\text{Ext}(next(x)), \text{ where rExt} = f\text{Ext}(x)$$

2. Expand $f\text{Ext}(next(x))$ by definition of $f\text{Ext}$, and simplify operations in the expanded expression that use $next(x)$.

3. Replace function calls in the simplified expression with retrievals of their values from the result rExt of $f\text{Ext}(x)$, or with recursive calls to the incremental function $f\text{Ext}'$.

The retrievals are based on equalities and exploit both data structures and control structures: the result of a function call may equal a part of a cached result in a data structure, and an equality may hold under a condition for a branch.

For the LCS example, we use and maintain the cached values in three steps as follows. In step 1, we introduce lcsExt'(i,j,rExt) to compute lcsExt(i+1,j), by setting up

$$\text{lcsExt'(i,j,rExt)} = \text{lcsExt(i+1,j), where rExt} = \text{lcsExt(i,j)}$$

In step 2, we expand lcsExt(i+1,j) based on the definition of lcsExt, simplify i+1-1 to i in the expanded expression, and remove the condition i+1=0 using the given constraint i>=0 from the definition of lcsExt:

```
lcsExt(i+1,j)
= if i+1=0 or j=0 then [0]                    || expanded by
    else let v := lcsExt(i+1,j-1) in          || definition,
        if x[i+1]=y[j] then [lcs(i,j-1)+1, v] || simplified
        else [max(1st(v),lcs(i,j)), v]        || i+1-1 to i

= if j=0 then [0]                    -- removed i+1=0 using i>=0
    else let v := lcsExt(i+1,j-1) in
        if x[i+1]=y[j] then [lcs(i,j-1)+1, v]
        else [max(1st(v),lcs(i,j)), v]
```

In step 3, we replace the three function calls lcsExt(i+1,j-1), lcs(i,j-1), and lcs(i,j) based on the following three equalities:

- by definition of lcsExt, we have lcs(i,j) = 1st(lcsExt(i,j)),

- by definition of lcsExt again, we have lcs(i,j-1) = 1st(lcsExt(i,j-1)), and

- by matching lcsExt(i+1,j-1) against lcsExt(i+1,j), and using the equation lcsExt(i+1,j) = lcsExt'(i,j,rExt), where rExt = lcsExt(i,j), from step 1, we have lcsExt(i+1,j-1) = lcsExt'(i,j-1,lcsExt(i,j-1)).

Obviously the value of lcsExt(i,j) used in the first equality can be retrieved from rExt, because lcsExt(i,j) = rExt. Now consider lcsExt(i,j-1) used in the second and third equalities; note that the uses are for a branch where j≠0. By definition of lcsExt, we know that lcsExt(i,j-1) = [0] if i = 0, and lcsExt(i,j-1) = 2nd(rExt) if i≠0 and j≠0. Thus we have

$$\text{lcsExt(i,j-1)} = \text{(if i=0 then [0] else 2nd(rExt))}$$

Because this value is used in two places, we hold it in a variable, rExt1. We obtain the following incremental function, where the underlines indicate replacements:

```
def lcsExt'(i,j,rExt):
  if j=0 then [0]
  else let rExt1 := (if i=0 then [0] else 2nd(rExt)) in
       let v := lcsExt'(i,j-1,rExt1) in           -- recursive call
       if x[i+1]=y[j] then [1st(rExt1)+1, v]
       else [max(1st(v),1st(rExt)), v]
```

It is easy to see that `lcsExt'(i,j,rExt)` takes $O(j)$ time and uses and builds a linear recursive structure of size $O(j)$, because the second argument is decremented by 1 in the recursive call until it is 0, and each call is performed by constant-time operations and uses and constructs one or two elements in a tuple structure.

Constructing results for base-case condition and initial argument

To construct the results of the extended function fExt for the base-case condition and initial argument, we expand fExt(x) by definition and simplify the expanded expression using the base-case condition and initial argument, yielding fExt0 specialized for the base-case condition and initial argument, respectively.

For the LCS example, expanding `lcsExt(i,j)` by definition, and simplifying under the base-case condition `i=0` or `j=0` and initial argument satisfying $i = 0$, respectively, we have `lcsExt(i,j)` $=$ `[0]` in both cases. Thus we obtain

```
def lcsExt0(i,j): [0]
```

The initial argument satisfies $i = 0$ because the condition `i=0` is always encountered when applying the decrement operation $prev(i,j) = $`[i-1,j]` repeatedly to the input; so we can construct the initial argument by setting `i` to `0`.

The definition of fExt0 is almost always extremely simple and can be simply expanded to replace calls to fExt0.

Exercise 4.6 (Incrementalizing edit distance) Derive an incremental version of the edit distance function you defined for Exercise 4.2 under the minimum increment you determined for Exercise 4.4.

Exercise 4.7 (Incrementalizing binomial coefficient*) Derive an incremental version of the binomial coefficient function under the minimum increment discussed in Section 4.2.

4.4 Implement: use linked and indexed data structures

Step Implement uses linked and indexed data structures for storing all the values cached and used for incremental computation. It is easy to see the following two simple ideas.

1. We can implement recursively constructed tree-like structures using linked data structures, and implement maps using indexed data structures, ensuring

that each data construction and retrieval operation takes worst-case constant time.

2. In the trivial case where there are only a constant number of primitive values to be cashed, each value can be held in a separate variable, avoiding the constant cost factor of manipulating any data structures.

This simplicity helps show that, for efficient implementations of recursive functions, Step Iterate and Step Incrementalize are essential and more sophisticated, while Step Implement is straightforward.

Using linked data structures

Recursively constructed tree structures are simply constructed data or tuples nested recursively. Each constructed data or tuple corresponds to a record. If a constructed data or tuple t_1 has another constructed data or tuple t_2 nested inside, then the record for t_1 has a field that points to the record for t_2. These records, with pointers for nested records, form a linked data structure.

For the LCS example, only recursively constructed tuples are used for incremental computation. They correspond to linked data structures straightforwardly as just described, so we do not display them. The final optimized program is the definition of lcsOpt and recursive or iterative definition of lcsExtOpt obtained in Section 4.2 plus the definition of lcsExt' obtained in Section 4.3. The time and space complexity is as analyzed near the end of Section 4.2.

Using indexed data structures

A map that maps possible values of the arguments of a function to the corresponding results of the function is a flat structure. It is implemented using an array by representing possible values of arguments using integers that pack as the smallest integer indices. This forms an indexed data structure. The 0-1 knapsack problem in Section 4.5 will show the use of indexed data structures.

Exercise 4.8 (Optimized edit distance) For the edit distance problem in Exercise 4.2, form the final optimized program using the minimum increment you determined for Exercise 4.4 and the incremental version you derived for Exercise 4.6.

Exercise 4.9 (Optimized binomial coefficient) For the binomial coefficient problem, form the final optimized program using the minimum increment discussed in Section 4.2 and the incremental version you derived for Exercise 4.7.

4.5 Example: combinatorial optimization

We consider a well-known combinatorial optimization problem, the 0-1 knapsack problem, expressed using recursive functions. The derivation illustrates the use of maps and indexed data structures, as opposed to nested tuples and linked data structures we have seen for the longest common subsequence problem.

0-1 knapsack

Given n items, where the i-th item has value v_i and positive integer weight w_i, and given a weight limit *weight*, the *0-1 knapsack* problem is to find the maximum total value for a subset of these items whose total weight does not exceed the given limit. This can be computed as $knap(n, weight)$, where $knap(i, u)$, the maximum value for a subset of the items 1 through i with a total weight not exceeding u, is defined recursively as, for $i \geq 0$, $u \geq 0$, and $w_i > 0$,

$$knap(i, u) = \begin{cases} 0 & \text{if } i = 0 \text{ or } u = 0 \\ knap(i-1, u) & \text{if } i > 0, u > 0, \text{ and } w_i > u \\ \max(v_i + knap(i-1, u-w_i), & \text{otherwise} \\ \quad knap(i-1, u)) \end{cases}$$

If $i = 0$ or $u = 0$, that is, either no item is left or no weight allowance is left, then no item can be taken, and the resulting value is 0. Otherwise, if $w_i > u$, that is, the i-th item is heavier than u, then it cannot be taken, and items 1 through $i-1$ are considered with the same weight limit u. Otherwise, the i-th item may be taken or not, so the maximum value from the two cases is returned; in the former case, items 1 through $i-1$ are considered with weight limit reduced by w_i, and the resulting value is increased by v_i; in the latter case, items 1 through $i-1$ are considered with the same weight limit u.

The function $knap$ can be written straightforwardly in our language as follows, where the arrays v and w, of values and weights, respectively, are implicit parameters:

```
def knap(i,u) where i>=0, u>=0, all i in 1..n | w[i]>0:
  if i=0 or u=0 then 0
  else if w[i]>u then knap(i-1,u)
  else max(v[i]+knap(i-1,u-w[i]), knap(i-1,u))
```

To understand the efficiency of this function, suppose each item is of weight 1. Then knap(i,u) calls knap(i-1,u-1) and knap(i-1,u), where the former calls knap(i-2,u-2) and knap(i-2,u-1), the latter calls knap(i-2,u-1) and knap(i-2,u), and everything repeats until i or u becomes 0. This grows exponentially and may take $O(2^i)$ time. We transform this program into an efficient dynamic programming algorithm that performs appropriate caching and takes $O(i \times u)$ time.

Iterate

For function `knap(i,u)`, recursive calls to `knap` are `knap(i-1,u)`, with two occurrences, and `knap(i-1,u-w[i])`. Among them, the tuple of arguments that changes minimally from the parameters `[i,u]` is `[i-1,u]`. Taking the opposite of this decrement, we obtain `[i+1,u]`, that is, $next(i,u) = [i+1,u]$.

Step Incrementalize will construct `knapExt` and its incremental version `knapExt'` to return an array where the value of `knap` is the first element, and construct `knapExt0(i,u)` for the base-case condition `i=0` or `u=0` and initial argument satisfying `i = 0`. We will then have $orig(\text{knapExtOpt}(i,u)) = \text{knapExtOpt}(i,u)[u]$ and `knapExt0(i,u) = array(0: u1 in 0..u)`, which can be simply expanded. So we form the following recursive optimized program:

```
def knapOpt(i,u): knapExtOpt(i,u)[u]

def knapExtOpt(i,u):
   if i=0 or u=0 then array(0: u1 in 0..u)   -- base case
   else let rExt := knapExtOpt(i-1,u) in      -- recursion
       knapExt'(i-1,u,rExt)                    -- incremental computation
```

and the following iterative optimized program:

```
def knapOpt(i,u): knapExtOpt(i,u)[u]

def knapExtOpt(i,u):
   if u=0: return array(0: u1 in 0..u)          -- base case, i=0 is removed
   i1 := 0; rExt := array(0: u1 in 0..u)        -- initialization
   while i1 != i:                               -- iteration
     i1 := i1+1; rExt:= knapExt'(i1-1,u,rExt)   -- incremental computation
   return rExt
```

In the base case of the iterative optimized program, condition `i=0` is removed because an input satisfying `i = 0` will cause the `while` loop to be skipped and the corresponding base-case result to be returned anyway.

Both versions of `knapExtOpt` call `knapExt'` a total of i times. Both use an auxiliary array of size `rExt`, as used and built by `knapExt'`; the recursive version uses also $O(i)$ stack space. We will see in Step Incrementalize that `knapExt'(i,u,rExt)` takes $O(u)$ time and uses and builds a structure of size $O(u)$. So the total time complexity of the optimized program is $O(i \times u)$, and the space complexity is $O(i + u)$ for the recursive version and $O(u)$ for the iterative version.

Note that the time complexity factor u is linear in the numeric value of u, but exponential in the size of u, because the size of u is $\log u$. The resulting algorithm is said to run in *pseudo-polynomial time*, meaning that the running time is polynomial in the numeric value of the input. The 0-1 knapsack problem is well known to be NP-complete, so it is so far not known to be computable in polynomial time in the size of the input.

Incrementalize

To derive an incremental version of knap under the increment $next(i,u) = [i+1,u]$, we first consider the computation of knap on the incremented input [i+1,u]. We expand knap(i+1,u) by definition, simplify i+1-1 to i, and remove condition i+1=0 using the given constraint i>=0, yielding

```
knap(i+1,u) = if u=0 then 0
              else if w[i+1]>u then knap(i,u)
              else max(v[i+1]+knap(i,u-w[i+1]), knap(i,u))
```

This needs knap(i,u) in the second branch and needs knap(i,u-w[i+1]) and knap(i,u) in the third branch. The value of knap(i,u) is just the return value of knap on the un-incremented input. The value of knap(i,u-w[i+1]), however, is not computed by knap on the un-incremented input, and thus should be computed and cached together with knap(i,u).

Consider knap(i,u-w[i+1]). Its second argument, u-w[i+1], may have a range of possible values, because it depends on the global variable w whose value is independent of i and u. We consider constraints on u-w[i+1] based on the definition of the function.

1. w[i+1]>0 holds by given constraints on the arguments of knap.

2. knap(i,u-w[i+1]) is computed in knap(i+1,u) in the third branch, where w[i+1]>u is false.

From these two constraints, we know that w[i+1]>0 and w[i+1]<=u, that is, w[i+1] may range from 1 to u, and thus u-w[i+1] may range from 0 to u-1. Therefore, we may only need the value of knap(i,u-w[i+1]) for any integer value of u-w[i+1] from 0 to u-1. That is, we may only need knap(i,u1) for u1=0, ..., u-1. We also need the original return value knap(i,u). So we cache knap(i,u1) for u1=0, ..., u in an auxiliary map, represented straightforwardly using an array, yielding

```
def knapExt(i,u): array(knap(i,u1): u1 in 0..u)
```

The original return value of knap(i,u) can be retrieved from the value of knapExt(i,u) as knapExt(i,u)[u].

We use and maintain the cached values in three steps as follows. In step 1, we introduce knapExt'(i,u,rExt) to compute knapExt(i+1,u), by setting up

```
knapExt'(i,u,rExt) = knapExt(i+1,u), where rExt = knapExt(i,u)
```

In step 2, we expand knapExt(i+1,j) based on the definition of knapExt, further expand the resulting expression based on the definition of knap, simplify i+1-1 to i in the expanded expression, and remove condition i+1=0 using the given constraint i>=0, yielding

```
knapExt(i+1,u) = array(knap(i+1,u1): u1 in 0..u)

              = array(if u1=0 then 0
                      else if w[i+1]>u1 then knap(i,u1)
                      else max(v[i+1]+knap(i,u1-w[i+1]), knap(i,u1))
                      : u1 in 0..u)
```

In step 3, we replace function calls knap(i,u1) and knap(i,u1-w[i+1]) with retrievals rExt[u1] and rExt[u1-w[i+1]], respectively, from the result rExt of knapExt(i,u), yielding the following, where the underlines indicate replacements:

```
def knapExt'(i,u,rExt):
  array(if u1=0 then 0
        else if w[i+1]>u1 then rExt[u1]
        else max(v[i+1]+rExt[u1-w[i+1]], rExt[u1])
        : u1 in 0..u)
```

It is easy to see that knapExt'(i,u,rExt) takes $O(u)$ time, and that it uses an array of size $O(u)$ to build a new array of size $O(u)$, because it computes each of the $u + 1$ elements of the new array, and each other operation takes constant time.

To construct the result for the base-case condition i=0 or u=0, we expand knapExt(i,u) by definition of knapExt under i=0 or u=0:

$$knapExt(i,u) = array(knap(i,u1): u1 \text{ in } 0..u)$$

and then expand knap(i,u1) in it by definition of knap under i=0 or u1=0, where u1=0 is obtained from u=0. This simplifies knap(i,u1) to 0, so we have

$$knapExt(i,u) = array(0: u1 \text{ in } 0..u)$$

To construct the result for the initial argument satisfying i = 0, we expand knapExt(i,u) as for the base case above, and then expand knap(i,u1) and simplify it to 0 using i = 0, yielding the same equation as above. Thus, we obtain

```
def knapExt0(i,u): array(0: u1 in 0..u)
```

Implement

The index of the auxiliary map ranges from 0 to u, and thus nothing needs to be done in languages where array indices start at 0. The final optimized program is the definition of knapOpt and recursive or iterative definition of knapExtOpt from Step Iterate plus the definition of knapExt' from Step Incrementalize. The time and space complexity is as analyzed at the end of Step Iterate.

Exercise 4.10 (Single-source shortest path) Given a graph where each edge has an associated weight, and given a vertex s in the graph, the *single-source shortest path* problem is to compute, for each vertex t in the graph, the minimum weight from s to t, summing the weights of edges following any path from s to t. Let n be the number of vertices in the graph. Let w_{ij} be the weight of the edge from vertex i to vertex j, and be ∞ if there is no edge from i to j. Assume that there are no negative-weight cycles. Then there is a simple recursion that computes the minimum weight from s to t as $d(s, t, n-1)$, where $d(i, j, m)$, the minimum weight of any path from i to j that contains at most m edges, is defined as, for $m \geq 0$,

$$d(i, j, 0) = \begin{cases} 0 & \text{if } i = j \\ \infty & \text{otherwise} \end{cases}$$
$$d(i, j, m) = \min_{1 \leq k \leq n}\{d(i, k, m-1) + w_{kj}\} \quad \text{for } m \geq 1$$

Write a straightforward program based on the given recursion. Note that the results computed from the above recursion can be used to check whether there are negative-weight cycles, as discussed in Exercise 4.15.

Exercise 4.11 (Minimum increment for shortest path) For the shortest path problem in the previous exercise, what is the minimum increment?

Exercise 4.12 (Additional values for shortest path) Continuing the shortest path problem in the previous exercise, what are additional values to maintain for incremental computation? Note that by definition, in the computation of $d(i, j, m+1)$, values $d(i, k, m)$ for $k = 1, \ldots, n$ are needed.

Exercise 4.13 (Incrementalizing shortest path) Continuing the shortest path problem in the previous exercise, derive an incremental version under the minimum increment you determined.

Exercise 4.14 (Optimized shortest path) Continuing the shortest path problem in the previous exercise, form the final optimized program using the minimum increment you determined and the incremental version you derived.

Exercise 4.15 (Cost analysis for shortest path) Continuing the shortest path problem in the previous exercise, what is the time complexity of the optimized program? If we strengthen the original recursive definitions to consider only k's such that $w_{kj} \neq \infty$, then in the resulting optimized program, for each j from 1 to n, only its predecessor nodes, not all n nodes, are considered. Suppose the number of edges in the graph is e, then the optimized program takes $O(ne)$ time. It is exactly the well-known Bellman-Ford algorithm except without the triangle inequality test for each edge at the end for checking whether there are negative-weight cycles.

4.6 Example: math and puzzles

We discuss four examples.

- The factorial example shows that our systematic method naturally transforms recursion to iteration without potential pitfalls of ad hoc methods.

- The Ackermann function example demonstrates that our method for identifying a minimum increment, even when the result is unexpected, leads to successful optimization, whereas ad hoc methods, even when the result appears best in some sense, fails. This example also shows repeated calls to an incremental function in the definition of the incremental function, which we have not seen in any other example.

- The Fibonacci numbers example shows the handling of two base cases, and more importantly, iterating at bigger increments than the minimum increment.

- The Tower of Hanoi example illustrates that our method can derive a linear-time algorithm that constructs a minimum linked structure from which an exponential-size solution can be read off.

Factorial

The *factorial* of a nonnegative integer n is the product of all positive integers less than or equal to n, except that the factorial of 0 is 1. Factorial is important for counting permutations in combinatorics and is also used extensively in probability theory. The standard recursive definition for factorial is as follows:

```
def fac(n) where n>=0:
  if n=0 then 1
  else n * fac(n-1)
```

The best-known iterative program for factorial uses an additional variable, named r below, to accumulate the result of the multiplications. Note that this iterative program changes the order in which numbers are multiplied, which requires knowing that multiplication is associative, that is, $a*(b*c) = (a*b)*c$.

```
def fac(n):
  r = 1
  while n > 0:
    r = n*r
    n = n-1
  return r
```

Does the method we described derive this program? No, it derives one that uses yet another additional variable, i, to iterate from 0 to n, and keeps the same order of multiplying the numbers without using associativity. The derivation is almost trivial, so we show the result directly:

```
def fac(n):
  n1 = 0; r = 1      -- initialization covering the base case
  while n1 != n:     -- iteration
    n1 = n1+1        -- next(n1)=n1+1
    r = n1*r         -- incremental version fac'(n1,r)=(n1+1)*r
  return r
```

One might expect our derived program to be slightly slower than the best-known version, because of the extra variable i and because the number of operations are basically the same. Also, one might expect that both versions are significantly faster than the original recursive program, because of the elimination of the allocation and deallocation of a linear stack.

You might be a bit surprised to learn that our derived program is actually faster than the best-known version, and much more surprised to learn that the best-known version is not only slower than our program, but also slower than the original recursive program. The reason? Factorials are big numbers. Changing the order of multiplying the numbers resulted in bigger numbers being multiplied first, and multiplying bigger numbers is more expensive than multiplying smaller numbers! It is no surprise that our derived program is indeed faster than the recursive program, because it does exactly the same multiplications as the recursion program but without using a stack.

Ackermann function

The *Ackermann function* is defined below. It is the best-known example of a function that is not primitive recursive, which implies that it grows more rapidly than any exponential, double exponential, and even any-fold iterated exponential function. It is sometimes used for benchmarking because of its extremely deep recursion.

```
def ack(i,n) where i>=0, n>=0:
  if i=0 then n+1
  else if n=0 then ack(i-1,1)
  else ack(i-1,ack(i,n-1))
```

Note that the running time of this recursive function grows even much more than the value of the function because of vastly many repeated recursive calls. Can our method derive an optimized version of Ackermann function? Yes, we can derive an optimal implementation in the sense that the running time is $O(\text{ack}(i, n))$, that is, linear in the value of the function; it is optimal because the only given operation in the function is increment by 1, and our method eliminates all repeated recursive calls.

Step Iterate considers all recursive calls to ack in the definition of ack(i,n). Even though two of them have i-1 as one of the arguments and might prompt us to iterate with the increment of $next$(i,n) = [i+1,n], we can see that the minimum increment determined using our method should be $next$(i,n)=[i,n+1], because it corresponds to the minimum decrement among arguments of all recursive calls. As it turns out, the former would quickly lead to failure in incrementalization, whereas the latter would lead to success. Step Iterate then forms the following iterative optimized program, where ackExt0 and ackExt' will be derived in Step Incrementalize:

```
def ackOpt(i,n): 1st(ackExtOpt(i,n))
```

```
def ackExtOpt(i,n):
    if i=0: return [n+1]                      -- base case
    n1 := 0; rExt := ackExt0(i,n1)            -- initialization
    while n1!=n:                              -- iteration
        n1 := n1+1; rExt := ackExt'(i,n1-1,rExt) -- incremental computation
    return rExt
```

Step Incrementalize derives `ackExt`, `ackExt'`, and `ackExt0`. First, we determine appropriate values to maintain. The main goal would be an incremental version of `ack` under the input increment operation $next(i,n) = [i,n+1]$, that is, a function `ack'(i,n,r)` that computes `ack(i,n+1)` incrementally using the previous result r of `ack(i,n)`. We have, by definition,

```
ack(i,n+1)  =  if i=0 then n+2               || expanded by definition,
               else if n+1=0 then ack(i-1,1) || simplified n+1+1 to n+2,
               else ack(i-1,ack(i,n))        || and simplified n+1-1 to n

            =  if i=0 then n+2            -- removed n+1=0 branch using n>=0
               else ack(i-1,ack(i,n))
```

It has two calls to `ack` when $i \neq 0$. The call `ack(i,n)` is just `ack` on the un-incremented input, so can be replaced with the previous result. The call `ack(i-1,ack(i,n))` can be computed incrementally starting from some `ack(i-1,x)` that is computed in `ack(i,n)` when $i \neq 0$, with x being 1 if $n = 0$ and being `ack(i,n-1)` otherwise based on the definition of `ack(i,n)`; the incremental computation is by calling the incremental version `ack'` repeatedly with the second argument ranging from `(x+1)-1` to `ack(i,n)-1`, that is,

```
ack(i-1,ack(i,n))  =  let v := ack(i-1,x)
                          for k := x+1 to ack(i,n):
                              v := ack'(i-1,k-1,v)
                      in v
```

where x is

```
if n=0 then 1 else ack(i,n-1)
```

The starting value of v, being `ack(i-1,1)` if $n = 0$ or `ack(i-1,ack(i,n-1))` otherwise, is the return value of `ack(i,n)`; this leaves `ack(i,n-1)` under $n \neq 0$ as an additional value to be cached for incremental computation. The recursive call `ack'(i-1,k-1,v)` when k=x+1, being `ack'(i-1,x,v)`, needs the corresponding additional value `ack(i-1,x)` recursively for argument v, for both $n = 0$ and otherwise. Therefore, `ack(i,n)` is extended to return also the intermediate result `ack(i,n-1)` under $n \neq 0$, and return `ack(i-1,x)` recursively for both $n = 0$ and otherwise, yielding

```
def ackExt(i,n) where i>=0, n>=0:
    if i=0 then [n+1]                    -- return [n+1] instead of n+1
    else if n=0 then ackExt(i-1,1)       -- do recursively for n=0
    else let v1 := ack(i,n-1) in         -- bind intermediate result
         let v2 := ackExt(i-1,v1) in     -- do recursively for n!=0
         [1st(v2), v1, v2]               -- return orig and additional values
```

Then, we derive ackExt'(i,n,rExt) that computes ackExt(i,n+1) using the cached result rExt of ackExt(i,n):

```
ackExt(i,n+1)
= if i=0 then [n+2]                   ||
    else if n+1=0 then ackExt(i-1,1)  || expanded by definition,
    else let v1 := ack(i,n) in        || simplified n+1+1 to n+2,
    let v2 := ackExt(i-1,v1) in        || and simplified n+1-1 to n
    [1st(v2), v1, v2]                  ||

= if i=0 then [n+2]           -- removed 2nd branch using n>=0
    else                      -- expanded v1, compute v2 incrementally
        let v2 := ackExt(i-1, if n=0 then 1 else ack(i,n-1))
            for k := (if n=0 then 1 else ack(i,n-1))+1 to ack(i,n):
                v2 := ackExt'(i-1,k-1,v2)  -- call ackExt' repeatedly
        in [1st(v2), ack(i,n), v2]

= if i=0 then [n+2]
    else                            -- lift test out of 2nd argument of ackExt
        let v2 := if n=0 then ackExt(i-1,1) else ack(i-1,ack(i,n-1)))
            for k := (if n=0 then 1 else ack(i,n-1))+1 to ack(i,n):
                v2 := ackExt'(i-1,k-1,v2)
        in [1st(v2), ack(i,n), v2]
```

and after replacing calls to ackExt and ack with retrievals from rExt, we obtain the following, where the underlines indicate replacements:

```
def ackExt'(i,n,rExt) where n>1, rExt=ackExt(i,n):
    if i=0 then [n+2]
    else let v2 := if n=0 then rExt else 3rd(rExt)
            for k := (if n=0 then 1 else 2nd(rExt))+1 to 1st(rExt):
                v2 := ackExt'(i-1,k-1,v2)
        in [1st(v2), 1st(rExt), v2]
```

Finally, we construct the result of ackExt(i,n) for the base-case condition i=0:

```
def ackExt0(i,n) where i=0: [n+1]
```

which is always expanded when used, and we construct the result of ackExt(i,n) for the initial argument satisfying n = 0:

```
ackExt(i,0) = if i=0 then [1]       || expanded by definition
                else ackExt(i-1,1)  || and simplified for n=0

            = if i=0 then [1]
                else ackExt'(i-1,0,ackExt(i-1,0))  -- incremental comp
```

which, by an easy incrementalization, yields the following iterative optimized program:

```
def ackExt0(i,n) where n=0:
    i1 := 0; rExt := [1]
    while i1!=i:
        i1 := i1+1; rExt = ackExt'(i1-1,0,rExt)
    return rExt
```

Step Implement needs to do nothing. The final optimized program is the definitions of ackOpt and ackExtOpt from Step Iterate where ackExt' and ackExt0 are as defined near the end of Step Incrementalize. The time complexity is $O(\text{ack}(i, n))$ because there are no repeated calls. The space complexity is $O(i)$ for the depth of the recursive calls. Repeated recursive calls to an incremental function in the definition of the incremental function, seen as calls to ackExt' in the for loop in the definition of ackExt', is what we have not seen in any other example.

Fibonacci number

Fibonacci numbers are the sequence of numbers where each number is the sum of the preceding two numbers with the first two numbers defined to be 1, and with the 0-indexed number defined conventionally to be 0. The sequence is found in many biological settings, in nature, and is used in many analysis problems, such as financial market analysis. The standard recursive definition of the Fibonacci function is as seen in Section 4.2, copied here:

```
def fib(n) where n>=0:
  if n=0 then 0
  else if n=1 then 1
  else fib(n-1) + fib(n-2)
```

Step Iterate determines easily that the minimum increment is $next(\text{n}) = \text{n+1}$, as discussed in Section 4.2. It then forms the following iterative optimized program, where fibExt'(n,rExt) for n>=1 and fibExt0(n) for n=0 and n=1, both expanded here, will be defined in Step Incrementalize:

```
def fibOpt(n): 1st(fibExtOpt(n))

def fibExtOpt(n):
  if n=0: return [0]        -- expanded fibExt0(n) for n=0 to [0]
  n1 := 1; rExt := [1,0]    -- expanded fibExt0(n) for n=1 to [1,0]
  while n1!=n:
    n1 := n1+1; rExt := let v := 1st(rExt) in    || expanded
                        [v+2nd(rExt), v]         || fibExt'(n1-1,rExt)
  return rExt
```

Step Incrementalize derives fibExt, fibExt', and fibExt0. It is easy to see by expanding fib(n+1), below, that fib(n-1) is needed for computing fib(n+1) when n=0 is false:

```
fib(n+1)  = if n+1=0 then 0        || expanded by definition,
              else if n+1=1 then 1 || simplified n+1-1 to n, and
              else fib(n)+fib(n-1) || simplified n+1-2 to n-1

          = if n=0 then 1          || simplified tests and
              else fib(n)+fib(n-1) || removed 1st branch using n>=0
```

So Step Incrementalize obtains fibExt below:

```
def fibExt(n):
  if n=0 then [0]              -- return a singleton tuple
  else if n=1 then [1,0]      || return also fib(n-1)
  else let v := fib(n-1) in   || when n=0 is false
    [v+fib(n-2), v]           ||
```

and derives an incremental version fibExt'(n,rExt), where n>=1 and rExt=fibExt(n), to compute fibExt(n+1), as follows:

```
fibExt(n+1) = if n+1=0 then [0]            || expanded by definition,
              else if n+1=1 then [1,0]     || simplified n+1-1 to n, and
              else let v := fib(n) in      || simplified n+1-2 to n-1
                [v+fib(n-1), v]            ||

            = let v := fib(n) in  || removed two branches using n>=1
              [v+fib(n-1), v]     ||
```

yielding, after replacing calls to fib with retrievals, indicated with underlines,

```
def fibExt'(n,rExt) where n>=1, rExt=fibExt(n):
  let v := 1st(rExt) in
  [v+2nd(rExt)), v]
```

Step Incrementalize also constructs fibExt0(n) for n=1 and n=2, by definition of fibExt, to return [0] and [0,1], respectively. Finally, because fibExt0 and fibExt' are non-recursive, they are expanded in fibExtOpt, as shown under Step Iterate; fibExtOpt can in turn be expanded in fibOpt, yielding

```
def fibOpt(n):
  if n=0: return 0     -- return only the first component
  n1 := 1; rExt := [1,0]
  while n1!=n:
    n1 := n1+1; rExt := let v := 1st(rExt) in
                        [v+2nd(rExt), v]
  return 1st(rExt)     -- return only the first component
```

Step Implement replaces the pair-valued variable rExt with two variables a and b, yielding the final optimized program

```
def fibOpt(n):
  if n=0: return 0
  n1 := 1; a := 1; b :=0
  while n1!=n:
    n1 := n1+1; v := a; a := v+b; b := v
  return a
```

Note that the use of variable v cannot be avoided, because the new value of a needs the old value of b, and the new value of b needs the old value of a.

When optimization using incrementalization under a smaller increment succeeds, a bigger increment may yield better optimization. Consider the increment $next(n) = n+2$ for this example. Step Iterate forms the following iterative optimized program, where fibExp0, fibExp', and fibExp2' will be derived in Step Incrementalize:

```
def fibOpt2(n): 1st(fibExtOpt2(n))

def fibExtOpt2(n):
  if n=0: return [0]        -- expanded fibExt0(n) for n=0 to [0]
  n1 := 1; rExt := [1,0]    -- expanded fibExt0(n) for n=1 to [1,0]
  while n1!=n and n1!=n-1:  -- extra test for one step before too
    n1 := n1+2; rExt := let v := 1st(rExt)+2nd(rExt)  || expanded
                        in [v+1st(rExt)), v]          || fibExt2'
  if n1=n-1: rExt := let v := 1st(rExt) in  || if one more step needed:
                     [v+2nd(rExt), v]       || expanded fibExt'
  return rExt
```

Step Incrementalize derives `fibExt`, `fibExt'`, and `fibExt0` that are the same as before, and derives `fibExt2'` below that computes `fibExt(n+2)`:

```
def fibExt2'(n,rExt) where n>=1, rExt=fibExt(n):
let v := 1st(rExt)+2nd(rExt) in
[v+1st(rExt)), v]
```

Expanding `fibExt0`, `fibExt'`, and `fibExt2'` in `fibExtOpt2`, defined in Step Iterate, and expanding `fibExtOpt2` in turn in `fibOpt2`, also defined in Step Iterate, yields

```
def fibOpt2(n):
  if n=0: return 0     -- return only the first component
  n1 := 1; rExt := [1,0]
  while n1!=n and n1!=n-1:
    n1 := n1+2; rExt := let v := 1st(rExt)+2nd(rExt) in
                        [v+1st(rExt)), v]
  if n1=n-1: rExt := let v := 1st(rExt) in
                     [v+2nd(rExt), v]
  return 1st(rExt)      -- return only the first component
```

Step Implement replaces the pair-valued variable `rExt` with two variables `a` and `b`, yielding

```
def fibOpt2(n):
  if n=0: return 0
  n1 := 1; a := 1; b :=0
  while n1!=n and n1!=n-1:
    n1 := n1+2; b:=a+b; a:=b+a   -- simplified from v:=a+b; a:=v+a; b:=v
  if n1=n-1: a:=a+b  -- need only a; simplified from v:=a; a:=v+b; b:=v
  return a
```

Note that variable v was removed, saving two copy operations in each of the $O(n)$ iterations, and that the number of iterations is reduced by half.

Tower of Hanoi

The *Tower of Hanoi* problem computes the sequence of moves needed to move a stack of n differently sized disks, one at a time, from one peg a, initially with no larger disks on top of smaller ones, to a second peg b via a third peg c, without ever putting a larger disk on top of a smaller one. This can be solved using a simple recursion that has one move operation, two recursive calls, and two concatenation operations, as follows, where move(a,b) is a constructor application denoting moving the top disk on peg a to peg b, and :: is a primitive function denoting concatenation:

```
def hanoi(n,a,b,c) where n>=1:
  if n=1 then move(a,b)
  else hanoi(n-1,a,c,b) :: move(a,b) :: hanoi(n-1,c,b,a)
```

Computing this recursive function for n disks takes $O(2^n)$ time, because of repeated recursive calls on the same arguments. One might notice that there are at most 6 ways of calling hanoi on n disks given 3 pegs—3 ways to choose the peg that holds the disks initially combined with 2 ways to choose the peg that holds the disks at the end—and decide to compute the result of all 6 of them for each n, yielding an algorithm that takes linear time. Our method yields an algorithm that computes the result of only 3 ways of calling hanoi for each n.

Step Iterate examines recursive calls in hanoi(n,a,b,c), which have [n-1,a,c,b] and [n-1,c,b,a] as arguments. Either one can be the minimum decrement because both change the same in the first argument, and switches two of the three remaining arguments. Say the first one is taken. So $next$(n,a,b,c) = [n+1,a,c,b], with an increment to n by 1 and a swap of the last two arguments. Step Iterate then forms the following recursive optimized program, where hanoiExt0 and hanoiExt' will be derived in Step Incrementalize:

```
def hanoiOpt(n,a,b,c): 1st(hanoiExtOpt(n,a,b,c))

def hanoiExtOpt(n,a,b,c):
  if n=1 then hanoiExt0(n,a,b,c)            -- base case
  else let rExt := hanoiExtOpt(n-1,a,c,b) in -- recursion
    hanoiExt'(n,a,c,b,rExt)                  -- incremental computation
```

An iterative optimized program is also possible but not as straightforward to form because the increment operation swaps the last two arguments, and the correct initial argument depends on whether n is odd or even.

Step Incrementalize derives functions hanoiExt, hanoiExt', and hanoiExt0. The main goal is to compute hanoi(n+1,a,c,b) incrementally using the previous result of hanoi(n,a,b,c). We have, by definition,

```
hanoi(n+1,a,c,b)
= if n+1=1 then move(a,b)                          || expanded by
  else hanoi(n,a,b,c)::move(a,c) :: hanoi(n,b,c,a) || definition

= hanoi(n,a,b,c) :: move(a,c) :: hanoi(n,b,c,a)
                      -- removed 1st branch using n>=1
```

It has two calls to hanoi. The first call, hanoi(n,a,b,c), can simply be replaced with the previous result. The second call, hanoi(n,b,c,a), however, is not computed previously, so we extend hanoi(n,a,b,c) to also compute and return this auxiliary value. In a similar fashion, one can see that computing the extended function will also need hanoi(n,c,a,b), so the final extended function is

```
def hanoiExt(n,a,b,c):
    [hanoi(n,a,b,c), hanoi(n,b,c,a), hanoi(n,c,a,b)]
```

Incrementalizing this extended function yields the following incremental function that computes hanoiExt(n+1,a,c,b) using the result rExt of hanoiExt(n,a,b,c):

```
def hanoiExt'(n,a,c,b,rExt):
    [1st(rExt) :: move(a,b) :: 2nd(rExt),
     3rd(rExt) :: move(b,c) :: 1st(rExt),
     2nd(rExt) :: move(c,a) :: 3rd(rExt)]
```

Constructing the base-case result for n=1 expands hanoiExt(n,a,b,c) by definition and then expands the three calls to hanoi in it by definition, yielding the following hanoiExt0(n,a,b,c) for n=1:

```
def hanoiExt0(n,a,b,c) where n=1:
    [move(a,b), move(b,c), move(c,a)]
```

Both hanoiExt0(n,a,b,c) and hanoiExt'(n,a,c,b,rExt) contain no function calls, whereas computing hanoiExt(n+1,a,c,b) from scratch requires an exponential number of recursive calls. We can expand both in the definition of hanoiExtOpt, yielding

```
def hanoiExtOpt(n,a,b,c):
    if n=1 then [move(a,b),move(b,c),move(c,a)]
    else let rExt := hanoiExtOpt(n-1,a,c,b) in
        [1st(rExt) :: move(a,b) :: 2nd(rExt),
         3rd(rExt) :: move(b,c) :: 1st(rExt),
         2nd(rExt) :: move(c,a) :: 3rd(rExt)]
```

Step Implement maps concatenation to pointer operations over a doubly linked list structure, so each concatenation operation takes $O(1)$ time. The final optimized program is the definition of hanoiOpt from Step Iterate and the definition of hanoiExtOpt at the end of Step Incrementalize. The time complexity is $O(n)$ because hanoiExtOpt is called recursively only $O(n)$ times. The space complexity is $O(n)$ for the depth of the recursive calls. That is, the resulting linear data structure can be constructed in linear time and space. Reading off the resulting sequence of moves takes exponential time following the pointers.

Exercise 4.16 (Fibonacci under bigger increment) For the Fibonacci number problem, derive the incremental version fibExt2' of fibExt under the input change of increment by 2.

Exercise 4.17 (Iterative Tower of Hanoi*) For the Tower of Hanoi problem, form an iterative optimized program.

4.7 Need for data abstraction

Recursive functions provide high-level control abstraction for recursive computations over primitive values, such as numbers, or recursively constructed values, primarily lists and trees. However, many problems are more easily described as high-level queries over sets and maps, rather than as recursive functions over lists and trees; if written as the latter, they can be unnecessarily hard to understand and optimize.

For example, the graph reachability example, described in Chapter 3, cannot be straightforwardly written using recursive functions, whereas it can be specified as a simple `while` loop or fixed-point expression over sets. In fact, it is not even clear how to represent the set of edges using lists and trees and still be efficient, or still be clear and allow powerful optimizations.

Exercise 4.18 (Graph reachability using recursive functions*) For the graph reachability problem, write a definition of it using recursive functions and recursive data structures but not loops and sets.

Exercise 4.19 (Shortest path using aggregate operation) For the single-source shortest path problem in Exercise 4.10, did your program use aggregate operations? If not, rewrite it using aggregate operations. If yes, rewrite it without using aggregate operations.

Bibliographical notes

Recursive functions are the core of functional programming languages, and are also supported in most other common programming languages. These languages include the earliest list processing language Lisp and its dialects Common Lisp and Scheme, typed functional languages ML and its dialects SML, CAML, and OCaml, lazy functional languages Haskell and Miranda, and all the other languages mentioned in Chapters 2 and 3 except for earlier versions of FORTRAN, BASIC, and SQL.

Transformation of recursive functions has been studied extensively since at least the 1970s. Burstall and Darlington [39] used a set of transformation rules and certain strategies. Many others studied more focused strategies or principles, including goal-directed transformations by Wegbreit [315], continuation-based transformations by Wand [311], internal specialization by Scherlis [276], redundant call elimination by Cohen [63], tupling by Pettorossi [252], promotion and accumulation by Bird [30, 31], deforestation by Wadler [309], fusion by Chin [54], partial evaluation by Jones et al. [156], grammar thinning by Webber [314], and morphisms by Hu et al. [145]. Many of these are summarized in books and surveys [83, 249, 253] and used in powerful transformation systems, such as CIP [38, 21, 249] and KIDS [287, 288]. The more systematic methods among these tend to apply to more limited classes of problems.

Transforming recursion to iteration, also called recursion removal, is a well-known subject studied extensively. Previous work includes program schematology and other ways to relate recursion with iteration [250, 97, 310, 117, 92, 85, 162], theorems formulated for Backus's FP or otherwise about linear forms [15, 165, 16, 20, 127, 128], and transformations based on various rules and strategies mentioned in the previous paragraph, among others [14, 129, 34]. For example, it is shown that general recursive scheme is more powerful than while loop scheme, and a linear recursive scheme is equivalent to a while loop scheme [250]; an extensive set of linear functions can be turned into iterative forms [20]; a certain class of nonlinear functions can be transformed into linear forms [127] and then into loops [128]. None of these are as simple and effective as iterating at a minimum increment as discussed in this chapter. Shao et al. [283] describe transformations for unrolling lists to recurse fewer times at larger steps.

Two well-known ways to achieve dynamic programming are memoization and tabulation [65, 197]. Memoization uses a table that is separate from the original program to save and reuse the results of function calls as the program executes [223, 93, 147, 226, 161, 257, 260, 249, 163, 1, 5]. The original program needs little or no change, and only values needed in the original execution are computed. However, the separate table has an interpretive overhead, and no general strategy for table management is space-efficient for all problems. Tabulation statically determines the shapes of tables needed to store the results of possibly needed function calls, introduces appropriate data structures for the tables, and computes table entries in an appropriate order so that the result of a function call is computed using available results of needed function calls [29, 63, 252, 249, 55, 57, 146, 56, 254, 58]. This overcomes shortcomings of memoization, even though it may compute values not computed by the original program. However, this requires a thorough understanding of the problem and a manual rewrite of the program. Incrementalization-based optimization provides a systematic method for this; it not only saves time asymptotically by avoiding repeated computations, but also saves space asymptotically by allowing space to be reused after computation on each increment.

There are various works on data structure selection in program refinement and program synthesis for problems specified using recursive functions [249, 287, 32]. Related transformations are discussed together with general transformations. For example, Darlington and Burstall [69] briefly discuss reusing discarded data cells, and Liu and Stoller [195] show that a powerful method for transforming recursion to iteration can achieve pointer reversal on low-level data structures.

Optimizing recursive functions using incrementalization was introduced by Liu and Stoller: determining minimum increments [194, 197], transforming recursion to iteration [195, 204], and using both indexed and recursive data structures [196, 204] are all built on incrementalization that exploits previous results [213], intermediate results [210], and auxiliary values [211]. These works also study certain more general and powerful aspects of the method than those described in this chapter. The method has also been extended to support the use of high-level aggregate operations in recursive functions [204], which helps make the programs clearer and the optimizations simpler.

Many problems in combinatorics and optimization can be solved straightforwardly using simple recursions [262, 65]. The idea of deriving dynamic programming algorithms using incrementalization was motivated by the examples in Cormen, Leiserson, and Rivest [65], where they give straightforward solutions expressed using recursive functions, before discussing memoization and tabulation. Additional issues in solving these problems include computing closed forms [219, 303] of recursive functions, as studied often for complexity analysis [333], discovering stronger invariants as those used by greedy or thinning strategies in greedy algorithms [28], and obtaining the original recursive function for a given optimization problem [27, 289].

The original recursive function for the longest common subsequence problem is copied from the textbook by Cormen, Leiserson, and Rivest [65, p. 316]. The one for the 0-1 knapsack problem is written in a similar way. For the 0-1 knapsack problem, additional invariants may be employed so that linked lists may be used instead of arrays, by keeping items in order of increasing value and decreasing weight [7]. This does not improve the worst-case time and space complexities but may take less actual time and space, depending on the particular input, because of sparsity of elements in the linked lists. The recursive function for the single-source shortest path problem in Exercise 4.10 is copied from [65, p. 553]; the Bellman-Ford algorithm is described before that [65, p. 532–533].

The factorial and Fibonacci numbers are widely used as examples, but the issues discussed about them in this chapter have been studied rarely [195] or not at all. The Ackermann function is used much less, but its optimization using incrementalization was studied before [200], albeit yielding a slightly more complicated program than the one in this chapter. Tower of Hanoi problem was from [6, p. 306–307] and [253]. Pettorossi and Proietti use tupling [252] to give a linear-time program for it [253]. The resulting program consists of 9 moves and 18 concatenations in a recursive equation and 3 moves and 6 concatenations together in five other non-recursive equations; it is 4 times the size of our derived programs and has worse constant factors in both time and space.

Anil Nerode asserted that optimization using incrementalization corresponds to integration by differentiation several years before I could understand it. He also asserted that incrementalization could optimize the Ackermann function several years before I was able to do it. Eventually, Alan Mycroft and Zhe Yang asked about the Ackermann function, which prompted me to look at it seriously to solve it. Joshua Goldberg discovered that incrementalization of the Fibonacci function can spare the temporary variable, after I tossed the idea of iterating at bigger increment and trying the increment of 2 for Fibonacci in a class. Olivier Danvy asked a question about transforming recursion to iteration, which led me to find an error in our paper [195], in the paragraph about associativity: `r = b(x0); while ... return r` should be `r = identity of a1; while ... return a1(r,b(x0))`. The old version happens to be correct for all the examples there because `b(x0)` happens to be the identity of `a1` in all of them.

What are all problems in NP, what are all problems in P, whether NP equals P, and many other related questions have been studied extensively for decades [138]. The theory of computation studies these problems as well as primitive recursive functions and general computable functions.

5

Rules: iterate, incrementalize, and implement

Many complex computational problems are most clearly and easily specified using logic rules. Logic rules state that if certain hypotheses hold then certain conclusions hold. These rules can be used to infer new facts from given facts. Example applications include queries in databases, analysis of computer programs, and reasoning about security policies. Datalog, which stands for Database logic, is an important rule-based language for specifying how new facts can be inferred from existing facts. Its fixed-point semantics allows the computation of the set of all facts that can be inferred from a given set of facts. It is sufficiently powerful for expressing many practical analysis problems.

While a Datalog program can be easily implemented using a logic programming system, such as a Prolog system, evaluated using various evaluation methods, such as well-established tabling methods, or rewritten using transformation methods for more efficient evaluation, such as using the well-known magic-sets method, these implementations are typically for fast prototyping. The running times of Datalog programs implemented using these methods can vary dramatically depending on the order of rules and the order of hypotheses in a rule. Even less is known about the space usage. Developing and implementing efficient algorithms specialized for any given set of rules and with time and space guarantees is a nontrivial, recurring task.

This chapter describes a method for generating efficient specialized algorithms and implementations from Datalog rules. Given any set of Datalog rules, the method

1. transforms, or compiles, the set of rules into an efficient specialized implementation that, given any set of facts, computes exactly the set of facts that can be inferred and does so with guaranteed worst-case time and space complexities, and

117

2. computes the guaranteed worst-case time and space complexities of the implementation from the set of rules and allows easy simplification of the complexity formulas based on characterizations of the set of facts.

The running time is optimal in the sense that only useful combinations of facts that lead to all hypotheses of a rule being simultaneously true are considered, and each such combination is considered exactly once in constant time. For space complexity, the method separately analyzes the output space and the auxiliary space. The auxiliary space may sometimes be reduced using scheduling optimizations to eliminate some summands in the space complexity formula.

These results are formally derived using our systematic design method. Step Iterate forms a fixed-point specification of the meaning of the rules and transforms it into a loop that handles a single new fact in each iteration. Step Incrementalize replaces expensive computations on sets of tuples in the loop with efficient incremental operations. Step Implement designs a combination of linked and indexed data structures for efficiently storing and accessing the values used by incremental computation. The analysis of the complexities is based on a thorough understanding of the transformation process, reflecting the time and space complexities of the generated implementation through the rules. The complexity analysis based on rules is easy and precise, greatly facilitating the understanding and comparison of implementations at the rule level.

These steps extend those described for transforming set expressions in Chapter 3. Step Iterate forms a fixed-point expression from rules, rather than requiring that it be given. Step Incrementalize maintains appropriate auxiliary maps as sets of tuples at first, to use for higher-level algorithm derivation, and as nested maps at the end, to prepare for data structure design. Step Implement adds extensive use of sophisticated indexed structures, because linked structures alone do not suffice.

We first describe the method together with illustration on the problem of computing the transitive closure of graphs. We then discuss two additional examples: program analysis and trust management. The first one shows decomposition of rules with more than two hypotheses into rules with at most two hypotheses, in order to achieve the best time complexity; the second one shows handling of extensions to Datalog. Finally, we describe the need for module abstraction regardless of whether data abstraction and control abstraction are used.

Example: transitive closure

Given a graph with a set of edges, each from a vertex to another, the *transitive closure* of the graph is the set of all pairs of vertices such that there is a path from the first vertex to the second vertex following a sequence of edges. Stated logically, we can have two rules that capture any pair of vertices u and v such that there is a path from u to v:

1. If there is an edge from vertex u to vertex v, then there is path from u to v.

2. If there is an edge from u to w, and there is a path from w to v, then there is path from u to v.

All pairs of vertices u and v such that there is a path from u to v form the transitive closure of the graph.

With such rules, for any given set of data as input, we want to efficiently compute the set of all data that can be inferred from the rules. These rules do not specify anything about how the computation should proceed, or how the data should be represented, let alone anything about efficient incremental computation. Thus, efficient computation requires all of Steps Iterate, Incrementalize, and Implement. We will generate a specialized efficient program from any given set of rules. A significant advantage of starting with rules, which are declarative in both data representation and computation process, is that we can provide precise time and space complexity guarantees on the generated implementations.

For the transitive closure example, our method will compile the two given rules into an efficient implementation whose worst-case time complexity is bounded by the number of edges times the number of vertices, whose output space is quadratic in the number of vertices, and whose auxiliary space is linear in the number of edges.

Exercise 5.1 (Transitive closure in other ways*) For the transitive closure problem, think of different ways to state the rules. The second rule discussed uses edge as the first hypothesis. Can we write one that uses edge differently? How about one that does not use edge at all? What are the advantages and disadvantages of these different ways compared with each other?

5.1 Logic rules—data abstraction and control abstraction

We describe logic rules that are in the form of Datalog rules, which are built using constants, variables, predicates, conjunctions, and logical implications. A predicate over a set of arguments is equivalent to a relation over these arguments. For example, a predicate west over two arguments Norway and Sweden, denoting that Norway is to the west of Sweden, is equivalent to a relation west relating Norway and Sweden.

Language

A *Datalog rule* is of the following form, where h is a finite natural number, each P_i or Q is a predicate of finite natural number a_i or a, respectively, of *arguments*, each argument X_{ij} or X_k is either a constant or a variable, and each variable in the arguments of Q must also be in the arguments of some P_i.

$$P_1(X_{11}, \ldots, X_{1a_1}), \ \ldots, \ P_h(X_{h1}, \ldots, X_{ha_h}) \ \text{->} \ Q(X_1, \ldots, X_a)$$

If $h = 0$, then there is no P_i or X_{ij}, and each X_k must be a constant, in which case $Q(X_1, \ldots, X_a)$ is called a *fact*. From now on, we use "rule" to refer only to the case where $h \geq 1$, in which case each $P_i(X_{i1}, \ldots, X_{ia_i})$ is called a *hypothesis* of the rule, and $Q(X_1, \ldots, X_a)$ is called the *conclusion* of the rule.

The intuitive meaning of a rule is that, if each hypothesis $P_i(X_{i1}, \ldots, X_{ia_i})$ holds, then the conclusion $Q(X_1, \ldots, X_a)$ holds. Precisely, a comma (,) separating two hypotheses denotes conjunction, an arrow (->) denotes logical implication, and the meaning of a rule is that, for all possible values of the variables in the rule, the conjunction of the hypotheses implies the conclusion. In other words, each rule is a logical implication, and all variables are universally quantified, that is, the implication is true for all substitutions of its variables with constants, where all occurrences of the same variable in a rule must be substituted with the same constant.

For the transitive closure example, we use edge(u,v) to denote that there is an edge from a vertex u to a vertex v, and we use path(u,v) to denote that there is a path from a vertex u to a vertex v following a sequence of edges. Then, the two rules that define path can be specified as the following Datalog rules:

```
edge(u,v) -> path(u,v)
edge(u,w), path(w,v) -> path(u,v)
```

The intuitive meaning of a set of rules and a set of facts is the least set of facts that contains all the given facts and all the facts that can be inferred using the rules. Precisely, given a set of rules and a set of facts, we call a rule with all its variables substituted with constants an instance of the rule, and we say that a fact can be *inferred* if it is a given fact or it is the conclusion of an instance of a rule whose hypotheses can all be inferred. With this precise definition, the meaning of a set of rules and a set of facts is simply the least set of all facts that can be inferred.

For the transitive closure example, given any set of facts of the edge relation, the meaning of the two rules and the given facts is the least set containing all facts of the edge relation and all facts of the path relation that can be inferred. The set of all pairs in the resulting path relation is the transitive closure of the given edge relation.

Note that Datalog rules operate over relations, that is, sets of tuples, and may involve recursion, that is, infer facts of a relation using facts of the same relation. For the transitive closure example, the two rules are over sets of pairs, and the second rule uses recursion. Such logic rules provide both data abstraction and control abstraction, because sets provide data abstraction, and recursion provides control abstraction.

Reduction to rules in simplified form

Even though a Datalog rule looks extremely simple, it is nontrivial for efficient computations to take care of the restrictions imposed by multiple occurrences of the same variable, both in the same hypothesis and among different hypotheses and the conclusion. We will give a formal derivation of the algorithms and complexities for a slightly simplified form of rules. Other rules can be reduced easily to the simplified form, as discussed in the following, or be handled with a slight extension to the derivation, as discussed at the end of Section 5.5; we will see that there are trade-offs between these two alternatives.

The *simplified form* consists of only rules with one or two hypotheses and where equal cards and wild cards, defined next, may occur only in rules with one hypothesis.

- A variable that occurs multiple times in a hypothesis is called an *equal card*; it forces a fact that matches the hypothesis to have the same value in those argument positions.

- A variable that occurs only once in a rule, in a hypothesis, is called a *wild card*; it can take on any value, and its name does not affect the meaning of the rule.

For ease of exposition, we write simplified rules, and the given facts, in the forms below, where arguments of relations appear to be grouped and possibly reordered. We will see through the derivation that grouping and reordering of arguments do not affect the results.

form 2: `P1(X1s,Ys,C1s), P2(X2s,Ys,C2s) -> Q2(X1s,X2s,Y's,C3s)`
form 1: `P(Zs,As) -> Q1(Z's,Bs)`
form 0: `Q(Cs)`

Each of X1s, X2s, Ys, Y's, Zs, and Z's abbreviates a group of variables. Each of C1s, C2s, C3s, As, Bs, and Cs abbreviates a group of constants. Variables in Y's and Z's are subsets of variables in Ys and Zs, respectively. In form 2, variables in Ys are exactly those shared between the two hypotheses. Each variable or constant may occur multiple times in a group, except for X1s, X2s, and Ys in the hypotheses in form 2; the exception ensures that there is no equal card in rules with two hypotheses. There is no wild card in rules with two hypotheses, because each variable occurs in both hypotheses or in a hypothesis and the conclusion.

Note that different relation names in these forms may refer to the same relation. We use different names for different occurrences of relations so that, in the description that follows, we can tell which occurrence is from where. For similar reasons, we use different names for different groups of constants and variables.

For the transitive closure example, the edge facts are of form 0, and there is one rule of form 1 and one rule of form 2, both with no constants. It is easy to see how the predicates and variables in the rules are represented using the two forms. For example, P and P1 represent predicate edge, and Ys represents variable w.

For any rule with more than two hypotheses, we can transform it into rules with two hypotheses. The transformation simply introduces auxiliary relations with necessary arguments to hold the results of combining two hypotheses at a time. Precisely, for each rule with more than two hypotheses, we apply the following transformations repeatedly until only two hypotheses are left:

1. Replace any two hypotheses, say H_i and H_j, with a new hypothesis, H, where H is a fresh relation applied to the set of variables in H_i and H_j that are also in other hypotheses or the conclusion of this rule, that is, variables that are only in H_i and H_j are not in H.

2. Add a new rule H_i, H_j -> H.

For equal cards and wild cards that occur in any rule with more than one hypothesis, we can eliminate them by simple transformations. If a hypothesis contains equal cards, we introduce an auxiliary relation that has only the variable arguments of the hypothesis and contains only one occurrence of each equal card. Precisely, for each hypothesis of a rule that contains equal cards, we do the following:

1. Replace the hypothesis, say H_i, with a new hypothesis, H, where H is a fresh relation applied to the set of variables in H_i, that is, H does not contain multiple occurrences of any variable.

2. Add a new rule H_i -> H. So equal cards occur only in rules with one hypothesis.

Similarly, if a hypothesis contains wild cards, we introduce an auxiliary relation that has only the variable arguments of the hypothesis that are not wild cards. Precisely, we do the same two transformations as for equal cards, except that variables in H are now variables in H_i that are not wild cards. Note that we must remove equal cards first and wild cards second, because removing equal cards may introduce wild cards.

We do not give examples here, because these transformations are quite straightforward, especially for handling equal cards and wild cards. The pointer analysis problem in Section 5.6 shows the transformation of rules with more than two hypotheses into rules with two hypotheses.

Cost model

For time complexity, we count the number of rule firings and consider the time needed for each firing, where a *firing* of a rule refers to a use of the rule where a combination of facts makes all the hypotheses of an instance of the rule true and the corresponding conclusion is inferred. For space complexity, we count the sizes of all linked lists and arrays used for storing the facts of predicates and the entries of auxiliary maps. We consider the total size of the rules as a constant, which includes the number of rules, the maximum number of hypotheses in a rule, and the maximum number of arguments of a predicate; these numbers are generally very small compared with the number of facts, but could be taken into account easily if needed.

Exercise 5.2 (Transitive closure using different rules) For the transitive closure problem, write Datalog rules for your different ways of stating the rules for Exercise 5.1.

Exercise 5.3 (Graph reachability using rules) Consider the graph reachability problem discussed in Chapter 3: Given a graph with a set e of edges and a set s of source vertices, we want to find the set r of vertices reachable from the vertices in s following the edges in e. Represent the sets e and s using predicates, and write Datalog rules for computing r.

Exercise 5.4 (Meaning of graph reachability rules) For the rules for the graph reachability problem in the previous exercise, describe the meaning of the rules, and describe what the set of reachable vertices is.

5.2 Iterate: transform to fixed points

All rules of the same form are processed in the same way, so we describe the compilation method for only one rule of form 1 and one rule of form 2.

We represent relations as sets of tuples. For relation arguments that are grouped in a simplified form of rules, we use the same grouping in the tuples and indicate this by omitting the commas between normal tuple components. Specifically, we represent a fact of the form Q(Cs) as [Q Cs], which abbreviates a tuple whose first component is a constant Q and whose other components are the constants in Cs. We represent a hypothesis of the form P(Zs,As) as [P Zs As], where P and the components in As are constants and those in Zs are variables. We represent other forms of hypotheses and conclusions in a similar fashion.

We capture rules and facts as set expressions. Let expression e0 capture the set of all given facts from givenFacts.

$$e0 \;=\; \{[Q \; Cs] \;:\; Q(Cs) \text{ in givenFacts}\}$$

For the rule of form 1, let expression e1(R) capture, for any given set of facts R, the set of facts Q1(Z's,Bs) such that P(Zs,As) is in R, that is, e1(R) is the set of facts that can be inferred from R using the rule of form 1 once.

$$e1(R) \;=\; \{[Q1 \; Z's \; Bs] \;:\; [P \; Zs \; As] \text{ in } R\}$$

For the rule of form 2, let expression e2(R) capture, for any given set of facts R, the set of facts Q2(X1s,X2s,Y's,C3s) such that P1(X1s,Ys,C1s) and P2(X2s,Ys,C2s) are in R, that is, e2(R) is the set of facts that can be inferred from R using the rule of form 2 once.

```
e2(R) = {[Q2 X1s X2s Y's C3s] : [P1 X1s Ys C1s] in R and
                                [P2 X2s Ys C2s] in R}
```

The meaning of the given set of rules and facts naturally forms a least fixed point, specified by the fixed-point expression

```
min R: e0 subset R, R + e1(R) + e2(R) = R
```

The fixed-point expression above is equivalent to the fixed-point expression below:

```
min R: e0 + R + e1(R) + e2(R) = R
```

Note that we allow sets to contain elements of different types, that is, facts of different relations. This allows simpler and clearer algorithm derivation at a high level in Step Incrementalize before data structure design in Step Implement.

The least fixed-point expression is then transformed into the following `while` loop such that, when the loop terminates, R is the desired result.

```
R := {}
while exists x in e0 + e1(R) + e2(R) - R:
  R add x
```

Note that the first fixed-point expression can be transformed into a similar loop except that R is initialized to e0, and e0 is removed from the condition of the loop; we do not use that loop, because it would yield much more complicated initialization and a very slightly simplified loop body, similar to what we have seen in the graph reachability example in Chapter 3.

For the transitive closure example, we obtain the fixed-point specification and `while` loop as given above where

```
e0    = {[edge,u,v] : edge(u,v) in givenFacts}
e1(R) = {[path,u,v] : [edge,u,v] in R}
e2(R) = {[path,u,v] : [edge,u,w] in R and [path,w,v] in R}
```

where `edge` and `path` are constants.

Exercise 5.5 (Least fixed point for different transitive closure rules) For the different transitive closure rules you wrote for Exercise 5.2, give a least fixed-point specification and a `while` loop transformed from it.

Exercise 5.6 (Least fixed point for graph reachability rules) For the graph reachability problem you specified using rules for Exercise 5.3, give a least fixed-point specification and a `while` loop transformed from it.

5.3 Incrementalize: exploit high-level auxiliary maps

We transform the `while` loop obtained from Step Iterate to compute expensive set expressions incrementally in each iteration. That is, we hold the values of expensive expressions in variables, initialize the values of these variables for the initial value of R before entering the loop, use the values of these variables where the values of the corresponding expressions are needed, and update the values of these variables incrementally as the value of R is updated. This eliminates repeated recomputations of expensive expressions in the loop body.

Determining expensive expressions and auxiliary maps

Set comprehension and set union and difference are expensive because they require iterating through one or more sets. Thus, the expensive expressions in the while loop from Step Iterate are e0, e1(R), e2(R), and e0 + e1(R) + e2(R) - R. We use fresh variables E0, E1, E2, and W to hold their respective values and maintain the following invariants:

```
E0 = e0    = {[Q Cs] : Q(Cs) in givenFacts}
E1 = e1(R) = {[Q1 Z's Bs] : [P Zs As] in R}
E2 = e2(R) = {[Q2 X1s X2s Y's C3s] : [P1 X1s Ys C1s] in R and
                                     [P2 X2s Ys C2s] in R}
W  = e0 + e1(R) + e2(R) - R = E0 + E1 + E2 - R
```

Expression e0 does not depend on R. So E0 can simply be initialized to e0, and it does not need to be updated when R is updated in the loop body.

Expression e1(R) depends on R but is simple. It is {} when R is {}, so E1 can be initialized to {} with the initialization R := {}. E1 can also be updated easily together with the update R add x: if x is of the form [P Zs As], then the corresponding [Q1 Z's Bs] is added to E1 if it is not already in E1, otherwise nothing needs to be done.

Expression e2(R) is formed by joining elements from two sets, so efficient incremental computation requires maintaining auxiliary maps. To update E2 incrementally with the update R add x, if x is of the form [P1 X1s Ys C1s], then we consider all matching tuples [P2 X2s Ys C2s] in R and add the corresponding tuple [Q2 X1s X2s Y's C3s] to E2. To form the tuples to add, we need to efficiently find the appropriate values of X2s, so we maintain an auxiliary map that maps values of the variables in Ys to values of the variables in X2s for all [P2 X2s Ys C2s] in R. We store this map in variable P2YsX2s, indicating that it is built from P2 and maps variables in Ys to variables in X2s:

$$P2YsX2s = \{[Ys\ X2s] : [P2\ X2s\ Ys\ C2s]\ in\ R\}$$

P2YsX2s may be omitted if arguments of the hypothesis P2(X2s,Ys,C2s) start with variables in Ys, followed by variables in X2s, and possibly followed by constants, because in this case, facts of P2 that are in R can be used in place of P2YsX2s to find the matching X2s. Having no shared variables, that is, Ys being empty, and having all constant arguments at the end is a trivial case of this.

Symmetrically, if x is a tuple of P2, we need to consider each matching tuple of P1 and add the corresponding tuple of Q2 to E2. To efficiently form the tuples to add, we maintain

```
P1YsX1s = {[Ys X1s] : [P1 X1s Ys C1s] in R}
```

We call the first set of arguments in an auxiliary map the *anchor*, and the second set of arguments the *non-anchor*. Being able to directly find only the matching tuples allows us to consider only combinations of facts that make both hypotheses simultaneously true and to consider each combination only once.

For the transitive closure example, E0, E1, E2, and W are defined straightforwardly. We also maintain the auxiliary map

```
edgewu = {[w,u] : [edge,u,w] in R}
```

which is an inverse map of edge. Auxiliary map pathwv is not needed, because facts of path that are in R can be used instead.

Maintaining invariants incrementally

Variables holding the values of expensive subexpressions and auxiliary maps are initialized together with the assignment R := {} and updated incrementally together with the assignment R add x in each iteration.

By definitions of E0, E1, E2, W, and auxiliary maps P2YsX2s and P1YsX1s, when R is initialized to {}, we can initialize these variables as follows:

```
E0 := {[Q Cs]: Q(Cs) in givenFacts}   -- given facts
E1 := {}                              -- inferred from R using rule 1
E2 := {}                              -- inferred from R using rule 2
W := {[Q Cs]: Q(Cs) in givenFacts}    -- work-set
P2YsX2s := {}                         -- aux map for rule 2 hypothesis 2
P1YsX1s := {}                         -- aux map for rule 2 hypothesis 1
```

and when x is added to R in the loop body, we can update these variables as follows:

```
if x of [P Zs As]:                             -- match rule 1 hypo
  E1 add [Q1 Z's Bs]                            || update E1,
  if [Q1 Z's Bs] not in R: W add [Q1 Z's Bs]   || update W
if x of [P1 X1s Ys C1s]:                        -- match rule 2 hypo 1
  E2 +:= {[Q2 X1s X2s Y's C3s]: X2s in P2YsX2s{Ys}}  || update E2,
  W  +:= {[Q2 X1s X2s Y's C3s]: X2s in P2YsX2s{Ys}   || update W,
        | [Q2 X1s X2s Y's C3s] not in R}         ||
  P1YsX1s add [Ys X1s]                           || update aux map
if x of [P2 X2s Ys C2s]:                        -- match rule 2 hypo 2
  E2 +:= {[Q2 X1s X2s Y's C3s]: X1s in P1YsX1s{Ys}}  || update E2,
  W  +:= {[Q2 X1s X2s Y's C3s]: X1s in P1YsX1s{Ys}   || update W,
        | [Q2 X1s X2s Y's C3s] not in R}         ||
  P2YsX2s add [Ys X2s]                           || update aux map
W del x                                          -- update W
```

Note that P2YsX2s{Ys} denotes the set of X2s such that [Ys X2s] is in P2YsX2s, and

P2YsX1s{Ys} is similar; they are examples of the image operation defined in Section 3.1. A command of the form `if` v `of` *tpat*: *cmd* matches the value of variable v against tuple pattern *tpat* and, if the match succeeds, binds the free variables in *tpat* using the match and executes command *cmd*.

Adding these initializations and incremental updates and using `W` in place of `e0+e1(R)+e2(R)-R` in the `while` loop from Step Iterate, we obtain the following incrementalized loop. It is easy to see that `W` serves as the work-set, that is, the set of facts to be worked on.

```
... -- initialize as shown above
R := {}
while exists x in W:
  ... -- update as shown above
  R add x
```

Eliminating dead code

To compute the value of `R`, only the values of `W`, `P2YsX2s`, and `P1YsX1s` are needed. So computations for variables `E0`, `E1`, and `E2` are dead and can be eliminated. Eliminating them from the incrementalized loop above, we obtain the following algorithm:

```
W := {[Q Cs] : Q(Cs) in givenFacts}
P2YsX2s := {}
P1YsX1s := {}
R := {}
while exists x in W:
  if x of [P Zs As]:
    if [Q1 Z's Bs] not in R: W add [Q1 Z's Bs]
  if x of [P1 X1s Ys C1s]:
    W +:= {[Q2 X1s X2s Y's C3s]: X2s in P2YsX2s{Ys}
           | [Q2 X1s X2s Y's C3s] not in R}
    P1YsX1s add [Ys X1s]
  if x of [P2 X2s Ys C2s]:
    W +:= {[Q2 X1s X2s Y's C3s]: X1s in P1YsX1s{Ys}
           | [Q2 X1s X2s Y's C3s] not in R}
    P2YsX2s add [Ys X2s]
  W del x
  R add x
```

Cleaning up

Finally, the code is cleaned up to contain only uniform element-level operations to prepare for data structure design in Step Implement. We first decompose `R` and `W`, because the different sets obtained will need different data structures. Specifically, we decompose `R` into `Ri`'s, where each `Ri` is for a single relation that occurs in the rules. Similarly, we decompose `W` into `Wi`'s. For a relation `Qi` that occurs in the conclusion of a rule, we also write `RQi` and `WQi` in addition to `Ri` and `Wi`, respectively.

We also eliminate relation names from the first component of tuples, and transform
the `while` clause and pattern-matching clauses to iterate over `Wi`'s.

For the transitive closure example, after representing R as `Redge` and `Rpath` and
representing W as `Wedge` and `Wpath`, we obtain the following algorithm. Note that the
first two cases in the general form of the loop body, for hypotheses of the forms
`[P Zs As]` and `[P1 X1s Ys C1s]`, are merged in this example because both rules for
this example have a hypothesis about `edge`. Also, `Rpath`—facts of `path` that are in
R—is used in place of an auxiliary map `pathwv`.

```
Wedge := {[u,v] : edge(u,v) in givenFacts}   || W split into
Wpath := {}                                   || Wedge and Wpath
edgewu := {}                                  -- inverse map for edge
Redge := {}                                   || R split into
Rpath := {}                                   || Redge and Rpath
while Wedge!={} or Wpath!={}:
  while exists [u,w] in Wedge:                -- match rule 1, rule 2 hypo 1
    if [u,w] not in Rpath: Wpath add [u,w]    -- update W for rule 1
    Wpath +:= {[u,v]: v in Rpath{w}           || update W for rule 2, and
               | [u,v] not in Rpath}          || use Rpath as aux map
    edgewu add [w,u]                          -- update inverse map
    Wedge del [u,w]
    Redge add [u,w]
  while exists [w,v] in Wpath:                -- match rule 2 hypo 2
    Wpath +:= {[u,v]: u in edgewu{w}          || update W for rule 2, and
               | [u,v] not in Rpath}          || use inverse map
    Wpath del [w,v]
    Rpath add [w,v]
```

Then, we do the following three sets of transformations.

1. Transform set-level operations (unions here) into loops that use element-
   level operations. Specifically, replace commands of the form `S +:= {exp: x
   in sexp | bexp}` with `for x in sexp: if bexp: S add exp`. Additionally, re-
   place enumeration of facts `Q(Cs)` from `givenFacts` with reading of facts `Q(Cs)`
   from input one at time, denoted `while read Q(Cs)`.

2. Replace tuples and tuple operations with maps and map operations. Specifically, replace tuples of more than two components with tail nested tuples
   of two components, for example, `[x,y,z]` becomes `[x,[y,z]]`. Then, replace
   `while exists [x,y] in M` with `while exists x in dom(M): while exists y in M{x}`
   and replace for loops similarly. Finally, replace `M!={}` with `dom(M)!={}`; replace
   `[x,y] not in M` with `x not in dom(M)` or `y not in M{x}`, where or uses *short-
   circuit semantics*, that is, the second operand is evaluated only if the first
   evaluates to true; replace `M add [x,y]` with `if x not in dom(M): M{x} := {}`
   followed by `M{x} add y`; and replace `M del [x,y]` with `M{x} del y` followed by
   `if M{x}={}: dom(M) del x`.

3. Make all element-level updates easy by testing membership first. Specifically, replace `S add x` with `if x not in S: S add x`, and replace `S del x` with

if x in S: S del x. There are four exceptions, corresponding to the following optimizations: (1) initial addition to Wi from given facts does not need the additional test if the given facts contains no duplicates; (2) removal from Wi does not need the additional test, because the removed element is retrieved from Wi; (3) addition to Ri does not need the additional test, because elements are moved from Wi to Ri one at a time and each element is put into Wi, and thus Ri, only once; and (4) addition to PiYsXis does not need the additional test if the corresponding hypothesis Pi(Xis,Ys,Cis) has no constant arguments, because the element to add corresponds to an element in some Wj and each element is put into Wj, and thus the corresponding element is put into PiYsXis, only once.

For the transitive closure example, after applying the three sets of transformations, we obtain the following algorithm. The comments show the corresponding code in the preceding algorithm.

```
Wedge := {}                                    || Wedge :=...
while read edge(u,v):                          ||
  if u not in dom(Wedge): Wedge{u} := {}  ||
  Wedge{u} add v                               || if input has no duplicates
Wpath := {}
edgewu := {}
Redge := {}
Rpath := {}
while dom(Wedge)!={} or dom(Wpath)!={}:   -- while Wedge != {} or ...
  while exists u in dom(Wedge):                || while exists [u,w] in Wedge
    while exists w in Wedge{u}:                 ||
      if u not in dom(Rpath) or w not in Rpath{u}:--if [u,w] not in Rpath
        if u not in dom(Wpath): Wpath{u} := {}  || Wpath add [u,w]
        if w not in Wpath{u}: Wpath{u} add w    ||
      for v in Rpath{w}:                        || Wpath +:=...
        if u not in dom(Rpath) or v not in Rpath{u}:||
          if u not in dom(Wpath): Wpath{u} := {}   ||
          if v not in Wpath{u}: Wpath{u} add v      ||
      if w not in dom(edgewu): edgewu{w} := {}    || edgewu add [w,u]
      edgewu{w} add u                            ||
      Wedge{u} del w                             || Wedge del [u,w]
      if Wedge{u} = {}: dom(Wedge) del u         ||
      if u not in dom(Redge): Redge{u} := {}     || Redge add [u,w]
      Redge{u} add w                             ||
  while exists w in dom(Wpath):                  || while exists [w,v] in Wpath
    while exists v in Wpath{w}:                  ||
      for u in edgewu{w}:                        || Wpath +:=...
        if u not in dom(Rpath) or v not in Rpath{u}:||
          if u not in dom(Wpath): Wpath{u} := {}   ||
          if v not in Wpath{u}: Wpath{u} add v      ||
      Wpath{w} del v                             || Wpath del [w,v]
      if Wpath{w} = {}: dom(Wpath) del w         ||
      if w not in dom(Rpath): Rpath{w} := {}     || Rpath add [w,v]
      Rpath{w} add v                             ||
```

Exercise 5.7 (Incrementalizing different transitive closure rules) For the different transitive closure rules you transformed into a least fixed-point specification for Exercise 5.5, derive an algorithm for incrementally computing the fixed point.

Exercise 5.8 (Incrementalizing graph reachability rules) For the graph reachability problem you transformed into a least fixed-point specification for Exercise 5.6, derive an algorithm for incrementally computing the fixed point.

5.4 Implement: design linked and indexed data structures

Data structures are designed based on how sets and set elements are accessed. We design sophisticated linked structures, whenever possible, so that each element-level operation can be performed in worst-case constant time and with at most a small constant factor of space overhead, as done in Chapter 3. However, to compile Datalog rules to achieve the best worst-case time complexity, indexed structures, that is, arrays, must also be exploited extensively, to allow each operation to be performed in worst-case constant time, although with possibly larger space overhead.

Precisely, we describe how to guarantee that each element-level operation from Step Incrementalize takes worst-case $O(1)$ time, by using a combination of records, arrays, and linked lists. The operations are of the following kinds:

- set initialization (s := {}) and emptiness test (s={}),
- element addition (s add x) and deletion (s del x),
- element retrieval (in while exists x in S and for x in S),
- domain operation (dom(M)) and image operation (M{x}), and
- membership test (x in S and x not in S).

As in Chapter 3, we use *associative access* to refer to membership test (x in S and x not in S) and image operation set (M{x}). Such an operation requires the ability to locate an element (x) in a set (S or dom(M)).

Need for indexed data structures

We repeat the motivation and description of *based representations* presented in Chapter 3 before describing the need for indexed data structures.

Consider using a singly linked list for each set, including the domain set and image sets of each map, and let each element in a domain set linked list contain a pointer to the element's image set linked list. In other words, represent a set as a linked list, and represent a map as a linked list of linked lists. Then, we have the following observation:

If associative access can be done in worst-case constant time, so can all other element-level operations. To see this, note that initialization and emptiness test are obvious; adding or deleting an element to or from a set can be done in constant time after doing an associative access of the element in the set; retrieving an element from a set only needs to locate any element or any next element in the set; and a domain operation simply returns a pointer to the set.

An associative access would take linear time if a linked list is naively traversed to locate an element. A classical solution to this problem is to use hash tables instead of linked lists, but this gives average-case, not worst-case, constant time for each operation, and it has the overhead of hash-related computations for each operation. Another solution is to use arrays, but this gives worst-case constant-time operations only when the sets do not change dynamically, and it may use asymptotically more space than necessary and may have bad memory performance when the arrays are large.

Based representations can be used to design linked structures that support associative access in worst-case constant time with little space overhead for a general class of set-based programs. The basic observation is that an access, x in s, in a program, is not isolated—the element x must be retrieved from some set w before the access, as in

```
...
... -- retrieve x from W
...
... -- access x in S
...
```

That is, we want to locate x in s after it has been located in w. The idea is to use a set B, called a *base*, to store values for both w and s, so that a retrieval of a value from w also locates this value in s.

- Base B is a set of records (this set is only conceptual), with a K field storing the key (i.e., value).

- Set s is represented using an s field of B: records of B whose keys are in s are connected by a linked list whose links are stored in the s field; records of B whose keys are not in s store a special value, null, indicating undefinedness in the s field. If set s is never retrieved from, then the s field can be a bit indicating whether the key is in s.

- Set w is represented as a separate linked list of pointers to records of B whose keys are in w.

Thus, an element of s is represented as *a field in* the record, and s is said to be *strongly based* on B; an element of w is represented as *a pointer to* the record, and w is said to be *weakly based* on B. This representation allows an arbitrary number of weakly based sets, but only a constant number of strongly based sets, because there can be any number of pointers to a record, but only a constant number of fields in a record. Essentially, base B provides a kind of indexing to elements of s starting from elements of w.

Need for indexed data structures arise when a non-constant number of sets must be strongly based for constant-time associative access. This is particularly the case here for compiling rules. Specifically, in the resulting algorithm from Step Incrementalize, there are three kinds of associative access, in the *domain*, that is, the set of possible values, of each component of the elements of the following three kinds of sets, respectively:

1. Result sets RQi's and work-sets WQi's for relations Qi's that occur in the conclusions of rules, by tests of whether a fact of Qi to be added to WQi is already in RQi or WQi.

2. Anchors of auxiliary maps PiYsXis's, by image operations PiYsXis{Ys}.

3. Auxiliary maps PiYsXis's, by tests of whether a tuple [Ys Xis] to be added to PiYsXis is already in it.

Because each value accessed in the domain of a non-last component yields an image set for the domain of the next component whose values need to be accessed efficiently again, and there are a non-constant number of values in the domain of a component, these non-constant number of image sets cannot all be strongly based directly on the set of possible domain values. Therefore, based representations do not apply. Nevertheless, we may extend them to use arrays for all the non-constant numbers of image sets, as described next. This still guarantees worst-case constant running time for each operation, unlike if hashing is used.

Data structures

The data structures need to support the three kinds of associative access described and the following two kinds of element retrieval, in the domain of each component of the elements of the following two kinds of sets, respectively:

1. Work-sets Wi's, by the while loops in the resulting algorithm from Step Incrementalize.

2. Non-anchors of auxiliary maps PiYsXis's, by the for loops in the resulting algorithm from Step Incrementalize that add elements to the work-sets Wi's.

We describe a uniform method for representing all these sets and maps, using an array for each non-constant number of sets that have associative access, a linked list for each set that is traversed by loops, and both an array and a linked list when both kinds of operations are needed.

Consider all domains from which arguments of relations take values. For each domain D, we map the values in D one-to-one to the integers from 1 to $\#D$, and use these integers to refer to the values in D. Recall that Qi's denote relations that occur in the conclusions of rules. We represent RQi's, WQi's and other Wi's, and PiYsXis's, respectively, as follows.

- Each RQi of, say, a components is represented using an a-level nested array structure. The first level is an array indexed by values in the domain of the first component of RQi; the k-th element of the array is null if there is no tuple of RQi whose first component has value k, and otherwise is true if a = 1, and otherwise is recursively an (a-1)-level nested array structure for the remaining components of tuples of RQi whose first component has value k.

- Each WQi is represented in the same way' as RQi with two additions. First, for each array, we add a linked list linking indices of non-null elements of the array. Second, to each linked list, we add a tail pointer, that is, a pointer to the last element, to form a queue. We combine the array, the head of the linked list, and the tail pointer in a record. Each other Wi is represented simply as a nested linked-list structure (without the underlying arrays or the tail pointers), one level for each component of Wi, linking the elements (which correspond to indices of the elements in the array) directly.

- Each PiYsXis for which associative access of the third kind is needed uses a nested array structure as RQi and WQi do and additionally linked lists (without the tail pointers) for each component of the non-anchor as WQi does. Each other PiYsXis uses a nested array structure only for the anchor, where elements of arrays for the last component of the anchor are each a nested linked-list structure (without the underlying arrays or the tail pointers) for the non-anchor. Finally, if an Ri is used in place of an PiYsXis, the corresponding data structure must be imposed on Ri.

Note that we did not discuss representations for relations Ri's that do not occur in the conclusion of any rule and are not used in place of any auxiliary map. These sets contain only given facts, not newly inferred facts. They are not used in any way by our derived algorithms, except that their elements are simply taken from the given facts via the Wi's. Elements of RQi's and other Ri's could be linked together as we do for WQi's and other Wi's if these result sets need to be traversed in subsequent computations.

A small natural improvement is to avoid using completely separate data structures for the different kinds of tuples in RQi's, WQi's, and PiYsXis's. For all kinds of tuples whose first components are from the same domain, we use a single 1st-level array of records, as a base, for the domain, and use a field for each kind of tuples that shares the 1st-level array. This does not change the asymptotic complexities but allows the use of a single indexing operator to locate the first component of multiple tuples that are always accessed next to each other, for example, RQi and WQi in each of the three branches in the resulting algorithm from Step Incrementalize, and P2YsX2s and P1YsX1s in each of the two branches for the rule of form 2. This also allows all the data structures to fall back completely to based representations when there is no associative access into a non-constant number of sets.

For the transitive closure example, we use integers 1 to V to refer to the vertices. A base for the domain of all vertices is used, because both arguments of both `edge` and `path` are from this same domain. The resulting data structure is explained below and is depicted for a small graph in Figure 5.1.

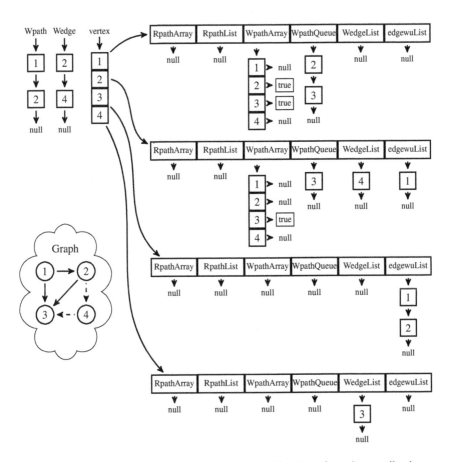

Figure 5.1 Data structure for the transitive closure algorithm. To reduce clutter, tail pointers for Wpath and queues in the WpathQueue field are not shown. In the graph, the edges drawn with solid lines are already processed, and the edges drawn with dashed lines are not yet processed.

Elements of the base are stored in an array indexed by the vertices 1 to V, for efficient access of the first component of Rpath, Wpath, and edgewu. Each element u of the base array is a record of six fields.

- An RpathArray field of u is for Rpath; it is null if no element of Rpath starts with u, and otherwise is an array for the second component of Rpath, indexed by the vertices and whose element at v is true if [u,v] is an element of Rpath and null otherwise. An RpathList field of u is a linked list of indices of non-null elements of the array in RpathArray.

- A similar WpathArray field of u is for Wpath. A linked list Wpath with a tail pointer is used to link indices of the base array elements whose WpathArray field is not null. A WpathQueue field of u is a linked list with a tail pointer linking indices of non-null elements of the array in WpathArray.

- A linked list Wedge with a tail pointer is used to link indices of vertices in the first component of Wedge. A WedgeList field of u is a linked list of indices of successor vertices of u.

- An edgewuList field of u is used for the inverse map edgewu; it is a linked list of indices of predecessor vertices of u.

Time and space trade-offs

When elements in a set are sparse over a domain, array representations may result in non-optimal use of space, but initialization of such arrays does not affect the time complexity, because an array entry can be initialized the first time it is accessed. To do this, one can maintain a pointer in each initialized entry to a back pointer on a memory stack; each time an entry is accessed, one can verify that the contents are not random by ensuring that the pointer in that entry points to the active region on the memory stack and that the back pointer points to the entry.

When a set over a domain is sparse, we could use linked lists instead of arrays for accessing the set elements. This makes the space usage for this domain optimal but incurs an extra factor of the length of the lists for time complexity. When worst-case time is not a concern, one could also use hash tables in place of arrays or linked lists, yielding another set of trade-offs involving also the overheads of hashing.

These trade-offs can be explored based on the sparsity of domain values in any specific applications. When space is not a concern, arrays are the most efficient. When space is a concern, but values are truly sparse, linked lists are best. Otherwise, when an overhead in either time or space or both is necessary, hash tables provide a good compromise.

Exercise 5.9 (Data structures for different transitive closure rules) For the different transitive closure rules that you transformed into an algorithm for incremental computation for Exercise 5.7, derive data structures for efficient access of facts.

Exercise 5.10   (Data structures for graph reachability rules) For the graph reachability problem that you transformed into an algorithm for incremental computation for Exercise 5.8, derive data structures for efficient access of facts.

5.5   Time and space complexity guarantees

We describe how to compute time and space complexities precisely from the rules, and express the complexities in terms of characterizations of the facts. The idea is to analyze precisely the number of facts actually used and produced, avoiding crude approximations that use only sizes of individual argument domains.

Size parameters and basic constraints

We use P.i to denote the set of values of the i-th argument of relation P, that is, P.i is the projection of P on its i-th argument. We use P.I, where $I = \{i_1, i_2, \ldots, i_k\}$, to denote the set of tuples of values for the i_1-th, i_2-th, ..., and i_k-th arguments of P, that is, P.I is the projection of P on its i_1-th, i_2-th, ..., and i_k-th arguments.

The analysis uses the following size parameters to characterize the set of given facts, called *relation size*, *domain size*, *argument size*, and *relative argument size*, respectively:

- #P: the number of facts that actually hold for relation P.

- #D(P.i): the size of the domain from which elements of P.i can take values.

- #P.i: the number of values actually in P.i.

  #P.I: the number of tuples of values actually in P.I. For $I = \emptyset$, we take #P.$I = 1$.

- #P.i/j: the maximum number of values that the i-th argument of P actually takes for each value that the j-th argument of P takes, where $i \neq j$.

  #P.I/J: the maximum number of tuples of values that arguments of P with indices in I actually take for each tuple of values that the arguments with indices in J take, where $I \cap J = \emptyset$. For $I = \emptyset$, we take #P.$I/J = 1$. For $J = \emptyset$, we take #P.$I/J = $ #P.I.

  If an argument or a tuple of arguments with indices in J can take only a particular constant value or tuple of values, we specify that with an equal sign in between the argument(s) and value(s).

In the transitive closure example, #edge is the number of pairs in relation edge, that is, the number of edges in the graph; #D(edge.1) is the number of vertices; #edge.1 is the number of vertices that are sources of edges; #edge.1/2 is the maximum number of predecessors of a vertex, that is, the maximum *in-degree* of vertices; and #edge.1/2 = c is the number of predecessors of a particular vertex c.

It is easy to see that the following basic constraints hold:

$\#\text{P} = \#\text{P}.\{1, \ldots, a\}$ for relation P of a arguments
$\#\text{P}.i \leq \#D(\text{P}.i)$
$\#\text{P}.I \leq \#\text{P}.J$ for $I \subseteq J$
$\#\text{P}.(I \cup J) \leq \#\text{P}.I \times \#\text{P}.J/I$ and $\#\text{P}.J/I \leq \#\text{P}.J$, for $I \cap J = \emptyset$

These imply commonly used constraints, including in particular

$$\#\text{P} \leq \#D(\text{P}.1) \times \ldots \times \#D(\text{P}.a)$$

for relation P of a arguments, which is especially useful when $\#\text{P}$ is not an input parameter, that is, when P occurs in the conclusion of a rule.

For the transitive closure example, let the set of vertices 1 to V be the domain of the arguments of edge, and thus also the domain of the arguments of path. We have

$$\#\text{path}.2/1 \leq \#\text{path}.2 \leq \#D(\text{path}.2) = V$$
$$\#\text{path} \leq \#D(\text{path}.1) \times \#D(\text{path}.2) = V^2$$
$$\#\text{edge}.1/2 \leq \#\text{edge}.1 \leq \#D(\text{edge}.1) = V$$
$$\#\text{edge} \leq \#D(\text{edge}.1) \times \#D(\text{edge}.2) = V^2$$

Time complexity and optimality

In our derived algorithms, each fact is added to W once and then moved from W to R once. Each fact that makes the hypothesis of a rule of form 1 true and each combination of facts that makes both hypotheses of a rule of form 2 simultaneously true is considered exactly once, leading to a firing of the corresponding rule; the concluded fact is added to W if it is not in R or W, that is, if it was never put into W. To see that each combination of facts that makes both hypotheses P1 and P2 of a rule simultaneously true is considered only once, note that the auxiliary map entry for a fact f of P1 or P2 is built after retrieving f from a work-set and used afterward. So, a fact f1 of P1 combines once with each fact of P2 retrieved before f1 is retrieved, and each fact of P2 retrieved after f1 is retrieved combines once with f1.

It is therefore easy to see that the time complexity is the time of reading in the given facts plus the total number of firings of all rules, analyzed below. Because each firing as defined above may imply a new fact as an instance of the conclusion, it must, in general, be considered at least once. In this sense, the running times of our derived algorithms are optimal.

For each rule r, let $r.firedTimes$ denote the total number of times r is fired. Let Ixs denote the set of indices of arguments xs. For a rule r of form 1, we have

$$r.firedTimes \leq \#\text{P}.$$

For a rule r of form 2, we have

$$r.firedTimes \leq \min(\#\text{P1} \times \#\text{P2}.I\text{X2s}/I\text{Ys},$$
$$\#\text{P2} \times \#\text{P1}.I\text{X1s}/I\text{Ys}).$$

Each size used can also be made more precise by making it relative to the values of the constant arguments. For example, the bound $\#\text{P}$ for a rule of form 1 can be $\#\text{P}.I\text{Zs}/I\text{As} = \text{As}$.

Consider any given set of rules. Let characteristics of facts be given in terms of the four kinds of size parameters defined above, and consider the constraints on these size parameters described above. The total time complexity is the input size plus the sum of *firedTimes* over all rules, minimized symbolically with respect to the given size parameters and the constraints. In particular, if a relative argument size is needed but not given, we use the corresponding non-relative argument size; if an argument size $\#\text{P}.I$ is needed but not given, we use the minimum of (1) the product of domain sizes for arguments of P that are in I and (2) the argument sizes of P for arguments that are a superset of I.

For the transitive closure example, the time complexity is the input size $\#\text{edge}$ plus the sum of $\#\text{edge}$ for the first rule and $\min(\#\text{edge} \times \#\text{path}.2/1, \#\text{path} \times \#\text{edge}.1/2)$ for the second rule. When only parameters $\#\text{edge}$ and V are given, where V is the number of vertices, this sum is bounded by $\min(\#\text{edge} \times V, V^3)$ based on the constraints above; simplifying it based on $\#\text{edge} \leq V^2$, we obtain the worst-case time complexity $O(\#\text{edge} \times V)$. When in-degrees of vertices are given, the second operand of min, $\#\text{path} \times \#\text{edge}.1/2$, indicates that the complexity is also bounded by the output size times the maximum in-degree.

Additional constraints that capture dependencies among relations and relation arguments can be constructed from the rules to further bound the sizes for symbolic minimization. They can provide more precise results of symbolic minimization for rules that have longer chains of non-circular dependencies among relations and relation arguments. They can also help understand the complexity in terms of output size, rather than input size alone. Basically, we can bound, for each rule, the number of instances of the conclusion based on the number of instances of the hypotheses combined, and we can bound the number of instances of a hypothesis by summing all the facts that are instances of the hypothesis based on the rules that can conclude these instances and on the given facts.

Space complexity

We consider the space needed besides the space taken by the input. The total such space is the sum of the space needed for each of the result sets RQi's and other Ri's, work-sets WQi's and other Wi's, and auxiliary maps PiYsXis's, described separately as follows:

- RQi's are for relations that occur in the conclusions of the rules, that is, relations for which new facts may be inferred. For each such relation Qi of, say, a arguments, the space for RQi is for the a-level nested array structure that RQi uses. These arrays are indexed by the values in the domains and thus take

$$\#D(\text{Qi.1}) \times \ldots \times \#D(\text{Qi.}a)$$

space. Other Ri's take the same amount of space as the given facts for the corresponding relations.

- WQi's use the same amount of space for their nested-array structures as RQi's use. The queues for WQi's take no more space than the arrays. The queues for other Wi's take the same amount of space as the given facts for the corresponding relations.

- PiYsXis's are for relations that occur in the hypotheses of rules of form 2. If associative access of the third kind is needed, then the space for PiYsXis is for the arrays used for accessing all the components; linked lists for the components in the non-anchor take no more space. Otherwise, the space is taken by the arrays for the components in the anchor, plus linked lists for the non-anchor.

Let the domains of Ys be DY1 to DYj and of Xis be DXi1 to DXik. If associative access of the third kind is needed, the total space for PiYsXis is

$$\#D\text{Y1} \times \ldots \times \#D\text{Yj} \times \#D\text{Xi1} \times \ldots \times \#D\text{Xik}.$$

Otherwise, the product after the anchor is replaced with the amount of space taken by the nested linked-list structures for the non-anchor, one such structure for each element of the arrays for the last component of the anchor; it is hard to sum the space used by these structures directly, but it is easy to express it as the difference between the space for a nested linked-list structure for all components and the space for a nested linked-list structure for the anchor. So the total space for PiYsXis is

$$\#D\text{Y1} \times \ldots \times \#D\text{Yj} + \#\text{Pi.}(I\text{Ys} \cup I\text{Xis}) - \#\text{Pi.}I\text{Ys}.$$

We call the space taken by result sets RQi's the *output space*, and the space taken by auxiliary maps PiYsXis's the *auxiliary space*. Work-sets WQi's take asymptotically the same space as RQi's, and other Wi's and Ri's take asymptotically no more space than the given facts.

In our data structures for the auxiliary map for each individual relation, and for the result set for each individual rule, arrays are used only where needed—each array supports constant-time associative access by index for a non-constant number of sets that have associative access—and linked structures with minimum space overhead are used for the rest. However, optimizations that schedule the order in which elements in the work-sets are considered may allow reuse of space by considering relations and rules in a certain order, so space taken by relations no longer needed can be reused; this may eliminate some summands in the space usage formula. Therefore the total space used may sometimes be reduced by using scheduling optimizations to eliminate some summands in the space usage formula.

For the transitive closure problem, the output path takes space $\#D(\text{path}.1) \times \#D(\text{path}.2)$, which is $O(V^2)$, where the set of vertices 1 to V is the domain of the arguments of edge, that is, $\{1, ..., V\} = \text{edge}.1 \cup \text{edge}.2$. The auxiliary space usage is $\#D(\text{edge}.2) + \#\text{edge}.\{2, 1\} - \#\text{edge}.2$, which is $O(V + \#\text{edge})$ and thus is $O(\#\text{edge})$.

Handling of rules not in simplified form

Recall that in the simplified form, each rule has at most two hypotheses, and equal cards and wild cards occur only in rules with one hypothesis. Rules not in the simplified form can either be reduced to the simplified form, as discussed in Section 5.1, or be handled with a slight extension to the derivation, with trade-offs, as discussed below.

Consider decomposing rules with more than two hypotheses into rules with two hypotheses. For a rule with h hypotheses, the number of ways of decomposing it into rules with two hypotheses is the double factorial of $2 \times h - 3$, shown below, although h is usually a small constant, often no more than two. Note that we are counting the number of distinct rooted binary leaf-labeled trees with h leaves, where $h \geq 2$. To prove the formula, note that a rooted tree topology with $h - 1$ leaves has $2 \times ((h - 1) - 1)$ branches. The h-th leaf may be added by picking any one of the branches to split and add the new leaf, or by making an outgrow to the existing tree, a total of $2 \times ((h - 1) - 1) + 1 = 2 \times h - 3$ possible choices, each leading to a different tree topology.

$$(2 \times h - 3)!! \quad = \quad 1 \times 3 \times \cdots \times (2 \times h - 3)$$

Each decomposition leads to certain time and space complexities, calculated from the rules using the method above; the only modification is that the space taken by the introduced auxiliary relations should be counted as auxiliary space, not output space. In principle, the complexities resulting from different decompositions can be compared to determine which one is best in terms of time and space; in practice, this needs heuristics. There may be many trade-offs, if no decomposition leads to the smallest complexities in all measures.

Although decomposing rules is higher-level, simpler, and clearer than handling more hypotheses in the derivation, the space taken by the auxiliary relations might be unnecessary. Handling three or more hypotheses directly in the derivation requires us to find matching facts of two or more additional hypotheses, when adding a fact of one hypothesis, without storing auxiliary relations. This in turn requires considering the additional hypotheses one at a time, repeatedly; considering each additional hypothesis is similar to finding matching facts for rules with two hypotheses, so the best running time that this approach can achieve is the same as the transformational method. However, avoiding storing auxiliary relations in handling three or more hypotheses reduces auxiliary space, except it may cause repeated computations when common intermediate facts inferred are not stored in auxiliary relation and trigger repeated further firings.

Handling equal cards and wild cards in rules with more than one hypothesis, either by reduction to rules in the simplified form or by extension to the derivation, results in essentially the same algorithms and complexities. Again, the reduction approach is higher-level, simpler, and clearer, and the only effect on space is that the space taken by introduced auxiliary relations should be counted as auxiliary space, not output space. This auxiliary space is asymptotically no more than the space needed for the original rules, and it can lead to savings in the time complexity. Specifically, in the derived algorithms for the simplified rules, when rules with two hypotheses are considered, instances of a hypothesis that differ only in the wild-card components are considered only once all together, and only instances whose equal-card components are equal are considered. The domain of an equal-card component is the intersection of the domains of all the components of the equal card.

As a final note, for rules with more than two hypotheses, relations used by these hypotheses can be first restricted to only facts that will contribute to the relation in the conclusion. This helps ensure that we consider only combinations of facts that lead to all hypotheses of a rule being simultaneously true.

Exercise 5.11 (Complexity analysis for different transitive closure rules) For the transitive closure rules that you wrote for Exercise 5.2, give the complexity formula for running time, output space, and auxiliary space.

Exercise 5.12 (Complexity analysis for graph reachability rules) For the graph reachability rules that you wrote for Exercise 5.3, give the complexity formula for running time, output space, and auxiliary space.

5.6   Example: program analysis

Program analysis is important for all kinds of program development and maintenance tasks, yet it is also a challenging field of study, because flows and dependencies for program control and data form complicated cyclic relations. Experience has shown that most program analyses can be easily specified as Datalog rules. We discuss one of the most commonly used and studied program analysis—pointer analysis. This example also shows the decomposition of rules with more than two hypotheses into rules with two hypotheses.

Pointer analysis

Pointer analysis determines memory locations that variables in a program point to. Perhaps the single most studied pointer analysis, and definitely one of the most studied analyses, is the context-insensitive and flow-insensitive may-point-to analysis for programs written in the C language. Context-insensitive means that functions and procedures are analyzed for all calling contexts together, rather than specialized for different calls. Flow-insensitive means all control flows are considered possible, rather than only flows among certain program points. May-point-to means an over-approximation of the actual points-to relation.

The analysis defines a points-to relation, denoted points_to, based on four kinds of assignment statements that involve pointers:

- taking address, $p = \&q$, denoted addr(p,q),

- making copy, $p = q$, denoted copy(p,q),

- taking content, $p = *q$, denoted cont(p,q), and

- assigning content, $*p = q$, denoted asgn(p,q).

The analysis can be specified straightforwardly using four Datalog rules, one for each kind of statement; the first column gives the rule number.

```
1   addr(p,q) -> points_to(p,q)
2   copy(p,q), points_to(q,r) -> points_to(p,r)
3   cont(p,q), points_to(q,r), points_to(r,s) -> points_to(p,s)
4   asgn(p,q), points_to(p,r), points_to(q,s) -> points_to(r,s)
```

In the resulting points-to relation, each variable can point to a set of memory locations.

Decomposing rules with more than two hypotheses

The last two rules both have three hypotheses. The most straightforward way of decomposing such a rule is to combine its first two hypotheses first, and then combine the resulting auxiliary relation with the third hypothesis. This transforms the last two rules into two rules each, yielding the following four rules, where new1 and new2 are two fresh auxiliary relations:

```
3a  cont(p,q), points_to(q,r) -> new1(p,r)
3b  new1(p,r), points_to(r,s) -> points_to(p,s)
4a  asgn(p,q), points_to(p,r) -> new2(q,r)
4b  new2(q,r), points_to(q,s) -> points_to(r,s)
```

Iterate, incrementalize, and implement

An efficient program can be generated from the six rules, 1, 2, 3a, 3b, 4a, and 4b. Step Iterate simply considers one fact at a time. Step Incrementalize maintains auxiliary maps for the inverses of copy, cont, and new1. These inverse maps are needed because in each of the rules 2, 3a, and 3b, when a fact of points_to is added, the second argument of copy, cont, or new1, respectively, is bound and is used to find the corresponding values of the first argument. All other relations are accessed with the first argument bound, and thus the relation itself can be used to find the matching values of the second component, and no auxiliary maps are needed. Step Implement designs a combination of records, linked lists, and arrays, similar to the transitive closure example, because the rule forms are the same except for the relation names and that there are more rules.

Time complexity

A bound on the number of firings for each of the six rules is calculated straight-forwardly as follows:

1	$\#\text{addr}$
2	$\min(\#\text{copy} \times \#\text{points\_to}.2/1, \#\text{points\_to} \times \#\text{copy}.1/2)$
3a	$\min(\#\text{cont} \times \#\text{points\_to}.2/1, \#\text{points\_to} \times \#\text{cont}.1/2)$
3b	$\min(\#\text{new1} \times \#\text{points\_to}.2/1, \#\text{points\_to} \times \#\text{new1}.1/2)$
4a	$\min(\#\text{asgn} \times \#\text{points\_to}.2/1, \#\text{points\_to} \times \#\text{asgn}.2/1)$
4b	$\min(\#\text{new2} \times \#\text{points\_to}.2/1, \#\text{points\_to} \times \#\text{new2}.2/1)$

By rules 3a and 4a, it is obvious that $\#\text{new1}$ and $\#\text{new2}$ are bound by the formula for 3a and 4a, respectively. Simply taking the first argument of each min expression, the total number of firings is bound by

$$\#\text{addr} + (\#\text{copy} + \#\text{cont} + \#\text{cont} \times \#\text{points\_to}.2/1$$
$$+ \#\text{asgn} + \#\text{asgn} \times \#\text{points\_to}.2/1) \times \#\text{points\_to}.2/1$$

Each firing takes constant time, so the total time complexity is

$$O(\#\text{addr} + \#\text{copy} \times \#\text{points\_to}.2/1 + (\#\text{cont} + \#\text{asgn}) \times \#\text{points\_to}.2/1^2)$$

The sum of $\#\text{addr}$, $\#\text{copy}$, $\#\text{cont}$, and $\#\text{asgn}$ is $O(n)$, where n is the size of the program being analyzed. The parameter $\#\text{points\_to}.2/1$ is the maximum number of locations that a single variable may point to, denoted *to*. So the time complexity is $O(n \times to^2)$. The resulting *to* is $O(n)$ in the worst case. So the time complexity is $O(n^3)$ in the worst case, as is well known for this problem.

However, the number of locations a single variable may point to is typically a very small constant, often zero, for most program variables, so the actual running time can be much better than the worst-case bound of $O(n^3)$, and can even be $O(n)$ when all but a small number of variables point to a small number of locations. This explains the typically much better than cubic and often linear time complexity observed in practice. Besides offering a simple and clear explanation of this well-known, puzzling symptom, the formula above also shows precisely how the running time depends on the number of each kind of statement in the program.

Space complexity

Both output space and auxiliary space are $O(var^2)$, where var is the number of variables in the program and is bound by $O(n)$.

The output space is for storing the resulting `points_to` relation. The domain of both arguments of `points_to` is the set of variables in the program, so the output space is $O(var^2)$.

The auxiliary space includes space for storing auxiliary relations `new1` and `new2` and auxiliary maps for the inverses of `copy`, `cont`, and `new1`. Both `new1` and `new2` are bounded by $O(var^2)$, because the domain of their arguments is the set of program variables. The inverse maps take space $O(\#\texttt{copy} + \#\texttt{cont} + \#\texttt{new1})$, which is bound by $O(var^2)$. So the total auxiliary space is $O(var^2)$.

Exercise 5.13 (Regular path queries) Given a graph with edge relation `edge` and source vertex `v0`, and a regular expression converted into a finite automata with transition relation `trans` and start state `s0`, a *regular path query* computes all vertices `v` in the graph such that there is a path from `v0` to `v` in the graph that matches a path from `s0` to a final state in the automata. The following rule, along with a simple rule for the base case and a simple rule for the return value, can be used for answering regular path queries:

```
match(v1,s1), edge(v1,v2), trans(s1,s2) -> match(v2,s2)
```

What are all ways of breaking this rule into rules with two hypotheses? For each way of breaking, give the complexity formula for its running time, output space, and auxiliary space. Which way gives the least time complexity? Which way gives the least space complexity? What are the two simple rules not given?

Exercise 5.14 (Graph reachability by even edges*) Given a graph with a set of edges and a set of source vertices, we want to find all the vertices that are reachable from the source vertices by following an even number of edges. How do you think this should be computed and how long should it take? Did you think about writing rules for computing the solutions? Please do. Then, use our method to find out the algorithm and data structures and analyze the complexities.

5.7 Example: trust management

Trust management is a unified approach to specifying and enforcing security policies in distributed systems. It has become increasingly important as systems become increasingly interconnected. At the same time, logic-based languages have been used increasingly for expressing trust management policies. For policy analysis and enforcement, a method for generating efficient algorithms and implementations from policies specified using logic rules is highly desired. We discuss the core problem of name resolution in a well-known trust management framework.

This example also shows the handling of an extension to Datalog, where arguments of relations may be sequences.

SPKI/SDSI name-reduction closure

SPKI/SDSI, which stands for Simple Public Key Infrastructure/Simple Distributed Security Infrastructure, is a well-known trust management framework based on public keys that is designed to facilitate the development of secure and scalable distributed systems.

It has two types of certificates. A name certificate defines a local name in the issuer's local name space. An authorization certificate is issued by an issuer to grant a set of permissions to a subject and possibly allows the subject to delegate the permission. The heart of authorization checking is to compute the name-reduction closure given a set of name certificates. It composes certificates to infer reduced certificates and can be expressed directly as a Datalog rule with a constraint that tests whether a name is the head of a sequence of names, and with a call to an external function that returns the tail of a sequence in the conclusion.

Let `cert(k1,n,k2,ns)` denote the name certificate stating that the entity known to principal `k1` by name `n` is the entity known to principal `k2` by name sequence `ns`. Then the name-reduction closure can be specified straightforwardly as

```
cert(k1,n1,k2,[n2,ns3]), cert(k2,n2,k3,[]) -> cert(k1,n1,k3,ns3)
```

For example, an instance of the rule may state that

if `cert(kyle,wife,kate,[boss,[mom,[]]])`, that is, `kyle`'s `wife` is `kate`'s `boss`' `mom`,
and `cert(kate,boss,kirk,[])`, that is, `kate`'s `boss` is `kirk`,
then `cert(kyle,wife,kirk,[mom,[]])`, that is, `kyle`'s `wife` is `kirk`'s `mom`.

It matches the rule above with the mapping of `k1` to `kyle`, `n1` to `wife`, `k2` to `kate`, `n2` to `boss`, `ns3` to `[mom,[]]`, and `k3` to `kirk`.

Iterate, Incrementalize, Implement

Step Iterate simply considers one fact at a time. Step Incrementalize maintains auxiliary maps for finding matching certificates, and must handle the sequence argument in incremental computation. When a fact of the first hypothesis is added, the value of its last argument is accessed to locate the head of the sequence, `n2`, and the values of `k2` and `n2` are used to find matching facts of the second hypothesis. When a fact of the second hypothesis is added, the values of `k2` and `n2` are used to find matching facts of the first hypothesis through the third argument and the head of the fourth argument. To add a newly inferred `cert` fact, comparison with existing facts needs to handle the sequence argument; note that the sequence argument is always a tail of the sequence argument of a given certificate, so the comparison needs to use only a reference to the tail, in constant time.

Step Implement decides to use nested arrays for both anchors and non-anchors of auxiliary maps, because new cert facts can be inferred. It also decides to use an array for the first two arguments, together, of cert, because these arguments are always together as in the given certificates, and to use nested arrays for the last two arguments, where the sequence argument is a reference to a tail sequence in the input.

Time complexity

Matching and manipulation with an empty sequence and the head of a sequence for each firing take constant time, so the asymptotic time complexity is bound by the number of rule firings.

The number of firings is bounded by the number of inferred facts of the first hypothesis multiplied by the number of matching facts of the second hypothesis, yielding the following:

$$\#\text{cert} \times \#\text{cert}.3/\{1,2,4 = \texttt{[]}\}$$

where $\#\text{cert}.3/\{1,2,4 = \texttt{[]}\}$ denotes the maximum number of key values of the third argument for each combination of values of the first and second arguments when the fourth argument is empty.

It is easy to see that $\#\text{cert}$ is the number of all certificates that can be inferred, some possibly multiple times, and $\#\text{cert}.3/\{1,2,4 = \texttt{[]}\}$ is the maximum number of keys a single local name reduces to. The first number, $\#\text{cert}$, is bounded by $in \times key$, where in is the size of the input, that is, the sum of the sizes of the given certificates, and key is the number of keys. This is because in any inferred cert fact, the third argument is a key, and all other arguments are from a given certificate. The second number, $\#\text{cert}.3/\{1,2,4 = \texttt{[]}\}$, may in the worst case include all keys that appear in the certificates. Thus, the worst-case time complexity is $O(in \times key^2)$. However, one can see that not all names reduces to all keys, for example, in our example, the name boss for kate reduces to only one key kirk. So our complexity analysis is more precise and informative than using only worst-case sizes.

Space complexity

The output space is for storing the relation cert. Let kn be the total number of key and name pairs in the given certificates. Let s be the sum of the lengths of all name sequences in the given certificates. Then, the output space is $O(kn \times key \times s)$.

The auxiliary space is for auxiliary maps, one for each of the two hypotheses. Let $name$ be the total number of names in the given certificates. Then, the map for the first hypothesis maps k2 and n2 to k1-n1 pairs and ns3, and takes $O(key \times name \times kn \times s)$ space; the map for the second hypothesis maps k2-n2 pairs to k3, and takes $O(kn \times key)$ space. Therefore, the total auxiliary space is $O(kn \times key \times name \times s)$.

Exercise 5.15 (Worst case for name-reduction closure*) For the SPKI/SDSI name-reduction closure problem discussed, give an example set of certificates for which the worst-case time complexity is realized.

Exercise 5.16 (Permission query using rules) In core RBAC, user-role relation UR represents the assignment of users to roles, and permission-role relation PR represents the assignment of permission to roles. The following set query returns the set of permissions for a given user user.

```
{p: [user,r] in UR, [p,r] in PR}
```

Write a rule to infer the same query result. Analyze the cost of evaluating this query using the method discussed.

5.8 Need for module abstraction

In all of the problems we have seen so far, loops with primitives and arrays, set expressions, recursive functions, and logic rules are all used for specifying essentially a single functionality, rather than a large system with many functionalities. Also, there is no module structure in the problem specification—specifications range from straight-line code to flat rules. For scaled-up applications, many functionalities must be provided over many kinds of data, and module structures are necessary for organizing all the data and operations.

For example, a complex system may have many components, each encapsulating some data and some functionalities. Some of the functionalities may be specified as set queries, while others may be specified using recursive functions.

Specifications that use module abstractions, as well as methods for deriving efficient implementations in the presence of module abstraction, are discussed in the next chapter.

Exercise 5.17 (Applications with multiple components) Think of an application where you would like to have multiple components, each having its own sets of queries and updates over its own data, independent of how other components' queries and updates are implemented. Can you think of queries that are easier to write using rules than using set comprehensions, and vice versa?

Bibliographical notes

Logic rules have been used for programming since as early as the 1970s. The best-known logic programming language is Prolog. Well-engineered logic programming systems include XSB [296], Yap [66], and some commercial systems [183]. Datalog [49, 3] is an important database query language based on the logic programming paradigm; it is also used increasingly in program analysis [230], model checking [60], security [180], networking [218], and many other applications.

Efficient implementation of Datalog and general logic programs has been studied extensively in logic programming and database areas [49, 3]. Smart evaluation methods include semi-naive evaluation for bottom-up evaluation [49, 228], tabling for top-down evaluation [297, 53], and static and dynamic filtering [168, 169]. Smart rewriting methods include magic-sets transformation [18, 26] and partial evaluation [217, 178]. Other methods include notably the Rete algorithm [89], which builds a network from rules and propagates facts through it, and variations or improvements, e.g., [224, 177, 41, 158]. There are also methods used in applications for efficient evaluation of Datalog queries using binary decision diagrams (BDD) [317, 174] and relational databases [125].

All these methods do not provide precise complexity guarantees, even though complexity measures and complexity classes for various query languages have been studied, e.g., [305, 173, 68, 109, 108]. In fact, such analysis can be very difficult [183]. For example, for top-down evaluation with tabling and indexing [297, 274, 53, 264], a graph reachability program may have one of several different time complexities between linear and quadratic, depending on the order of the rules, the order of the hypotheses in a rule, the indexing used, and so on. It is well known that a Datalog program runs in $O(n^k)$ time where k is the largest number of variables in any single rule, and n is the number of constants in the facts and rules, but such a bound is too loose for most problems.

McAllester [222] introduced an evaluation method for capturing precise time complexity of logic programs, by counting the number of prefix firings, that is, combinations of facts that make all prefixes of the hypotheses of a rule true. Ganzinger and McAllester generalized this method to handle priorities and deletion of rules [95] and furthermore priorities of instances of the same rule [96]. Their time complexity is still sensitive to the order of hypotheses in the rules. Space complexity is not discussed. Hashing is used, which incurs extra time overhead, and possibly space overhead, and gives no tight worst-case guarantees on time and space. A follow-up work [231] discusses how to automate the complexity analysis.

The method in this chapter is by Liu and Stoller [199, 203]. What distinguishes it is (1) direct transformation of any set of Datalog rules into a complete algorithm and data structures specialized for those rules, and (2) precise analysis of worst-case time and space complexities supported by the algorithm and data structures. It is not an evaluation method because it transforms the rules rather than evaluating them. Nor is it a rewriting method in that it does not transform within the frameworks of rules. It compiles the rules into an optimized program in a standard imperative programming language. The program can be plugged in any application, not relying on any rule engine. The program performs a kind of bottom-up computation based on careful incremental updates with data structure support. The time and space complexities of the program are easy to analyze based on the rules.

The idea of considering one new fact at a time and finding other facts using indexing to form firings of rules is quite straightforward, and is used in many implementations. For example, in compilation of constraint handling rules [135, 278], the active constraint corresponds to the new fact considered, although constraints are more general. Reducing the time complexity to the number of firings of rules is used at least as early as the 1970s by Beeri and Bernstein [25], where they give a linear-time algorithm for solving the attribute closure problem that is expressed using rules. The idea of initializing an array entry the first time its is accessed is suggested in [6, Exercise 2.12]. Willard shows that relations in multiple-join queries can be first restricted to help ensure that only combinations of facts that lead to all hypotheses of a rule being simultaneously true are considered [324].

Compared with method described for sets in Chapter 3, Datalog rules are easier and clearer than fixed-point specifications [44] to start with. The derivation of incremental maintenance handles sets of tuples of any length and sets with different element types, not just sets and maps of uniform element types handled previously [236, 243, 238]. The derivation of data structures handles general sets of tuples, and yields more general and sophisticated combinations of arrays, linked lists, and records than allowed by the based representation before [239, 42, 110]. Precise complexity formulas are generated from Datalog rules, but were not from fixed-point specifications previously.

The context-insensitive and flow-insensitive may-point-to analysis for C programs was proposed by Andersen [12] and formulated using rules by Heintze and Tardieu [132]. It has been implemented and experimented with extensively and compared with other variants of the analysis, e.g., [90, 133, 294, 104]. Even though its worst-case asymptotic time complexity is known to be $O(n^3)$, various experiments show that it appears to be between linear and quadratic in practice. The more precise complexity formula in Section 5.6 was given previously [203]. Following the same method, similar pointer analysis for Java programs [294] can also be implemented efficiently and analyzed precisely [301].

SPKI/SDSI [80] is a well-known trust management framework. Trust management has become increasingly important [115, 35], and logic-based languages have been used increasingly for expressing security and trust management policies [152, 181]. SPKI/SDSI name-reduction closure algorithms are studied in [59, 182, 153, 144]. The bound of $O(in \times \#\texttt{key}^2)$ on $\#\texttt{cert}$ was given by Jha and Reps [153], and the time complexity was analyzed using worst-case sizes [59, 153]. The more precise time complexity in Section 5.7 was given by Liu and

Stoller [203], but the space complexity in that paper is incorrect, underestimating the sequence sizes.

The method discussed in this chapter has been applied to other application problems in program analysis, model checking, and security, e.g., [142, 143, 144], leading to improved algorithms for some problems and greatly simplified complexity analysis for all problems. There are many other methods for program analysis, model checking, and so on, which use equations, constraints, automata, formal languages, and so forth [67, 131, 267, 8, 82], but using rules is typically more direct and more general. Formal derivation of algorithms and implementations using a systematic method helps provide correctness assurance, in contrast to ad hoc development of algorithms. Precise complexity analysis, using detailed size characterizations of the given facts, helps significantly in understanding the performance of the generated implementations.

The method discussed in this chapter is limited to inferring all facts and considering only Datalog. Given certain queries, inferring only facts that are useful for answering the queries, that is, computing on demand, is important for performance [18, 26]; Tekle and Liu [300, 301] extended the method in this chapter to solve this problem cleanly, using a new demand transformation. The method in this chapter applies also to Datalog with stratified negation [203], but not general negation. The SPKI/SDSI example uses Datalog extended with sequences, but all sequences used are from given inputs, and there is no dynamically constructed sequences.

6

Objects: incrementalize across module abstraction

For building large systems, it is essential to build them from components and use *module abstraction*, that is, abstraction of both data and control in modules or components, to separate *what* functionalities are provided by a component from *how* the functionalities are implemented inside the component. Module abstraction is best supported as abstract data types. An *abstract data type* is an interface for a certain set of operations on a certain kind of data, that is, the "what", shielding users from having to know how the data are represented and how the operations are implemented, that is, the "how". It is a fundamental concept in modern high-level programming languages, particularly object-oriented languages.

Unfortunately, clear and modular implementations of the modules or components result in poor performance when nontrivial query operations are frequently performed and values of query parameters are gradually updated. At the same time, efficient implementations that incrementally maintain the query results with respect to updates to parameter values are much more difficult to develop and to understand, because the code grows significantly and is no longer clear or modular. Because the definitions and uses of queries and updates can cross multiple components, transforming clear implementations of the queries into efficient incremental implementations requires incrementalization across module abstraction.

We describe a powerful and systematic design method that first allows the "what" of each component to be specified in a clear and modular fashion and implemented straightforwardly in an object-oriented language; then analyzes the queries and updates, across object abstraction, in the straightforward implementation; and finally derives the sophisticated and efficient "how" of each component by incrementally maintaining the results of repeated expensive queries with respect to updates to their parameter values. We explain the method using an example with two components and then show additional applications in electronic health records and robot games. We also describe a rule language for specifying transformations for incrementalization, as well as invariant-driven transformations in general. We end with a simple and powerful language for more easily expressing a large class of queries over complex object graphs.

Example: wireless protocols

Consider a wireless protocol that, among other things, needs to keep a set of signals and find, frequently, the set of signals whose strength is above a certain threshold. This may involve two components, Protocol and Signal, as shown below. Each component has its own kind of data and set of operations, including the relevant ones shown in text below; the ellipses indicate that there are possibly other data and operations in these two components, and there are possibly other components.

```
component: Protocol
    data:
        signals: set of signals
        threshold: threshold for a signal to be strong
        . . .
    operations:
        addSignal: add a given signal to the set of signals
        findStrongSignals: return the set of signals whose strength is above
                           the threshold
        . . .
component: Signal
    data:
        strength: strength of the signal
        . . .
    operations:
        setStrength: set the strength to a given value
        getStrength: return the strength
        . . .
    . . .
```

First, we need a language to describe components that encapsulate data and operations. Then, for components and systems specified in the language, we need to analyze all dependencies among the components, as well as within each component. For example, the operation findStrongSignals is provided in the Protocol component, but it needs to know the strengths of signals, which are in the Signal component. Finally, for efficient incremental computation of frequent expensive queries, we need to decide, besides what values to maintain and how to do incremental maintenance, which components store what values and how to coordinate maintenance among the components. For example, when the strength of a signal is updated in the Signal component, the query result of findStrongSignals in the Protocol component needs to be updated, and the two components must coordinate to achieve this.

Exercise 6.1 (Component design and optimization) For the wireless protocol example, think of how to program it and how to maintain the result of findStrongSignals efficiently.

6.1 Objects with fields and methods—module abstraction

To express components that encapsulate data and operations, we use an object-oriented language. Both straightforward and efficient implementations can be written in this language.

Language

A program is a set of class definitions, each defining some kinds of data, called *fields*, and some kinds of operations, called *methods*, for a collection of objects. A *class definition* is of the form below. It defines a class named c that contains zero or more field declarations and method definitions, as described below.

```
class c:
    field_declarations
    method_definitions
```

An *object* of class c is an instance of c; it is an encapsulated entity that contains the fields and methods defined in c. Objects are accessed through references. Multiple variables may refer to the same object, in which case we say that these variables are *aliases* of one another. Objects are created during program execution. Once created, we can access the fields and invoke the methods of the object, as explained below. For simplicity of understanding, we consider every value to be an object.

A *field definition* is of the form below, where f is the name of a field, and *type* is the data type of the field. A data type may be any common type, such as int for integer, a class name, such as Protocol, or a compound type, such as set(Protocol), whose components are, recursively, types.

```
f : type
```

A *method definition* is of the form below, where m is the name of a method, v_1 through v_k, if any, are names of variables, called *parameters*, and command *cmd* defines the effect of invoking m on an object given values of v_1 through v_k. Types may be specified not only for fields but also for method parameters, return values, and local variables of methods, although we omit those for simplicity. We generally omit types when they can be inferred from the program.

    def $m(v_1, \ldots, v_k)$: cmd

Commands may be loops, conditionals, sequencing, and assignments as described in Chapter 2, except that commands may also be for object creation, assignment to a field of an object, and invocation of a method on an object, and may also use additional kinds of expressions, as described below.

Expressions may involve arithmetic, Boolean, and comparison operations, as in Chapter 2; set expressions, as in Chapter 3; and additionally, self object reference, object class test, field access, and method invocation, explained next. Note that method invocations subsume function calls from Chapter 4, except with the additional self object reference. We can include rules and queries from Chapter 5 too, even though our examples here do not need them.

The *self object reference expression*, self, refers to the object on which the method being defined is invoked. Although any name could be used, we always use self for consistency.

An *object class test*, isinstance(exp,c), returns true if the object returned by evaluating expression exp is an instance of class c, and false otherwise.

A *field access expression* is of the form below. It evaluates expression exp to obtain an object, retrieves the value of field f of the object, and returns the value.

    $exp.f$

A *method invocation expression* is of the form below, where m is the name of a method. Method m must have no side effect, that is, update only local variables of m, and its body must be a command in which every flow of control ends with a return command. The method invocation evaluates the expression exp to an object, invokes method m of the object, with the object as the argument value for self, and with values of expressions exp_1 through exp_k, if any, as additional arguments, evaluates the body of m, and returns the value of the expression in the return command encountered.

    $exp.m(exp_1, \ldots, exp_k)$

An *object creation command* is of the form below. It creates and returns an object of class c. It is both a command and an expression because it both changes the state and returns a value. The values of expressions exp_1 through exp_k, if any, are passed as arguments to a specially named method in c that is invoked when an object of c is created. This specially named method can be defined by the programmer just as any other method, and defaults to doing nothing if it is not defined.

    new $c(exp_1, \ldots, exp_k)$

A *field assignment command*, also called an *assignment command*, is of the form below. It evaluates expression exp to obtain an object and assigns the value of exp_1 to field f of the object.

$$exp.f := exp_1$$

A *method invocation command* is of the form below. It is of the same form as a method invocation expression, except that the method invoked in an expression must have no side effect. The command evaluates exp to obtain an object, invokes method m of the object, with the object as the argument value for `self`, and with values of expressions exp_1 through exp_k, if any, as additional arguments, and executes the command in the body of m. For a method invocation command to achieve anything besides consuming time, it must have some side effect.

$$exp.m(exp_1,\ldots,exp_k)$$

In expressions and commands for field access, field assignment, and method invocation, if the first expression exp is `self`, we omit `self` and the dot that follows when there is no ambiguity.

We make substantial use of sets, because they are well suited for expressing queries and updates at a very high level and are well supported in object-oriented languages. We use set expressions as in Chapter 3, except that they may contain additional kinds of expressions as described above. We use the following object-oriented notation for operations from a set class:

- `new Set()`, set object creation, creates and returns an empty set object.

- `S.add(x)`, element addition, adds x to set S.

- `S.del(x)`, element deletion, deletes x from set S.

- `S.contains(x)`, membership test, returns `true` if x is in set S and `false` otherwise.

- `S.size()`, size of set S, returns the number of elements in set S.

We make the following assumptions based on well-known principles about straightforward, clear, and modular programs, and we do not consider concurrency here.

- Fields are initialized at object creation time. So it is safe to access the fields any time after an object is created.

- Fields are updated only in the class where they are declared, and sets are updated only in the class where they are created. So one only needs to look for updates to a field or set inside the class that declares or creates it.

For the protocol example, the following straightforward implementation can be constructed. Note that we show only portions of the classes relevant to our current discussion.

```
class Protocol:
  signals: set(Signal)
  threshold: float
  ...
  def addSignal(s): signals.add(s)
  def findStrongSignals():
    return {s in signals | s.getStrength() > threshold}
  ...
class Signal:
  strength: float
  ...
  def setStrength(v): strength := v
  def getStrength(): return strength
  ...
...
```

Cost model

Because objects only provide organization of data and operations, not new kinds of data structures or control structures, the costs of operations involving loops, sets, recursion, and rules are the same as in previous chapters. Because programs can use operations from library classes, we also need to know the costs for library operations. Furthermore, because methods of classes may be invoked from outside, we also need to consider the frequencies of these operations. Finally, as before, what cost is considered expensive in the application should be specified explicitly.

To summarize from previous chapters: for loops, the cost is linear in the number of iterations through the loops; for operations on sets, the cost is linear in the number of elements to be enumerated for operations other than those that involve a single element; for functions, the cost is linear in the number of function calls; for rules, the cost is linear in the number of rule firings. Operations that require iteration, enumeration, and recursion are considered expensive, whereas operations that take constant time are considered inexpensive.

Costs of operations from library classes should be given based on the implementation of the library, just as the costs of built-in operations on primitive values is given based on the underlying machine hardware implementation. Frequencies of operations, at least those directly invoked by users of the application or an external system in the environment of the application, should also be provided if possible.

For the protocol example, the findStrongSignals operation requires enumeration and thus is expensive; also, depending on the implementation of the set class, either the set operations used here are all constant-time and thus inexpensive or the size operation can be expensive.

Exercise 6.2 (Attribute-based access control) Suppose RBAC needs to be extended to query attributes of users, but these user attributes are manipulated largely independently of usage by access control. How should you design the components?

Exercise 6.3 (Attribute-based permission query) In core RBAC, user-role relation UR represents the assignment of users to roles, and permission-role relation PR represents the assignment of permission to roles. Suppose user objects have an integer attribute age. Write a query that returns the set of permissions that any user under 18 years old has.

6.2 Queries and updates: clarity versus efficiency

Although components separate *how* operations are implemented inside from *what* these operations are to the users outside, there is a conflict between clarity and efficiency in implementing the operations. To resolve this conflict, we will need to analyze queries and updates.

Queries and updates

What operations are to the users of a system or component can be classified as, or decomposed into, two kinds: queries and updates. *Queries* compute results using data but do not change data, and are sometimes called views or observations. *Updates* change data.

For a simple example, consider the LinkedList class in Java 7.[1] It has a query method size that returns the number of elements in the list, 23 methods that add or remove elements, and 16 other query methods that return elements, their indices, membership test results, and so on.[2]

For the protocol example, in class Protocol, findStrongSignals is a query, and addSignal is an update; in class Signal, getStrength is a query, and setStrength is an update.

Conflict between clarity and efficiency

How to implement the queries and updates can vary significantly, which reflects a fundamental conflict between clarity and efficiency.

- A straightforward implementation lets each operation do its respective query or update and is clear and modular. For example, in the LinkedList class, size can iterate over elements in the list to count them, and each of the 23 update methods would do exactly the specified addition or removal of elements. However, this can have poor performance, because queries may be repeated

---

[1] http://download.oracle.com/javase/7/docs/api/java/util/LinkedList.html (Jan. 29, 2013)
[2] These numbers have been increasing since LinkedList was introduced in Java 1.2. For example, in Java 5, there were 15 methods that add or remove elements and 13 other query methods.

and many are expensive. For example, `size` takes time linear in the number of elements in the list, and if it occurs in a loop, the overall running time blows up quickly.

- A sophisticated implementation can have good performance, by storing the results of expensive queries appropriately and maintaining them incrementally when the data are updated. For example, the `LinkedList` class may maintain the result of `size` in a field and simply return it when `size` is queried. However, this is less clear, less modular, and more error-prone, because each update that may affect any of the query results must be augmented with appropriate updates to those query results. In the `LinkedList` class, each of the 23 update methods must also update the field for `size` appropriately.

Clearly, there is a conflict between clarity and efficiency, even for the simple `LinkedList` example. The situation becomes much worse for complex systems that may have many queries and updates, where queries may cross multiple classes, and updates may be spread in many places in many classes. A query can be affected by many updates, and an update can affect many queries. It poses a serious challenge to consider all the complex dependencies and trade-offs and to decide where and how to maintain what results, and the resulting code can become significantly more difficult to understand.

For the protocol example, each of the queries `findStrongSignals` and `getStrength`, and the updates `addSignal` and `setStrength`, can be constructed modularly and clearly in a straightforward fashion, as shown near the end of the previous section. Efficient implementations are much more complicated because the expensive query `findStrongSignals` must have its result stored and incrementally maintained for use in class `Protocol` when the strengths of signals are updated by `setStrength` in class `Signal` and when the set of signals is updated by `addSignal`.

This conflict between clarity and modularity, and thus software productivity and cost on one side and program efficiency and system performance on the other side, manifests itself widely in complex systems and components. To resolve this conflict, a powerful method for developing systems and components must support not only creation of module abstraction but also incrementalization across such abstraction, where the former is needed for clarity and modularity, and the latter is needed for performance.

Analyzing expensive queries and updates to parameter values

To perform incrementalization across module abstraction, we need to identify expensive queries and determine updates to their parameter values across the abstraction, and we need to analyze their costs and frequencies.

There are two kinds of expensive computations: (1) built-in or library operations that are specified as expensive in the cost model, such as a library operation that sorts a list, and (2) compound computations that require repeated operations, including set comprehensions, aggregate expressions, iterations, and recursions. For each expensive computation, three things must be determined: (1) containing class and method—the class and method where the computation appears, (2) parameters read—variables and fields that the computation depends on, and (3) primary cost consideration—asymptotic running time of the computation. Note that expensive computations may have expensive subcomputations; we identify all expensive computations, including all expensive subcomputations, and use the results of the subcomputations as parameters read by the enclosing computation.

Expensive computations are easy to identify given the cost model. For any expensive computation, its cost can be analyzed based on the cost model. Its containing class and method are easy to analyze. Its parameters must be analyzed using a precise analysis that can select parts of members of compound values. For example, for the query findStrongSignals in the protocol example, we want to avoid including all parts of the signals in signals as parameters read, but only the parts that are actually used, which include only the strength field of the signals. So, we need to refine the notion of parameters when dealing with objects and sets that can be arbitrarily nested. Precisely, *parameter*s are of the form of (1) a variable, (2) a sequence of field accesses starting with a variable, or (3) a comprehension representing a set of parameters where the sets enumerated are of the form of (1) or (2).

For the protocol example, in the straightforward implementation given, all built-in operations used are inexpensive. The only expensive computation is the following set comprehension:

```
{s in self.signals | s.getStrength() > self.threshold}
```

class: Protocol
method: findStrongSignals
parameters read: self.signals, self.signals.members,
                 {s.strength: s in self.signals}, self.threshold
cost: $O(\#signals)$

The containing class and method are obvious. The parameters include: the set to be enumerated, self.signals, which accesses the field signals on variable self; members of this set, self.signals.members; and parameters of the condition, {s.strength: s in self.signals} and self.threshold. The cost is linear in the number of signals in self.signals, because the condition only uses constant-time operations.

All updates to the value of each parameter of each expensive computation must be determined. To minimize coordination effort and facilitate atomicity, we identify only the most basic updates. There are two kinds of such basic update operations: (1) an assignment command that writes to a field or variable, and (2) a call to a library operation that writes to some fields. For each update operation, three things need to be determined: (1) containing class and method, (2) parameters written—the fields or variables being updated, and (3) cost—asymptotic running time of the update operation.

To determine whether a particular update is an update to the value of a particular parameter of a query, we need to determine whether the variable or object field being updated and a variable or object field appearing in the parameter are aliases of each other, that is, refer to the same object. This uses *alias analysis*, which computes variables and object fields that are aliases of one another. We can use any conservative analysis of the possible aliases during program execution, and guard the incremental maintenance code with a runtime check for actual aliasing. For a library operation, we assume that information about which parts of its arguments are updated by the operation is given.

For the expensive query in the protocol example, in the straightforward implementation, there is an update to the value of its parameter `self.signals.members`:

> `self.signals.add(s)`
>
> class: `Protocol`
> method: `addSignal`
> parameters written: `self.signals.members`
> cost: $O(1)$

and an update to the value of its parameter `{s.strength: s in self.signals}`:

> `self.strength := v`
>
> class: `Signal`
> method: `setStrength`
> parameters written: `self.strength`
> cost: $O(1)$

The update `self.signals.add(s)`, in method `addSignal`, may update the value of parameter `self.signals.members` of the expensive query, in method `findStrongSignals`, due to the following. Let `self`$_a$ and `self`$_f$ denote variable `self` in `addSignal` and `findStrongSignals`, respectively. Then, `self`$_a$ may alias `self`$_f$, because the elided part of the program, denoted by ellipses, may call `addSignal` and `findStrongSignals` on the same instance of `Protocol`. Thus, because `self`$_a$`.signals.add(s)` updates the value of `self`$_a$`.signals.members`, it may update the value of `self`$_f$`.signals.members`.

Exercise 6.4 (Query parameters and cost) In core RBAC, user-role relation UR represents the assignment of users to roles. Suppose user objects have an attribute `location`. The following query returns the set of roles for users located in `antarctica`.

> `{r: [u,r] in UR, | u.location = antarctica}`

What are the parameters of the query? What is the cost of the query if executed straightforwardly?

Exercise 6.5 (Updates to parameter values) Consider the query in the previous exercise. Suppose that a program can do arbitrary updates. What are all possible updates to the values of the parameters of this query?

6.3 Incrementalize: develop and apply incrementalization rules

Once expensive queries and updates to parameter values are determined, we must examine where to store the query results, and where and how to update them. For the expensive query in the protocol example, it is relatively easy to decide to store the result in a field of class Protocol. For updates, there are more issues to consider. In particular, the update by setStrength in class Signal may affect the query result. We want to incrementally maintain the stored query result as follows: if the strength of the signal is changed from above threshold to below, then the signal is removed from the query result; and if the strength is changed from below threshold to above, then the signal is added. However, object abstraction makes this more difficult.

Should setStrength in class Signal or some method in class Protocol take care of the update? Clearly setStrength should initiate the update because it changes the signal strength. However, recall the restriction that fields should be accessed directly only in the class where they are declared. Thus, setStrength cannot or should not directly access and update the query result in Protocol, or access other data that is needed for the update but is not in Signal, whereas a method in Protocol can. Rather than giving setStrength access to those, a method can be defined in Protocol and called from setStrength to perform the update.

Now, how can a Signal object get a reference to the Protocol object to call the defined method? Note that all and only members of signals need to get such references. So when a Signal object is added to the signals field of a Protocol object, a reference to the Protocol object, that is, self, can be passed to the Signal object. To do this, the Signal class must define a method for taking the reference to a Protocol object. Additionally, because a Signal object may be added to signals of multiple Protocol objects, a Signal object must maintain a *set* of references to these Protocol objects.

Finally, cost must be considered. Under what conditions will the transformations to achieve the aforementioned improve performance? In the straightforward implementation, each query takes $O(\#\texttt{signals})$ time and each update takes $O(1)$ time; after the transformations, each query takes $O(1)$ time and each update takes $O(\#\texttt{protocols})$ time, where $\#\texttt{protocols}$ is the number of protocols whose signals field contains the signal being updated. So there is a trade-off. In an application that has several or many signals but one or a few instances of Protocol, and where the query is performed at least as frequently as the signal strengths change, the transformed implementation is much more efficient.

The preceding discussion considers only one expensive query and one kind of update. In general, there may be many expensive queries and many kinds of updates that are interdependent. Even for the tiny program fragments in the straightforward implementation of the protocol example, we can see that the query result of findStrongSignals needs to be updated also in addSignal of Protocol. How to incrementally maintain all the invariants involved under all updates in a coordinated way, using a systematic and even automatic method?

The idea is to maintain invariants one at a time, just as in Chapter 3, but the maintenance of an invariant at a set of updates may be much more sophisticated, so a declarative language is desired for specifying the transformations and application conditions. We describe incrementalization rules for specifying coordinated maintenance of a query result at a set of updates to the values of the query parameters. Then we describe how to apply incrementalization rules, to maintain the result of a single query as well as the results of any number of queries. Finally, we discuss how to systematically develop incrementalization rules and build a library of rules.

The resulting incrementalized implementation for the protocol example is shown below. All commented lines are added lines compared to the straightforward implementation, except that the one-line query in findStrongSignals has been replaced with a retrieval from the maintained query result.

```
class Protocol:
  signals: set(Signal)
  threshold: float
  strongSignals: set(Signal)                    -- query result
  ...
  def addSignal(signal):
    signals.add(signal)
    signal.addProtocol(self)                    -- add a query object
    if signal.getStrength() > threshold:        || maintain result under
      strongSignals.add(signal)                 || element addition
  def findStrongSignals(): return strongSignals -- retrieve query result
  def signalModified(signal):                   ||
    if signals.contains(signal):                ||
      if strongSignals.contains(signal):        || define method for
        if not signal.getStrength() > threshold: || maintaining
          strongSingals.remove(signal)          || query result under
      else:                                     || element modification
        if signal.getStrength() > threshold:    ||
          strongSingals.add(signal)             ||
  ...
```

```
class Signal:
  strength: float
  protocols: set(Protocol)                -- query-object set
  ...
  def addProtocol(protocol):              || define method for
    protocols.add(protocol)               || adding a query object
  def setStrength(v):
    strength := v
    for protocol in protocols:            || maintain result under
      protocol.signalModified(self)       || element modification
  def getStrength(): return strength
  ...
...
```

Clearly, this implementation is significantly more complicated than the straight-forward, clear, and modular implementation, even though the original expensive query findStrongSignals is now much more efficient. Automated support for such incrementalization is highly desired.

Incrementalization rules: core form

An *incrementalization rule* specifies how to incrementally maintain the invariant that a result variable holds the result of an expensive query given a set of different kinds of updates to the values of the parameters of the query; it specifies the maintenance work to be done at each kind of updates. The *core form* of an incrementalization rule is

$$
\begin{aligned}
&\textbf{inv } r = query \\
&(\textbf{at } update \\
&\quad \textbf{do } maint)+
\end{aligned}
$$

where *query* and *update* are patterns for matching queries and updates, respectively, that are determined as described in the previous section, and *maint* is a sequence of commands. The plus sign (+) around update and maintenance indicates that, for a given query, there may be one or more kinds of updates to the values of its parameters and corresponding maintenance.

In the core form above, the maintenance work corresponding to an update can be done either before or after the update; this is correct if the maintenance code does not use the values of the variables updated. For many kinds of queries and updates, the maintenance work must be done before the update, not after, because it uses values of variables before the update, and the update may change the value of such a variable. Symmetrically, some maintenance work must be done after the update, not before. To accommodate this, we allow the **do** clause to have the form

$$
\begin{aligned}
&\textbf{do } (maint)? \\
&(\textbf{before } maint_1)? \\
&(\textbf{after } maint_2)?
\end{aligned}
$$

where *maint* can be done either before or after the update, *maint*$_1$ must be done before, and *maint*$_2$ must be done after. A question mark (?) after a clause indicates that the clause may be omitted.

To facilitate cost consideration, an incrementalization rule may specify the costs of the query, updates, and maintenance, by including a **cost** clause of the following form after each of them:

cost *cost*

where **cost** is a keyword, and *cost* is the cost of the corresponding query, update, or maintenance operations. For ease of reading, we omit the keyword **cost** and align the costs to the right.

For example, the following rule expresses that, to maintain the invariant $r = $ `s.size()` when all updates that may affect the size of s are s `:= new set()`, `s.add(`x`)`, and `s.del(`x`)`, the respective maintenance is setting r to `0`, incrementing r by 1 if x is not in s before the addition, and decrementing r by 1 if x is in s before the removal; the cost of the original query is linear in the size of s, and the cost of each update and maintenance is constant.

$$
\begin{array}{lll}
\textbf{inv } r = \texttt{s.size()} & \quad & O(\#s) \\[4pt]
\textbf{at } s := \texttt{new set()} & & O(1) \\
\textbf{do } r := \texttt{0} & & O(1) \\[4pt]
\textbf{at } \texttt{s.add(}x\texttt{)} & & O(1) \\
\textbf{do before} & & O(1) \\
\quad \texttt{if not s.contains(}x\texttt{):} & & \\
\quad\quad r := r + 1 & & \\[4pt]
\textbf{at } \texttt{s.del(}x\texttt{)} & & O(1) \\
\textbf{do before} & & O(1) \\
\quad \texttt{if s.contains(}x\texttt{):} & & \\
\quad\quad r := r - 1 & &
\end{array}
$$

At each update, the maintenance cost is no more than the update cost, so the linear-time `size` query can be replaced by a constant-time retrieval from r at no asymptotic cost increase in maintenance, regardless of the frequencies of queries and updates.

Variables in the rules in italic font are called *meta-variables*. They are different from variables in the program that is being transformed.

- A meta-variable in a query or update pattern may match any program segment, except restricted by the context of the specific occurrence of the variable in the pattern. For example, in the rule for set size above, s and x are meta-variables in the query and update patterns; s `:= new set()` restricts s to match a variable or field in the program being transformed, and `s.add(`x`)`

restricts x to match an expression. Other parts of patterns are displayed in teletype font and match program text exactly.

- The scope of a meta-variable in the query pattern is the entire rule, and the scope of a meta-variable in an update pattern is the update clause and the corresponding maintenance clause. For example, in the set size rule above, all occurrences of s must match the same program segment, but occurrences of x in two different update patterns need not match the same program segment. When matching occurrences of a variable, the scoping rules of the program being transformed are taken into account.

- In the presence of aliasing, we allow a meta-variable to match different program variables that are aliases for the same object. This is because these variables have the same value. For example, if s1 and s2 are aliases at an update s2.add(x), then this update affects the invariant r1 = s1.size(), just like s1.add(x) does.

- Meta-variables, including r, used in maintenance but not in the query and update patterns denote distinct names not used for other purposes in the program being transformed in the scopes of these names. Such a name can be defined in any scope that contains all uses of the name in maintenance, but for program clarity and modularity, by default, it is defined in the smallest of these scopes.

- Standard substitution is used to replace meta-variables in patterns with program text: $p[v \mapsto t]$ denotes p but with each occurrence of variable v in p replaced with t. We always rename bound variables beforehand so they are distinct.

Conditions and declarations

In general, an incrementalization rule may specify additional conditions on the matched query and update patterns and may declare new variables, fields, methods, and classes for incremental maintenance. The conditions and declarations may use meta-variables in the query and update patterns as well as other information about the matched query and update. For convenience, a special meta-variable, *query*, is used to refer to the matched query, and a special meta-variable, *update*, is used after an **at** clause to refer to the matched update. Other information used includes results from the following analyses:

> read(*exp*): set of parameters read by expression *exp*
> write(*cmd*): set of parameters written by command *cmd*
> type(*exp*): type of expression *exp*
> vars(*exp*): set of free variables in expression *exp*
> class(x): enclosing class of a program segment x
> method(x): enclosing method of a program segment x
> isfieldof(x, c): whether x is a field in class c
> isupdatedin(x, c): whether field x of class c is updated in class c

A condition that must be satisfied by a query or an update, matched by the **inv** clause or an **at** clause of a rule, respectively, may be specified by an **if** clause of the following form, immediately after the **inv** clause or **at** clause, respectively, where *condition* is a Boolean expression in the rule language that may use meta-variables and analysis functions; an unbound meta-variable in a condition denotes a variable to be instantiated.

if (*condition*)+

A declaration that is used by maintenance under multiple **at** clauses or a single **at** clause may be specified by a **de** clause of the following form after the **inv** clause or the **at** clause, respectively, where *class* is an expression in the rule language that returns the name of a class, and *declaration* is a field or method declaration to put in that class, except that, when the query and all updates are in the same method, a variable is declared in that method instead of declaring a field. When *class* is unspecified, the default is the class of the current query or update, respectively.

de ((**in** *class*)? (*declaration*)+)+

For example, the rule in Figure 6.1 maintains the result of a basic form of set comprehension. In particular, as shown in the **if** clauses, it handles set initialization and element addition and removal that are in the same class as the query, but element modification, that is, change in a field of an element, in the class of the element objects that is different from the class containing the query.

The first three **at** clauses are for updates in the same class as the query and are simple: for $r = \{v \text{ in } s \mid e\}$, when s is initialized, r is too; and when an element x is added to or deleted from s, the condition e is tested for x and, if it holds, x is added to or removed from r, respectively.

The fourth **at** clause handles element modification. It matches any command that is an update to the value of a parameter of the query. The condition is that s is a field of class(*query*), elements of s are from class(*update*), class(*update*) $\neq$ class(*query*), a field f of the elements is used in the query, and the *update* updates the field f of the self instance of class(*update*). The transformations for maintenance do two things.

1. In class(*update*), a field *qos* is declared to hold the set of class(*query*) objects

inv $r = \{v \text{ in } s \mid e\}$ $O(\#s \times time(e))$
if $\text{vars}(e) \subseteq \{v, \texttt{self}\}$

at s := new set()   -- set initialization $O(1)$
if $\text{class}(update) = \text{class}(query)$
do r := new set() $O(1)$

at s.add(x)   -- element addition $O(1)$
if $\text{class}(update) = \text{class}(query)$
do if $e[v \mapsto x]$: $O(time(e))$
    r.add(x)

at s.del(x)   -- element deletion $O(1)$
if $\text{class}(update) = \text{class}(query)$
do if $e[v \mapsto x]$: $O(time(e))$
    r.del(x)

at cmd -- element modification $O(time(cmd))$
if $\text{isfieldof}(s, \text{class}(query))$, $\text{type}(s) = \texttt{set}(\text{class}(update))$,
    $\text{class}(update) \neq \text{class}(query)$,
    $\{v.f : v \text{ in } s\} \in \text{read}(query)$, $\text{write}(update) = \{\texttt{self}.f\}$

de in $\text{class}(update)$
        qos: $\texttt{set}(\text{class}(query))$ -- query-object set
        def $addqo$(qo): || define method for
          qos.add(qo) || adding a query object

    in $\text{class}(query)$
        def $elementmodified$(x): ||
          if s.contains(x): || define method for
            if r.contains(x): || maintaining
              if not $e[v \mapsto x]$: || query result r
              r.del(x) || under element
            else: || modification to x
              if $e[v \mapsto x]$: ||
              r.add(x) ||
do after $O(\#qos \times time(e))$
    for qo in qos: || maintain query result
      qo.$elementmodified$(self) || under element modification

at s.add(x) $O(1)$
if $\text{type}(s) = \texttt{set}(c)$, $c \neq \text{class}(query)$, $\text{isfieldof}(f, c)$, $\text{isupdatedin}(f, c)$
do x.$addqo$(self)   -- add a query object $O(1)$

Figure 6.1 Rule for basic set comprehension.

o_q whose field s contains this class(*update*) object o_u. In other words, the rule maintains the additional invariant

$$o_q \in o_u.qos \text{ if and only if } o_u \in o_q.s$$

A method *addqo* is defined for adding an object to *qos*. The last **at** clause of the rule inserts code that calls *addqo* when an element is added to s.

2. In class(*query*), a method *elementmodified* is defined for updating r given a class(*update*) object x: if x is not in s, do nothing; otherwise, if x is in r but does not satisfy the condition e, remove x from r, and if x is not in r but satisfies e, add x to r. Code is inserted after the element modification: for each object qo in *qos*, *elementmodified* is called on qo with the self class(*update*) object as argument.

The new methods *addqo* and *elementmodified* and field *qos* work together as follows. Recall that the goal is to incrementally maintain, in a class(*query*) object, the result of a query over a set of class(*update*) objects when a class(*update*) object is updated. First, when a class(*update*) object is added to the set queried by the class(*query*) object, method *addqo* of the class(*update*) object is called to add the class(*query*) object to *qos*—the set of class(*query*) objects that query over sets containing the class(*update*) object. Then, when the class(*update*) object is updated, it calls method *elementmodified* for all class(*query*) objects in *qos* to update the query results in those objects.

The **cost** clauses say that a straightforward implementation of the set query takes $O(\#s \times time(e))$ time, because testing the condition in the set comprehension takes $O(time(e))$ time. An incremental implementation that maintains the query result at each update can return a reference to the query result in $O(1)$ time. The query result can be maintained in $O(1)$ time at initialization, in $O(time(e))$ time at element addition and deletion, and in $O(\#qos \times time(e))$ time at any update to an element's field that the query depends on.

This rule is complicated. Indeed, just the fourth and last **at** clauses alone, without the incremental maintenance code in the body of method *elementmodified*, already capture, precisely and at a meta level, the observer pattern. The observer pattern allows an object, called the subject, here a class(*update*) object, to maintain a list of its dependents, called observers, here class(*query*) objects, and notify them automatically about state changes, by calling a method of theirs. It is one of the most important design patterns used in object-oriented programs, especially in distributed event handling systems.

Incrementalization rules: general form

Back to the rule language, in general, work can also be done at the query to help with incremental maintenance. Such work can be specified as a **do** clause below the **inv** clause. For example, to incrementally maintain the average of a set, one may incrementally maintain the sum and the count, and do a division right before the query, instead of doing the division immediately after maintenance of sum and count.

Finally, in the **do** clause after an **at** clause, one could use the keyword **instead** to indicate that the original update in the **at** clause is to be removed. This is especially useful when an original update needs to be transformed. For example, the rule for set size indeed has a problem: x might not be a variable, in which case all of add, del, and maintenance have the cost of computing x. Rather than adding a condition to limit x to a variable, we can reduce the cost of maintenance to $O(1)$ by replacing the **do before** clause under add with the following, and similarly for del:

> **do instead**
> ```
> v := x
> if not s.contains(v):
>     r := r + 1
> s.add(v)
> ```

Altogether, the *general form* of an incrementalization rule is

> **inv** $r = query$
> (**if** *condition* +)?
> (**de** ((**in** *class*)? *declaration* +)+)?
> (**do** (*maint*)? (**before** *maint*)? (**after** *maint*)?)?
> (**at** *update*
>   (**if** *condition* +)?
>   (**de** ((**in** *class*)? *declaration* +)+)?
>   (**do** (*maint*)? (**before** *maint*)? (**after** *maint*)? (**instead** *maint*)?)?)+

where *query*, *update*, *declaration*, and *maint* are program text in the language of the program being transformed, except that they may contain meta-variables, and *condition* and *class* are a Boolean expression and a class-valued expression, respectively, in the rule language.

Applying incrementalization rules

Given the meaning of each clause in an incrementalization rule as explained above, we describe here how all clauses in a rule are applied together, and how to apply any number of rules.

For performance improvement, the application of rules needs to use not only the times but also the frequencies of the operations involved. We use *freq*(x) to denote the frequency of executing a program segment x in its context.

An incrementalization rule applies if a query matches *query*, every update to the values of the parameters of the query matches at least one *update*, and the corresponding conditions, including the cost conditions in item 3 below, hold; all transformations for the matched query and updates must be applied altogether, or none at all. Assuming that the meta-variables in a rule of the general form have been instantiated for a specific query and for all updates to the query, the semantics of applying the rule is:

1. Declare variable r in method($query$), if method($update$) = method($query$) for all $update$'s; declare field r in class($query$), otherwise. Also,
   - add the corresponding *declaration*'s as specified, and
   - insert the corresponding *maint*'s before or after the *query* as specified.

2. Replace each occurrence of *query* in the same scope as the *query* with r.

3. At each *update*, where the corresponding *condition*'s hold, and either $time(maint) \leq time(update)$ or the sum of $time(maint) \times freq(update)$, over all *update*'s where $time(maint) > time(update)$, is less than $time(query) \times freq(query)$,
   - add the corresponding *declaration*'s as specified, and
   - insert the corresponding *maint*'s before, after, or in place of the *update* as specified.

For the protocol example, applying the rule for basic set comprehension in Figure 6.1, the incrementalized implementation is obtained from the straightforward implementation. The query findStrongSignals in Protocol in the straightforward implementation can be incrementally maintained at updates addSignal in Protocol and setStrength in Signal. Testing the condition in the original findStrongSignals query takes $O(1)$ time. Thus it is easy to see, based on the rule for basic set comprehension, that the original query takes $O(\#\text{signals})$ time, while the new query takes $O(1)$ time, and incremental maintenance takes $O(1)$ time at all updates except for $O(\#\text{protocols})$ time at element modification. The cost condition of this rule is satisfied when $O(\#\text{protocols} \leq time(\text{setStrength}))$, that is, there are only a few protocols instances, or $O(\#\text{protocols}) \times freq(\text{setStrength}) \leq O(\#\text{signals}) \times freq(\text{findStrongSignals})$, that is, the query is sufficiently frequent.

Now, consider applying incrementalization rules to maintain the results of multiple queries. If these queries are independent, that is, the parameters of one query do not depend on the results of other queries, then the results of these queries can be maintained simply by applying the rules independently to all the queries, either simultaneously or one query at a time in any order.

To maintain the results of multiple queries that are not independent, that is, queries where the parameters of some query depend on the results of other queries, chains of dependencies among the queries must be followed. Dependencies arise when an expensive computation has expensive subcomputations, but these dependencies are acyclic, because they are between two nested computations or two sequential computations. Incrementalization first maintains results of queries that do not depend on results of other queries, with respect to updates to the values of its parameters, and then maintains queries that only depend on queries whose results have already been updated, with respect to updates to those results. Following the chain of dependencies in this fashion is like applying the chain rule in calculus, as we have seen in Chapter 3. This can be achieved by applying all the rules to expensive queries following a topological order of the dependencies among expensive queries.

In general, there may be multiple rules that apply to a query and all updates to the values of its parameters. Because all the application conditions, including cost considerations, are specified explicitly in rules, systematic methods and automated tools can be and should be developed to support the selection of the rule or rules that lead to the best performance. At the lowest level, this includes data structure selection. Declarative incrementalization rules facilitate the study of a general method that works at all levels.

Developing incrementalization rules

We see that incrementalization rules can capture important program design and development knowledge that is used repeatedly in constructing complex software systems. This knowledge for refined and efficient designs and implementations can be general-purpose or domain-specific. While some rules are easy to write, others are nontrivial to develop. Therefore, three kinds of effort are needed:

1. Rules should be developed systematically, following general methods for maintaining invariants, whenever possible.

2. A library of rules should be built to include also rules that we do not yet know how to systematically develop.

3. The correctness of rules should be verified rigorously.

Methods described in previous chapters for deriving incremental maintenance, for loops and arrays, set expressions, recursive functions, and logic rules, can be used for developing large classes of incrementalization rules systematically, but these methods must be extended to handle objects. Recall that objects do not add fundamentally new constructs for either data or control, but merely provide encapsulation through modularity. This encapsulation can be removed by transforming fields of objects into sets of tuples and transforming methods of objects into functions that have an additional argument for the target object. Then, transformations described previously for sets and functions can be used to derive incremental maintenance for the transformed program. Finally, the resulting incremental maintenance can be transformed back to fields and methods of objects, now incrementalized.

Some incrementalization rules will be developed manually, for example, to capture new data structures. However, once developed, they can be put in a library of rules and reused from application to application, as opposed to being rediscovered and manually embedded in scattered places in each application program. In fact, there is no limit on the range of rules that can be included in the library, whether manually or automatically derived. For example, the library may include rules for arithmetic operations, as used for strength reduction, rules for bitwise operations, as needed in hardware design, and rules for relational operations, as performed in databases. Furthermore, depending on the operations on data, different data structures can be used, such as heaps for element addition and minimum-element deletion, and red-black trees for arbitrary element addition and deletion. Clearly, the larger the library is, the more powerful incrementalization may become.

It is important to verify the correctness of incrementalization rules, especially those developed manually, in that they correctly maintain the specified invariants and capture the costs. Verifying invariants in programs is, in general, a very hard problem, but three features make verifying incrementalization rules much easier than invariants in programs. First, an incrementalization rule specifies an invariant with all updates of certain kinds that may affect the invariant and the corresponding maintenance together. Second, an incrementalization rule may explicitly specify applicability conditions about the queries and the updates, and the conditions are assumed to hold and are checked only when the rules are applied to programs. Third, an incrementalization rule is usually much smaller than application programs that perform incremental maintenance.

Exercise 6.6 (Incrementalizing join query across components*) Suppose two relations R1 and R2 are maintained in two different classes, and a third class has the following join query over R1 and R2:

```
{[x,y]: x in o1.R1, y in o2.R2 | if f(x) = g(y)}
```

What is the incremental maintenance code under an update that adds a new element in R1? Write that in an incrementalization rule that handles this update. Is this as simple, or as hard, as you had thought?

Exercise 6.7 (Incrementalizing attribute-based RBAC query*) Consider maintaining the result of the query in Exercise 6.4. Can you design efficient incremental maintenance code that handles the update that assigns a new location to a user?

6.4 Example: health records

Creating large-scale electronic health record (EHR) databases at a national level has been under heated discussion and development for quite a number of years in countries including the United States and United Kingdom. Clearly, there could be millions or billions of objects of many kinds in such a system, and thus components that encapsulate data and operations on objects are critical for the development and organization of such a system. However, objects and classes are important even for much smaller aspects of such a system—the security and privacy policies of such a system.

Security and privacy concerns are, in fact, among the most important hurdles for the creation of such large-scale databases, and how to specify and implement the policies still poses research challenges. We discuss how to address the challenges by considering a formal policy for the proposed national EHR service of the United Kingdom. The formal EHR policy consists of 375 rules in a variant of Datalog with constraints, taking about 1,500 lines and 30 pages.

EHR service policy specification

Although a formal specification in Datalog with constraints provides good data abstraction and control abstraction, two main problems make this specification difficult to understand, use, and maintain:

1. The entire specification is a flat list of rules with no formal structure, and all names are global, because the rule language used has no support for module abstraction.

2. All dynamic updates are expressed indirectly as role activation and deactivation, the two updates predefined outside the rule language, because the language cannot express updates.

We show that the use of objects provides the module abstraction that is extremely important for understanding such a large policy piece by piece, and the use of direct updates makes it easy to tell what changes dynamically from what remains unchanged in such a system.

The policy has an informal structure, used to group rules under sections and subsections, each with a heading in English. Overall, there are four sections: spine, patient demographics service, local health organizations, and registration authorities. Each section has a first subsection about main roles and one or more other subsections, including consent, permissions, registration, sealing off data, referrals, and a few others.

Fundamentally, each section really corresponds to a component; the main roles, as well as a large number of other roles and relations, in that section should be the data in that component; and the rules in that section essentially define the query operations and implicit update operations. Clearly, these correspond to objects, fields, and query and update methods. In the policy, most of the roles have data about themselves and operations about themselves too, and therefore are also best modeled as objects with fields and methods.

For example, the following rule in the spine section of the policy specifies that the count-conceal-requests predicate about the count of y and the patient pat is true if some entity x has activated the Conceal-request role with y as a parameter, y is a 4-tuple $(what, who, start, end)$, $what$ is a 7-tuple as specified, and who is

a 3-tuple as specified. So, for example, calling `count-conceal-requests`(n, `john`)
would find the number n of conceal requests about patient `john`.

$$\text{count-conceal-requests}(\text{count}\langle y \rangle, pat) \leftarrow$$
$$\text{hasActivated}(x, \text{Conceal-request}(y)),$$
$$what = (pat, ids, orgs, authors, subjects, from\text{--}time, to\text{--}time),$$
$$who = (orgs1, readers1, spectys1),$$
$$y = (what, who, start, end)$$

Structurally, a role for a `Conceal-request` operation should be an object of a class,
say called `Conceal-request`, that has 4 fields, one for each component of the 4-
tuple, and the first two fields are objects of two classes, say called `What` and `Who`,
respectively, with fields as specified:

```
class Conceal-request:        class What:         class Who
    what: What                    patient: ...         ...
    who: Who                      ...
    start: time
    end: time
```

The set of entity-role pairs where the entity has activated the role, as captured by
the `hasActivated` predicate, should be kept in a relation, say called `hasActivated`, of
the spine component. Then, the following method counts the number of conceal
requests about patient `pat`.

```
def count-conceal-requests(pat):
    return {y: [x,y] in hasActivated
               | isinstance(y,Conceal-request), y.what.patient = pat}.size()
```

One can see here that representing data using objects and relations not only makes
the data in a component clearer but also makes the query simpler, clearer, easier
to write, and easier to read.

Efficient implementation for policy analysis and enforcement

Queries in the specification are the basis for policy analysis and enforcement.
Queries that involve computing aggregates and set expressions over an unbounded
number of objects, possibly across multiple classes, are expensive. Queries that
use recursion can be expensive too, although the recursive definitions used in the
EHR policy rules do not involve an unbounded number of recursive calls.

There are two ways in which our method for generating efficient implementations for expensive queries is important: (1) make queries efficient, as for the
join query in Section 3.6, when computing from scratch, and (2) make queries
incremental with respect to updates, as for RBAC in Section 3.5, when the values
of the query parameters change slightly at a time and the queries are performed
sufficiently frequently.

For example, consider the count query above. Clearly, the value of query parameter `hasActivated` changes. To make the query efficient, we may maintain two

direct inverse maps: one from each patient to the set of What objects it is in, and one from each What object to the set of Conceal-request objects it is in. This avoids blindly enumerating hasActivated in the query, but enumerates it in a more focused way using the two inverse maps starting with any patient. Maintaining these two direct inverse maps, each mapping the value of a field to the containing object, takes constant time at each update.

Alternatively, we may maintain instead a single inverse map from each patient to the set of Conceal-request objects it is in. This also avoids enumerating hasActivated in the query, but enumerates it using the single inverse map, making the query much more efficient, taking time proportional to the size of the resulting set. However, maintaining this map requires an iteration at each update, similar to the iterations needed to maintain the CheckAccess query in Section 3.5.

Finally, we may maintain, in addition to the single inverse map, a result map from each patient to the resulting count, that is, the size of the set of Conceal-request objects it is in. This introduces a constant-time overhead at each update to the resulting set in the query, but allows the query to be answered in constant time. Of course, which map or maps to incrementally maintain depends on the frequencies of operations and total cost considerations.

Exercise 6.8 (Comparing object query and rule query*) Compare the count-conceal-requests query specified using objects and sets with the same query specified using rules. You may notice that the query using objects looks simpler, or at least is shorter. What do you think is the reason for this? Specifically, look at things in the query using rules that are not present in the query using objects, and where those things go. Which way do you think is better, and why?

Exercise 6.9 (Incrementalizing EHR policy query) For the count-conceal-request query specified using objects and sets, how to maintain the result of the query efficiently when elements are added and removed from hasActivated? Is that as obvious for the same query specified using rules?

6.5 Example: robot games

Many games and simulations model real-world objects, such as players in a large role-playing game, aircraft in an air traffic control simulation, or atoms in a protein-folding simulation. Queries about the state of the system may combine the positions, orientations, speeds, and other attributes of the objects. At the same time, objects may be added and deleted, and their attributes may change in many ways. If there are n kinds of expensive queries and on average m kinds of updates that might affect a query result, then a straightforward implementation would have $n + m$ clear and modular operations, each one performing exactly one kind of query or update, but this may be inefficient when the queries and updates are repeatedly performed. An efficient, sophisticated implementation could store some of the query results and, at each kind of update, incrementally maintain each of the stored results, yielding $n \times m$ kinds of incremental maintenance in the worst case.

Robocode score calculation

We use one of the robot games, Robocode, as an example, and we consider the queries that calculate the scores; other kinds of queries can be specified and implemented in a similar way. Robocode is an open-source programming game, where competitors write programs, in an object-oriented language, that control a robot tank that battles against other robot tanks in a playing field. Robots move, scan for each other, shoot at each other, and hit the walls or other robots if they are not careful. Although the idea of this game may seem simple, the actual strategy needed to win is not. Some of the more successful robots use techniques such as statistical analysis and neural networks in their designs.

Robocode keeps a collection of scores at any time during the game for use by the game strategy and displays them in a table at the end of the game. The scores are:

- `totalScore`: This is the sum of all scores and bonuses described below, and it determines a robot's rank in the battle.

- `survivalScore`: A robot that is alive scores 50 points every time another robot dies. This score is the total of such points.

- `survivorBonus`: The last robot alive scores 10 additional points for each robot that died. This bonus is the total of such points.

- `bulletDamageScore`: A robot scores 1 point for each point of damage it does to an enemy. This score is the total of such points.

- `bulletKillBonus`: When a robot kills an enemy, it scores an additional 20% of all the damage it did to that enemy. This bonus is the total of such points.

- `rammingDamageScore`: A robot scores 2 points for each point of damage it does by ramming an enemy. This score is the total of such points.

- `rammingKillBonus`: When a robot kills an enemy by ramming, it scores an additional 30% of all the damage it did to that enemy. This bonus is the total of such points.

- `totalFirst`, `totalSecond`, `totalThird`: These do not actually contribute to score. They are the number of rounds that a robot was placed 1st, 2nd, and 3rd, respectively.

We represent the basic data that a robot uses for calculating scores as follows.

The first two are kept globally and the rest are kept in the robot, indicated by the prefix self.

all: all robots

live: live robots

self.allDamage[r]: damage to robot r by self, for each robot r

self.allKilled: set of robots killed by self

self.ramDamage[r]: damage to robot r by self through ramming, for each robot r

self.ramKilled: set of robots killed by self through ramming

Then the scoring calculation can be specified based on the given definitions using the following queries.

```
totalScore  =  survivalScore + survivorBonus
                + bulletDamageScore + bulletKillBonus
                + rammingDamageScore + rammingKillBonus
survivalScore  =  50 * #(all - live)
survivorBonus  =  if #live = 1 then 10 * #(all - live) else 0
bulletDamageScore  =  sum{1 * allDamage[r]: r in all}
bulletKillBonus  =  sum{0.2 * allDamage[r]: r in allKilled}
rammingDamageScore  =  sum{2 * ramDamage[r]: r in all}
rammingKillBonus  =  sum{0.3 * ramDamage[r]: r in ramKilled}
```

For real-time gaming, these scores are maintained incrementally in Robocode at each event that affects the values that the scores depend on. The incremental calculation is programmed in different methods, to be called at corresponding events. Even though all the methods for calculation are defined in one file, the invocations of these methods are spread over different places in different files that handle different events.

Incrementalize

Using the method described in this chapter, these scores can be incrementally maintained, automatically, as the basic data in the state of the robots change, and the incremental maintenance code can be derived automatically. For the queries above, the following additional values are maintained:

```
deadCount  =  #(all - live)
liveCount  =  #live
```

These values and the scores must be incrementally maintained. For example, at a DeathEvent, of a robot r, killed by robot s, through ramming, the following basic data will be updated:

```
live -:= {r}
s.allKilled +:= {r}
s.ramKilled +:= {r}
```

and the following incremental update code will be derived, where the three groups correspond to the three updates above:

```
deadCount +:= 1
liveCount -:= 1
survivalScore +:= 50
totalScore +:= 50
if liveCount = 1:
    survivorBonus +:= 10
    totalScore +:= 10

bulletKillBonus +:= 0.2 * allDamage[r]
totalScore +:= 0.2 * allDamage[r]

rammingKillBonus +:= 0.3 * ramDamage[r]
totalScore +:= 0.3 * ramDamage[r]
```

Such incremental maintenance must be done at all possible updates to all basic data.

Automatically deriving such incremental maintenance helps improve both the correctness of programs and the productivity of program development, especially when the method is used for more critical applications, such as telecommunication networks or medical devices, that require complicated event handling with fast response time.

Exercise 6.10   (Cost analysis for Robocode score calculation) In Robocode score calculation, what is the cost of computing totalScore from scratch? What is the cost of computing it incrementally after a DeathEvent?

Exercise 6.11   (Dead code in incrementalized Robocode score calculation) In Robocode score calculation, why do we maintain deadCount and liveCount? You may note that it is not necessary to maintain deadCount. Why?

6.6   Invariant-driven transformations: incrementalization rules as invariant rules

Incrementalization rules express coordinated transformations driven by the need to maintain invariants. Although they were meant for design and optimization, that is, transforming clear high-level specifications into efficient low-level implementations, they can also be used in the reverse direction, that is, understanding low-level programs and reverse engineering them into high-level specifications. They can also be used in validating and verifying low-level programs against high-level specifications, and in general transformations, including program refactoring, and program instrumentation for runtime monitoring, profiling, and debugging.

Invariant rules

Before discussing different usages of incrementalization rules, we first interpret incrementalization rules as *invariant rules* by giving them a declarative semantics.

Recall that an incrementalization rule is of the following core form, with three key components: invariant, updates, and maintenance. Conditions help specify the queries and updates to be matched, and declarations help specify the maintenance.

$$
\begin{aligned}
&\textbf{inv } r = query \\
&\quad (\textbf{at } update \\
&\quad \textbf{do } maint)+
\end{aligned}
$$

We say that such a rule preserves the invariant $r = query$, if (1) $r = query$ holds after initialization of r and (2) for each pair of *update* and *maint*, if $r = query$ holds, then it still holds immediately after execution of *update* and *maint*, for all instances of *query*, *update*, and *maint*. It is easy to see that preserving an invariant is a property that can be checked individually for each rule.

The declarative semantics of an invariant-preserving rule is: for a variable and a query that match r and the *query* pattern, respectively, the value of the variable equals the result of the query if every update to the values of the parameters of the query matches at least one of the *update* patterns, and at each update that matches an *update* pattern, the maintenance that matches the corresponding *maint* pattern is performed.

Maintaining invariants for design and optimization

Obviously, invariant rules can be used for incrementalization, as we have seen earlier in this chapter. That is, according to invariant rules, efficient implementations of expensive queries can be obtained by (1) introducing variables to hold the results of the queries, (2) inserting code that corresponds to each update to incrementally maintain the results of queries at all updates to the values of the parameters of the queries, and (3) replacing the queries by retrievals from the variables that hold the results of the queries. The invariant maintained is that the value of a variable introduced to hold a query result always equals the result of the query.

Such incrementalization is at the center of design and optimization in the program development process, because it transforms high-level specifications containing queries that are easy to understand but inefficient to execute into sophisticated but efficient implementations containing low-level maintenance operations. Such design and optimization methods are an essential part of formal methods for program synthesis and refinement. Invariant rules specify not only all the query, update, and maintenance operations, but also costs of all of them, making it possible to give clear performance guarantees, which are generally lacking in program development methods.

As we have seen in Section 6.3, expressing coordinated incremental maintenance of invariants using invariant rules is high-level and declarative, which helps make complex general transformations easier to understand, use, extend, and verify. The semantics of the rules encapsulates many low-level details. For example, all updates to the values of the parameters of a query must be detected, one way or another, even in the presence of object aliasing, and maintenance must be performed at all updates. While it may be difficult to manually maintain queries under scattered updates, doing so by automatically applying a library of invariant rules is easy. Thus, languages and frameworks that facilitate the specification and application of invariant rules help increase developers' productivity.

Discovering invariants for understanding and reverse engineering

While transforming straightforward implementations into efficient implementations is important for developing new programs, it does not help with existing programs, which are generally not at all straightforward. Key challenges in dealing with existing real-world programs are program understanding and reverse engineering, which are the opposite of optimization and refinement. Can invariant rules help with such design recovery activities?

In real-world programs, for acceptable performance, results of expensive queries that are frequently performed are already incrementally maintained, but the invariants are implicit in the program, perhaps not even mentioned in the documentation, so the much harder problem is how to discover the invariants. For example, we may see that the value of a certain variable is returned at some places in the program and is updated in various ways at other places, and it could have any name and appear without comments, how do we know that it might be holding the size of a list, or the result of some more complicated query?

Because invariant rules are high-level and declarative, they allow us to observe that, given an incrementalization rule, if, at every update to the values that the invariant depends on, the corresponding maintenance is performed, then the invariant holds. For example, according to the invariant rule for maintaining the size of a set, if at all updates to a set, the corresponding maintenance operations in the rule are performed on a certain variable, and the variable is not updated anywhere else, then we can conclude that the variable holds the size of the set. While it is not hard to make this observation given invariant rules, it is much harder to make this observation if the transformations are expressed as lower-level rewrite rules with certain strategies for tree walking, program analysis, and rule applications.

Understanding and reverse engineering real-world programs is not at all so simple. In particular, the maintenance corresponding to an update is often not done immediately before or after the update, that is, they are decoupled; in fact, maintenance for different updates may be batched together. Discovering all invariants for arbitrary programs is in general impossible. However, a framework for discovering invariants can try to take such decoupling into account. In fact, such decoupling is a common source of errors in programs, and detecting violations of even simple patterns of coupling is effective for finding bugs.

Checking invariants for validation and verification

Program verification is an important and extensively studied topic. A central problem is to verify or check that certain invariants are preserved by a program. This is different from either optimization or reverse engineering. How can invariant rules help?

For program verification, both the program and the invariant to be verified are given, and the program contains updates and maintenance. In terms of invariant rules, we can see that optimization yields incremental maintenance given the invariant and updates, reverse engineering leads to discovery of the invariant given the updates and maintenance, and verification boils down to checking consistency when all three of the desired invariant, updates, and maintenance are given. For example, we may be given a program where the value of a certain variable is returned at some places and updated at other places, and an invariant that the value of the variable equals the size of a linked list at a certain place, and we are asked to prove that the invariant holds at that place.

While one could use traditional verification methods—collecting relevant facts about the program and proving the invariant using theorem provers, doing abstract forms of exhaustive checking using model checkers, or adding checks for runtime verification, invariant rules provide three additional ways. First, one could start with the invariant and all updates, as for invariant maintenance, and then verify more locally that the corresponding maintenance is performed at each update. Second, one could search for relevant updates and maintenance in the program, as for invariant discovery, and then verify more simply that the discovered invariant is equivalent to the desired one. Third, one could insert incremental maintenance code for efficient runtime verification. For example, to verify that a variable v holds the size of a list at a program point p at runtime, one can insert code that maintains the size in a fresh variable, say v', incrementally at each update according to the rule and checks that $v = v'$ at p; this avoids having to compute the size of the list at p. The first two methods must address the general problem that maintenance is often not done immediately at each update, the same problem of decoupling as for discovering invariants.

There is an advantage in using invariant rules for verification. When verification fails because of an error in the program or the invariant, a challenging problem is to find fixes to the program or the stated invariant. Invariant maintenance based on invariant rules can help find fixes to the program based on correct maintenance code, and invariant discovery based on invariant rules can help find a correct invariant.

General program transformations

While invariant rules are designed to express coordinated transformations that together preserve invariants, they can also express general program transformations that do not require such strong coordination. Nevertheless, it is important to note that general program transformations also preserve various kinds of invariants, albeit generally done implicitly. Invariant rules can help make the invariants more explicit, and help express these transformations more easily and declaratively. We discuss examples in program instrumentation for profiling, runtime invariant checking, and debugging, and in program refactoring.

Program instrumentation transforms a program to do additional logging, checking, and so on at runtime. It is important for addressing performance, security, and general correctness issues, by profiling frequencies of operations, monitoring accesses to data, and so forth. The invariants are that the behavior of the involved program fragments is preserved and the additional logging, checking, and so on are done when certain conditions hold. For example, to profile the frequencies of queries and updates, to help justify incremental maintenance of invariants, an invariant rule can match the queries and updates and increment a corresponding counter when a query or update is executed. For another example, to monitor and check a complex invariant efficiently at runtime, an invariant rule can be used to incrementally maintain the results of expensive computations needed for checking the invariant. Invariant rules for these two examples can in fact be generated automatically from the invariant rules for incremental maintenance.

Debugging is one of the most involved and often tedious programming activities, because one has to do all kinds of tracing and logging to help understand code details and determine the causes of bugs. Instrumentation to help debugging, for example, to log specified kinds of events, can easily be inserted with invariant rules. For example, to track where the value of a variable was last changed to a bad value, an invariant rule can match all assignments to that variable and appropriately record the program point when the variable is last assigned the bad value. In general, powerful queries can help debugging significantly, and invariant rules can incrementally maintain the results of expensive queries.

Program refactoring generally refers to transformations that improve code quality, for example, readability, extensibility, or modularity. Typical examples are renaming variables and turning blocks of code into subroutines. It is not hard to observe the invariants. For example, for renaming variables, the invariant is that the value of the old variable in a desired context always equals that of the new variable. For introducing subroutines, the invariant is that the original block of code is equivalent to the introduced subroutine call. A nontrivial issue in refactoring is the preservation of semantics. For example, when one wants to rename variable i to interest in a certain context or scope, other occurrences of i should not be changed. Invariant rules preserve such semantics because scoping rules of the programs transformed are taken into account.

Exercise 6.12 (Runtime invariant checking*) Write an incrementalization rule for efficiently checking the invariant that a variable v holds the size of a set s at a given program point, while s can be initialized to empty and have an element added or removed, and reporting an error when this invariant is violated. You may assume that a statement, x := s.size(), where x is a fresh variable, has been inserted at the given program point.

Exercise 6.13 (Profiling query and updates*) Write an incrementalization rule for profiling the frequencies of size queries and updates for each set by counting the number of queries and the number of each kind of updates for each set.

6.7 Querying complex object graphs

Objects are related to each other, and the relationships can be complex. These relationships among objects form a graph, called *object graphs*, where the objects are vertices, and the relationships are edges. Objects may include all attribute values and even classes. Relationships may include attribution, which relates objects and their attribute values, instantiation, which relates classes and objects of those classes, and subclassing, which relates classes and their subclasses.

While queries over objects and their relationships can be written using set expressions, recursive functions, and logic rules, a large class of queries can be expressed more easily as regular path expressions. A *regular path expression* is an extended regular-expression pattern, defined below, over paths in object graphs, where a path is a sequence of the form [vertex$_1$] edge$_1$ [vertex$_2$] edge$_2$ ... [vertex$_k$].

A *regular expression* is a concise way of representing a set of sequences of constant symbols, where segments of a sequence may be concatenated, may have alternatives, and may be repeated. For example, a(b|c)d* represents the set of sequences where each sequence is a followed by b or c (denoted by b|c) followed by zero or more d's (denoted by d*). The concatenation, alternative, and repetition can also be nested. For example, (ab|cd)* denotes a sequence of zero or more pairs, where each pair is either a followed by b or c followed by d.

An *extended regular-expression pattern* is a regular expression extended with variables and a number of convenient notations. Thus, vertices and edges to be matched can be expressed with not only constant symbols but also variables. If a vertex does not matter to the query, the vertex with its enclosing [] can be omitted from the query. In the examples below, we assume that x, y, and z are variables, and all other symbols are constants.

For an example query, consider an object graph that captures a social network, where vertices include people and other values of interest, such as email addresses, cities, and jobs, and edges include relationships, such as friend, relative, location, and affiliation, among people and other values. Suppose kay is moving to the city ithaca, to attend Cornell University, but she does not have any friend there, and she would like to find whether there is any friend's friend there. She can use the following query to return the set of people x who is a friend of a friend of kay and whose city is ithaca:

```
x: [kay] friend friend [x] city [ithaca]
```

Expressing this query using a path expression is slightly easier and clearer than using a set comprehension, such as the following:

```
{ x: x in kay.friend.friend | x.city = ithaca }
```

Of course, kay could also find the intermediate friend whose friend lives in ithaca, by inserting [y] in between the two occurrences of friend and returning the pair x,y instead of x. Also, she could check not only friends but also relatives by using friend|relative in place of friend. Expressing these queries using set comprehensions is more complex.

For a more interesting query, we show the use of repetition. Suppose tom would like to find all relatives whose hometown is not usa. Because all relatives include relatives' relatives, repeatedly, he can use the following query:

```
x: [tom] relative relative* [x] hometown [y] and y!=usa
```

Because of the use of repetition, it is impossible to write this query using a set comprehension. It is possible to write it using Datalog with constraints, as follows, but this is more complicated and less clear.

```
relative(x,y) -> allrelative(x,y)
relative(x,z), allrelative(z,y) -> allrelative(x,y)
allrelative(tom,x), hometown(x,y), y!=usa -> return(x)
```

Graph queries can in fact be implemented by transforming them into set comprehensions or Datalog with constraints, and then applying our methods for implementing these other kinds of queries.

Exercise 6.14 (Simplifying graph query*) Consider the graph query discussed that computes relatives of tom whose hometown is not usa. Recall that negation of an expression e can be expressed as not e. Can you make the query simpler?

Exercise 6.15 (Slightly changed graph query) Consider the graph query discussed that computes relatives of tom whose hometown is not usa. How to return the set of hometowns of relatives of tom that are not from usa?

Bibliographical notes

Module abstraction is a central concept in computer science and was proposed in the early 1970s [134, 247, 75, 184]. Abstract data types were first formulated by Liskov and Zilles [184]. While object abstraction is most commonly used with imperative languages, such as C++ and Java, it is also used with database languages, such as OQL, functional languages, such as OCaml, and logic languages, such as Flora [326, 327]. The language constructs described in Section 6.1 are supported in all common object-oriented languages, including Python, Java, and C++. The assumptions about straightforward programs are either enforced in high-level programming languages or accepted as good programming practices.

Many analyses and optimizations have been studied for object-oriented programs, e.g., [71, 17, 318, 77, 279, 11], especially virtual method resolution [71, 17] that enables further optimizations through method inlining. Optimizations involving incrementalization have been studied more recently [227, 205, 282, 273, 325], by decomposing queries to apply incremental computation [227], incrementalizing queries under updates via incrementalization rules [205], memoizing results of method calls [282], generating incremental implementations [273], and caching and incrementalizing queries over a single set in JQL [325].

The method for analyzing queries and updates and for developing and applying incrementalization rules described in this chapter is based on the methods described in Liu et al. [205]. Incrementalization rules can be derived using the methods described separately [214, 273, 271]. In particular, Rothamel and Liu [273] describe a method for automatically deriving and invoking incremental maintenance code for efficiently computing queries with respect to updates in an object-oriented language; the method can be used to generate large classes of incrementalization rules. The observer pattern, as embedded in the example incrementalization rule, is one of the most widely used design patterns [94].

The electronic health record (EHR) policy example [23] is from Becker's dissertation [22] at Cambridge University. The policy is based on specification documents of the UK National Health Service (NHS) project. It is expressed in the dissertation using a trust management language called Cassandra [24]. Many other languages have also been proposed for expressing trust management policies, especially languages based on Datalog with constraints [180], e.g., [154, 74], but they have only been used in relatively small and simple applications. The formal specification of the EHR policy in Cassandra provides a real-world policy example that is both large and complex.

Robocode [232] is an open-source educational game originally provided by IBM. The game is designed to help people learn to program in Java and enjoy the experience. It is very easy to start, where a simple robot can be written in just a few minutes, but perfecting a robot can take months or more. Besides course projects in teaching computer programming, the game has also been used to develop and teach ideas from artificial intelligence [130] as well as in other research [325].

While maintaining invariants is fundamental in program design and optimization, and has been studied by many, e.g., [159, 120, 238, 290], developing a precise language and framework for it, at a meta level, that applies to different languages and can be used also for discovering and checking of invariants, was not studied until more recently [190]. Gorbovitski et al. exploit invariant rules for efficient runtime invariant checking [106], including its application for query-based debugging [107]. Decoupling of operations in maintaining invariants is a common source of errors, and detecting violations of even simple patterns of coupling, like pairing of operations, is effective for finding bugs [81]. As pointed by Smith [290], maintaining invariants also underlies aspect-oriented programming (AOP) [164]. Gorbovitski et al. slightly extend invariant rules for program instrumentation in general and study composition of invariant rules [103].

Graph query languages have been studied especially for querying database and XML data [328, 2], as well as for analyzing computer programs and checking computer systems [70, 192]. The language discussed in the last section of this chapter is described in more detail in Liu and Stoller [201], and its efficient implementation is described in Tekle et al. [299]. Despite preliminary studies, ideas in regular-path-query-based frameworks [192, 201] have been used by more recent works for querying programs, for example, in JunGL for Java [306] and Condate for GCC [308], and are considered a powerful and convenient framework, compared to hand-coding the analyses [141].

7

Conclusion

We have shown a systematic method that succeeds in designing efficient implementations for many problems in many application domains starting with clear specifications of these problems using high-level language constructs. The method is systematic by being based on the language constructs used in the specifications and being guided by the cost considerations taken from the application domains.

The method, even though consisting of Steps Iterate, Incrementalize, and Implement in order, is driven by the middle step—Step Incrementalize. Because efficient computations on nontrivial input must proceed repeatedly on incremented input, Step Incrementalize aims to make the computation on each incremented input efficient by storing and reusing values computed on the previous input. Steps Iterate and Implement are enabling mechanisms: to maximize reuse by Step Incrementalize, Step Iterate determines a minimum input increment to take repeatedly; to support efficient access of the stored values by Step Incrementalize, Step Implement designs a combination of linked and indexed data structures to hold the values.

We first take a deeper look at incrementalization, showing how to systematically exploit the previous result, intermediate results, and auxiliary values for incremental computation. This will use simple examples specified using recursive functions, followed by several different sorting programs as additional examples. We then discuss abstractions in general, focusing on the importance of and principles for not only building up, but also breaking through, abstractions. The latter may sound surprising at first, but it is natural when query functions are incrementalized with respect to updates. We then describe issues with implementations and experiments for the method, including in particular the analyses needed and their automation. Finally, we point out current limitations and future directions.

Notations

For ease of reading in generic discussions and in examples, this chapter uses a few new notations.

- The operation $\oplus$ denotes a generic increment operation. It takes a previous input x and a change parameter y and returns a new input, denoted $x \oplus y$.

- The functions $\bar{f}$, $\hat{f}$, and $\tilde{f}$ denote extended versions of f that return additional values—*all* intermediate results, *useful* intermediate results, and useful intermediate results *and* auxiliary values, respectively—besides the return value of f.

- In examples, following tradition, we use $cons(h, t)$ to construct a list with head element h and tail list t; use $hd(l)$ and $tl(l)$ to select the head and tail, respectively, of list l; use nil to construct an empty list; and use $null(l)$ to test whether l is an empty list. For complexity analysis, we use n to denote the length of the input list.

Additionally, in examples, we use boldface font for keywords and italic font for the rest, rather than all in teletype font.

7.1 A deeper look at incrementalization

We describe the essence of a transformational approach that exploits the previous result, determines intermediate results, and discovers auxiliary values for incrementalization in a general and systematic way.

We first define the notion of incremental program precisely using the notation $\oplus$. Given a program f and an operation $\oplus$, a program f' is called an *incremental version* of f under $\oplus$ if f' computes $f(x \oplus y)$ efficiently by making use of $f(x)$, in addition to x and y. Here are some examples:

- Suppose f is a program *sort*, x is a list of numbers, and $\oplus$ prepends a number y to the old input x, that is, $x \oplus y$ is $cons(y, x)$. Then f' can be a program *sort'* that inserts y at the appropriate place in the sorted list $sort(x)$. If $r = sort(x)$, then $sort'(y, r) = sort(cons(y, x))$. While computing $sort(cons(y, x))$ from scratch takes $\Omega(n \log n)$ time, computing $sort'(y, r)$ by inserting y into r takes only $O(n)$ time.

- Suppose we write computer programs that are compiled into code in some machine language before running, where f is a compiler, x is a program, and $\oplus$ performs changes to the program. Then f' is an incremental compiler that compiles a new program by updating the old compiled code rather than compiling from scratch.

- For general iterative computer programs, f is a loop body, x is the loop variable, and $\oplus$ increments the loop variable. Then f' is a general strength-reduced version, like one from strength reduction, that computes each iteration incrementally based on the result of the previous iteration.

Given a program f and an operation $\oplus$, the goal is to derive an incremental program that computes $f(x \oplus y)$ efficiently by using

P1. the previous result $f(x)$, that is, the return value of $f(x)$,

P2. the intermediate results of $f(x)$, that is, values computed in computing $f(x)$, not necessarily the return value, and

P3. auxiliary values for $f(x)$, that is, values not computed in computing $f(x)$ and that can be inexpensively maintained for efficiently computing $f(x \oplus y)$.

Using the value of $f(x)$ gives incrementality, that is, ability to reuse, in contrast to computing $f(x \oplus y)$ from scratch; using the intermediate results of $f(x)$ gives greater incrementality than using only the value of $f(x)$; using auxiliary values gives even greater incrementality than using only the return value and the intermediate results. We use P1, P2, and P3 to denote these three subproblems. Although P2 is much harder than P1, and P3 is much harder than P1 and P2, we will see that solution to P2 is reduced to solution to P1, and solution to P3 is reduced to solutions to P1 and P2.

We use the program *cmp* in Figure 7.1 as a small example to illustrate our approach. It compares the sum of odd positions and the product of even positions of list x. We use the same language to describe the operation $\oplus$. For example, we may have $x \oplus y = cons(y, x)$.

---

def $cmp(x)$: $sum(odd(x)) \leq prod(even(x))$

def $odd(x)$: **if** $null(x)$ **then** nil
         else $cons(hd(x), even(tl(x)))$

def $even(x)$: **if** $null(x)$ **then** nil
         else $odd(tl(x))$

def $sum(x)$: **if** $null(x)$ **then** 0
         else $hd(x) + sum(tl(x))$

def $prod(x)$: **if** $null(x)$ **then** 1
         else $hd(x) * prod(tl(x))$

Figure 7.1 An example program.

P1: exploiting the previous result

Suppose that we have computed $f(x)$ and obtained its result r, as depicted on the left of Figure 7.2, and that we want to compute $f(x \oplus y)$ on the right. Clearly, all subcomputations of $f(x \oplus y)$ depend on either x or y. For those that depend on y—a new parameter—we do not attempt to reuse the old result r. For those that depend only on x, for example, $f(x)$, as shown in the box for $f(x \oplus y)$, we avoid recomputation by replacing them with retrievals from the old result r. Thus, the idea is to symbolically transform $f(x \oplus y)$ to separate subcomputations on

x from those on y and replace those on x with retrievals from r. The resulting program f' may depend on x, y, and r, and it satisfies that if $f(x \oplus y) = r'$ then $f'(x, y, r) = r'$, as shown on the right at the bottom of Figure 7.2. To summarize,

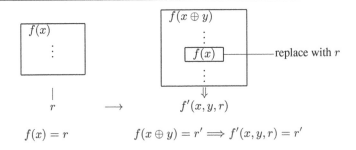

$$f(x) = r \qquad\qquad f(x \oplus y) = r' \Longrightarrow f'(x, y, r) = r'$$

Figure 7.2 Exploiting the previous result.

we first introduce function f' to compute $f(x \oplus y)$, with the cached result r of $f(x)$ as an extra argument besides x and y. Then, we do two things to obtain a definition of the incremental version: (1) *unfold* (i.e., expand $f(x \oplus y)$ using definitions of f and $\oplus$) and simplify, and (2) replace subcomputations using the cached result (based on identity, for the case that $f(x)$ appears in the expanded $f(x \oplus y)$). Finally, we replace a function call to f with a call to the incremental version f'. Replacement of a subcomputation may cause other subcomputations on which the replaced subcomputation depends to become dead code. Thus, dead code elimination is performed at the end.

We can do much better than only directly using the value of $f(x)$. We exploit the semantics of each program construct, that is, data structures and control structures. For example, if the return value r of $f(x)$ is a tuple, and $g(x)$ is a component of the tuple, then the value of $g(x)$ can be retrieved from r, as depicted by $g(x)$ sitting on the bottom of the box for $f(x)$ on the left of Figure 7.3. Thus, a subcomputation $g(x)$ in $f(x \oplus y)$ on the right can be replaced with a retrieval from r, based on equality reasoning. Also, subcomputation $g(x)$ in $f(x \oplus y)$ on the right may appear in certain context, for example, in the true branch of a conditional expression. If $f(x)$ on the left can be specialized to $g(x)$ under the same condition, by *auxiliary specialization*—specialization of $f(x)$ to help transform $f(x \oplus y)$, then the value of $g(x)$ on the right can be retrieved from r in this branch, even if it may not be retrievable in the other branch. The transformation steps are as previously summarized, except that replacements using the cached result are based also on equality reasoning and auxiliary specialization, as discussed above.

A number of important analyses and transformations are used here. Unfolding and algebraic simplification are among the most basic transformations, while equality reasoning and auxiliary specialization, which can be regarded as equality

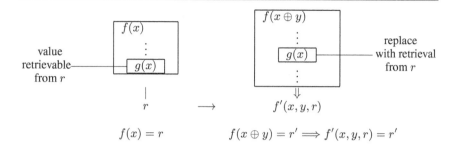

Figure 7.3 Exploiting the previous result (continued).

reasoning under conditions, could be arbitrarily powerful. However, limiting the power of these transformations, by using simple rewrite rules on data structures and control structures, such as $hd(cons(a, b)) = a$ and (**if** *true* **then** a **else** b) $= a$, and using fully automatable analyses for arithmetic and Booleans, we are able to derive incremental programs for all the examples discussed in this book and many more. Two efficient static analyses are also used: a forward dependence analysis to identify subcomputations depending only on x, and a backward dependence analysis to identify dead code.

As for most program transformation techniques, it should be noted that the quality of the resulting program depends on that of the original program. In the worst case, if no replacement with retrievals can be done, then $f(x \oplus y)$ is computed from scratch. We will show in the next section how our method derives different incremental programs for three different sorting programs.

For example, consider the given function *sum* and the operation $\oplus$ below.

> **def** $sum(x)$: **if** $null(x)$ **then** 0
>   **else** $hd(x) + sum(tl(x))$
> $x \oplus y = cons(y, x)$

We introduce $sum'(x, y, r)$, where $r = sum(x)$, to compute $sum(cons(y, x))$. Expanding $sum(cons(y, x))$ yields

> **if** $null(cons(y, x))$ **then** 0
> **else** $hd(cons(y, x)) + sum(tl(cons(y, x)))$

where the condition is simplified to false, the first operand of $+$ is simplified to y, and the argument of *sum* is simplified to x. Then replace $sum(x)$ with r. We obtain

> **def** $sum'(y, r)$: $y + r$

where parameter x to sum' is dead and eliminated. We have, if $r = sum(x)$, then $sum'(y, r) = sum(cons(y, x))$. While $sum(cons(y, x))$ takes $O(n)$ time to compute, $sum'(y, r)$ takes only $O(1)$ time and needs one unit of space to hold the old result.

P2: caching intermediate results

Often, intermediate results of $f(x)$ that are not retrievable from the return value are useful for efficient incremental computation. This is illustrated in Figure 7.4, which is the same as Figure 7.3 except for the two additional boxes for $g_1(x)$ and the additional line of formulas for $\widehat{f}$ at the bottom. Basically, a subcomputation $g_1(x)$ in $f(x \oplus y)$ on the right may also be computed in computing $f(x)$ on the left, but its value is not retrievable from the result r of $f(x)$. If we know which intermediate results of $f(x)$ are useful for the incremental computation, then we can extend $f(x)$ to $\widehat{f}(x)$ that returns also these results in $\widehat{r}$, as shown on the left of the bottom line in Figure 7.4; then an incremental version $\widehat{f}'$ of $\widehat{f}$ under $\oplus$ can use these results in $\widehat{r}$ and compute the corresponding results for $\widehat{f}(x \oplus y)$, as shown on the right of the bottom line in Figure 7.4. The hard problem is that $f(x)$

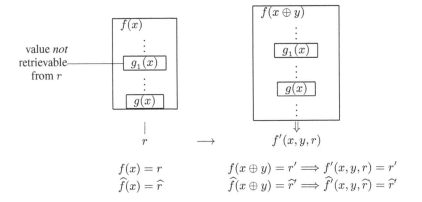

$$f(x) = r \qquad\qquad f(x \oplus y) = r' \implies f'(x, y, r) = r'$$
$$\widehat{f}(x) = \widehat{r} \qquad\qquad \widehat{f}(x \oplus y) = \widehat{r}' \implies \widehat{f}'(x, y, \widehat{r}) = \widehat{r}'$$

Figure 7.4 Caching intermediate results.

may compute a huge number of intermediate results. How can we identify useful intermediate results?

We can use a three-stage method called *cache-and-prune*. Stage I constructs a function $\bar{f}$ that extends f to return all intermediate results computed by f. The return value of $\bar{f}$ is a tree structure, mirroring the control structure incurred by (recursive) function calls, where the original value of f is, for convenience, the leftmost child of the root. Now that all intermediate results are cached in the return value of $\bar{f}$, Stage II incrementalizes $\bar{f}$ under $\oplus$ to obtain an incremental version $\bar{f}'$ that can use all of them, as done for P1. Function $\bar{f}'$ computes a new tree of intermediate results, but only the result corresponding to the new value of f—the value of $f(x \oplus y)$, at the leftmost child of the new tree—is originally desired. Stage III analyzes $\bar{f}'$ to determine all cached values needed for computing the desired value and prunes out the rest in both $\bar{f}$ and $\bar{f}'$, yielding $\hat{f}$ and $\hat{f}'$, respectively.

The cache-and-prune method for P2 consists of three relatively independent stages and thus is modular. Stage I enables maximum speedup via reuse by providing all intermediate results possibly used by Stage II. Stage II uses these intermediate results for the exclusive purpose of incrementalization and is reduced to P1. Stage III yields minimum space usage by preserving only intermediate results used by Stage II. Thus, the overall method for P2 has a kind of optimality—the best any caching method can do—with respect to the method used in Stage II. The analyses and transformations used for Stages I and III are simple and efficient.

The method for P2 can be used for general program optimization via caching, by incrementalizing the body of a loop or recursion. Because intermediate results are computed by the original program anyway, caching and using them will not increase the asymptotic running time of the transformed program. It can drastically decrease the running time if the original program performs repeated subcomputations, as we have seen in the examples in Chapter 4.

For example, consider the given function cmp and the operation $\oplus$ below.

$$
\boxed{
\begin{aligned}
&\textbf{def } cmp(x) : \ sum(odd(x)) \leq prod(even(x)) \\
&x \oplus [y_1, y_2] \ = \ cons(y_1, cons(y_2, x))
\end{aligned}
}
$$

Clearly, if we cache intermediate results $sum(odd(x))$ and $prod(even(x))$, then an incremental version only needs to add y_1 to the former and multiply y_2 by the latter.

Let us use cache-and-prune. First, caching all intermediate results yields function $\overline{cmp}$ below, where functions $\overline{odd}$, $\overline{sum}$, $\overline{even}$, and $\overline{prod}$ return their intermediate results in a similar fashion and are omitted. Recall that we use [] to denote a tuple, and selectors $1st$, $2nd$, and so on to select the corresponding components of a tuple. Then, incrementalizing $\overline{cmp}$ under the given $\oplus$ yields function $\overline{cmp}'$ below, such that if $\bar{r} = \overline{cmp}(x)$, then $\overline{cmp}'(y_1, y_2, \bar{r}) = \overline{cmp}(cons(y_1, cons(y_2, x)))$.

def $\overline{cmp}(x)$:
  let $u_1 := \overline{odd}(x)$ **in**
  let $u_2 := \overline{sum}(1st(u_1))$ **in**
  let $u_3 := \overline{even}(x)$ **in**
  let $u_4 := \overline{prod}(1st(u_3))$ **in**
  $[\, 1st(u_2) \leq 1st(u_4), \ u_1, \ u_2, \ u_3, \ u_4\,]$

def $\overline{cmp}'(y_1, y_2, \bar{r})$:
  let $u_1 := [\, cons(y_1, 1st(2nd(\bar{r}))), \ 2nd(\bar{r})\,]$ **in**
  let $u_2 := [\, y_1 + 1st(3rd(\bar{r})), \ 3rd(\bar{r})\,]$ **in**
  let $u_3 := [\, cons(y_2, 1st(4th(\bar{r}))), \ 4th(\bar{r})\,]$ **in**
  let $u_4 := [\, y_2 * 1st(5th(\bar{r})), \ 5th(\bar{r})\,]$ **in**
  $[\, 1st(u_2) \leq 1st(u_4), \ u_1, \ u_2, \ u_3, \ u_4\,]$

Finally, pruning all returned components not needed for computing $1st(u_2) \leq 1st(u_4)$ in $\overline{cmp}'(y_1, y_2, \bar{r})$, we obtain functions $\widehat{cmp}$ and $\widehat{cmp}'$ below. They satisfy that, if $\hat{r} = \widehat{cmp}(x)$, then $\widehat{cmp}'(y_1, y_2, \hat{r}) = \widehat{cmp}(cons(y_1, cons(y_2, x)))$, and

$cmp(x) = 1st(\widehat{cmp}(x))$.

---

def $\widehat{cmp}(x)$: **let** $v_1 := sum(odd(x))$ **in**
           let $v_2 := prod(even(x))$ **in**
           $[\, v_1 \leq v_2,\ v_1,\ v_2\,]$

def $\widehat{cmp}'(y_1, y_2, \widehat{r})$: **let** $v_1 := y_1 + 2nd(\widehat{r})$ **in**
           let $v_2 := y_2 * 3rd(\widehat{r})$ **in**
           $[\, v_1 \leq v_2,\ v_1,\ v_2\,]$

While $cmp(cons(y_1, cons(y_2, x)))$ takes $O(n)$ time, $\widehat{cmp}'(y_1, y_2, \widehat{r})$ takes only $O(1)$ time and needs two additional units of space for two intermediate results.

P3: discovering auxiliary values

Sometimes, auxiliary values not computed by $f(x)$ at all are useful for efficient computation of $f(x \oplus y)$. However, it is difficult to discover such values. Even for manually derived incremental algorithms, only a small number of special auxiliary data structures have been studied. We propose a systematic method that can discover a general class of auxiliary values. The idea is illustrated in Figure 7.5 and is explained below. Note that Figure 7.5 is the same as Figure 7.4 except for the additional box for $h(x)$ on the right and the different bottom line of formulas.

The method has two phases. In Phase A, we transform $f(x \oplus y)$, shown on the right of Figure 7.5, to separate subcomputations on x from those on y, as done for P1. If the value of a subcomputation, for example, $g(x)$ or $g_1(x)$ in the box for $f(x \oplus y)$, can be retrieved from the return value of $f(x)$ or an intermediate result of $f(x)$, for example, as $g(x)$ or $g_1(x)$ respectively in the box for $f(x)$ on the left, then it is left alone. However, if the value of a subcomputation depending only on x, for example, $h(x)$ in the box for $f(x \oplus y)$, cannot be retrieved from either, then it is collected as a candidate auxiliary value. In Phase B, we determine whether such values can be used and maintained for efficient incremental computation, as done for P2. We extend $f(x)$ to compute and cache the candidate auxiliary values, as well as intermediate results, incrementalize the resulting program, and prune out useless values and computations. This yields the resulting programs $\bar{f}$ and $\widetilde{f}'$, where $\bar{f}$ returns useful intermediate results as well as auxiliary values, and $\widetilde{f}'$ incrementally uses and maintains them, as shown in the bottom line of Figure 7.5.

The overall method for P3 is composed of analyses and transformations similar to those used for P1 and P2. Phase A uses transformations as those for P1, followed by a forward dependence analysis to identify subcomputations depending on x but not replaced with retrievals from the result of $\bar{f}(x)$, that is, subcomputations that are not the return value or intermediate results. Phase B uses the transformations for P2, except that $\bar{f}(x)$ is further extended to compute the candidate auxiliary values. Thus, we have reduced a difficult problem to modular steps

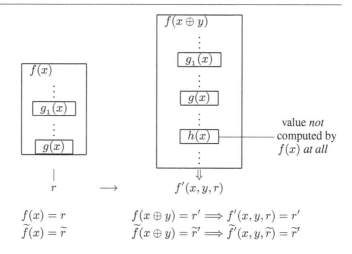

Figure 7.5 Discovering auxiliary values.

where solutions to previous problems can be used. Even though the overall method is complex, each step is relatively simple.

Because auxiliary values are not computed by the original program, we use such values only if we can conservatively determine that they can be efficiently computed and maintained. Actually, to obtain incremental programs that are asymptotically at least as fast as the original program, we only need to require that auxiliary values be computed initially as fast as the original program. Usually, the cost of this initial computation is amortized over repeated computation using the incremental program, and efficient use and maintenance of the auxiliary values allow the overall computation to be much faster.

For example, consider the given function *cmp* and the operation ⊕ below.

$$
\begin{array}{l}
\textbf{def } cmp(x) : \; sum(odd(x)) \le prod(even(x)) \\
x \oplus y \; = \; cons(y, x)
\end{array}
$$

After an input change, the sublists for the odd positions and even positions are swapped. Caching only intermediate results is useless for the incremental computation. We need to compute and save also the values of $sum(even(x))$ and $prod(odd(x))$. Then, an incremental version can use and maintain each of these values by a single addition, multiplication, or copy.

Using the two-phase method, we obtain functions $\widetilde{cmp}$ and $\widetilde{cmp}'$, such that if

$\tilde{r} = \widetilde{cmp}(x)$, then $\widetilde{cmp}'(y, \tilde{r}) = \widetilde{cmp}(cons(y, x))$, and $cmp(x) = 1st(\widetilde{cmp}(x))$.

def $\widetilde{cmp}(x)$:   **let** $v_1 := odd(x)$ **in**   **let** $u_1 := sum(v_1)$ **in**   **let** $v_2 := even(x)$ **in**   **let** $u_2 := prod(v_2)$ **in** $[\, u_1 \leq u_2,\ u_1,\ u_2,\ sum(v_2),\ prod(v_1)\,]$ **def** $\widetilde{cmp}'(y, \tilde{r})$: $[\, y + 4th(\tilde{r}) \leq 5th(\tilde{r}),$ $y + 4th(\tilde{r}),\ 5th(\tilde{r}),\ 2nd(\tilde{r}),\ y * 3rd(\tilde{r})\,]$

While $cmp(cons(y, x))$ takes $O(n)$ time, $\widetilde{cmp}'(y, \tilde{r})$ takes only $O(1)$ time and needs another two additional units of space for two auxiliary values.

7.2 Example: sorting

We use three different sorting programs, for insertion sort, selection sort, and merge sort, to illustrate the power of our method for deriving incremental programs.

The following table shows the running times of both the batch versions and the incremental versions (with respect to the given $\oplus$ operations) for the examples sum and cmp discussed above and the three sorting programs discussed next, where n is the size of the input list.

Problem	Batch	Incremental
sum, cmp	$O(n)$	$O(1)$
insertion sort	$O(n^2)$	$O(n)$
selection sort	$O(n^2)$	$O(n)$
merge sort	$O(n \log n)$	$O(n)$

Insertion sort

Insertion sort takes a list, recursively sorts the tail of the list, and then inserts the first element into the appropriate place in the sorted tail. Consider its definition below and a change operation that adds an element y to the input list.

def $sort(x)$: **if** $null(x)$ **then** nil **else** $insert(hd(x), sort(tl(x)))$ **def** $insert(i, x)$: **if** $null(x)$ **then** $cons(i, nil)$ **else if** $i \leq hd(x)$ **then** $cons(i, x)$ **else** $cons(hd(x), insert(i, tl(x)))$ $x \oplus y \ = \ cons(y, x)$

We introduce $sort'(x, y, r)$, where $r = sort(x)$, to compute $sort(cons(y, x))$. Expanding $sort(cons(y, x))$ yields

$$\text{\textbf{if} } null(cons(y, x)) \text{ \textbf{then} } nil$$
$$\text{\textbf{else} } insert(hd(cons(y, x)), sort(tl(cons(y, x))))$$

The condition is then simplified to false, the first argument of *insert* is simplified to y, and the argument to *sort* is simplified to x. Then replace $sort(x)$ with r. We obtain

$$\boxed{\textbf{def } sort'(y,r) : insert(y,r)}$$

where parameter x to *sort* is dead and eliminated. We have, if $r = sort(x)$, then $sort'(y,r) = sort(cons(y,x))$. While $sort(cons(y,x))$ takes $O(n^2)$ time, $sort'(y,r)$ takes $O(n)$ time. This result is easy to obtain. Function $sort'$ simply calls the given function *insert*.

Selection sort

Selection sort takes a list, selects the least element in the list, puts it in the first place, and then recursively sorts the rest of the list. Consider its definition below and a change operation that adds an element y to the input list. It is nontrivial how selection sort applied to the new list can be transformed to use the previously sorted list. Our approach to P1 allows us to derive a definition of insertion not given in the original program.

$$\boxed{\begin{array}{ll}
\textbf{def } sort(x) & : \textbf{if } null(x) \textbf{ then } nil \\
& \quad \textbf{else let } k := least(x) \textbf{ in} \\
& \qquad cons(k, sort(rest(x,k))) \\
\textbf{def } least(x) & : \textbf{if } null(tl(x)) \textbf{ then } hd(x) \\
& \quad \textbf{else let } s := least(tl(x)) \textbf{ in} \\
& \qquad \textbf{if } hd(x) < s \textbf{ then } hd(x) \textbf{ else } s \\
\textbf{def } rest(x,k) : & \textbf{if } k = hd(x) \textbf{ then } tl(x) \\
& \quad \textbf{else } cons(hd(x), rest(tl(x),k)) \\
x \oplus y = & cons(y,x)
\end{array}}$$

We introduce $sort'(y,x,r)$ to compute $sort(cons(y,x))$, where $r = sort(x)$. First, expand $sort(cons(y,x))$ and simplify:

$$
\begin{aligned}
& sort(cons(y,x)) \\
& = \textbf{if } null(cons(y,x)) \textbf{ then } nil \qquad\quad = \textbf{let } k := least(cons(y,x)) \textbf{ in} \\
& \quad \textbf{else let } k := least(cons(y,x)) \textbf{ in} \qquad\quad cons(k, sort(rest(cons(y,x),k))) \\
& \qquad cons(k, sort(rest(cons(y,x),k)))
\end{aligned}
\tag{7.1}
$$

Then, expand $least(cons(y,x))$ in (7.1) and simplify:

$$
\begin{aligned}
& least(cons(y,x)) \\
& = \textbf{if } null(tl(cons(y,x))) \textbf{ then } hd(cons(y,x)) \qquad = \textbf{if } null(x) \textbf{ then } y \\
& \quad \textbf{else let } s := least(tl(cons(y,x))) \textbf{ in} \qquad\qquad \textbf{else let } s := least(x) \textbf{ in} \\
& \qquad \textbf{if } hd(cons(y,x)) < s \textbf{ then } hd(cons(y,x)) \textbf{ else } s \qquad \textbf{if } y < s \textbf{ then } y \textbf{ else } s
\end{aligned}
\tag{7.2}
$$

and expand (7.2) into (7.1) and simplify:

$$
\begin{aligned}
& (7.1) \\
& = \textbf{let } k := \textbf{if } null(x) \textbf{ then } y \qquad\qquad = \textbf{if } null(x) \textbf{ then } cons(y, sort(rest(cons(y,x),y))) \\
& \qquad\qquad \textbf{else let } s := least(x) \textbf{ in} \qquad\qquad \textbf{else let } s := least(x) \textbf{ in} \\
& \qquad\qquad\quad \textbf{if } y < s \textbf{ then } y \textbf{ else } s \textbf{ in} \qquad\quad \textbf{if } y < s \textbf{ then } cons(y, sort(rest(cons(y,x),y))) \\
& \quad cons(k, sort(rest(cons(y,x),k))) \qquad\qquad\qquad \textbf{else } cons(s, sort(rest(cons(y,x),s)))
\end{aligned}
\tag{7.3}
$$

Then, expand $rest(cons(y,x),y)$ and $rest(cons(y,x),s)$ in (7.3) and simplify:

$$
\begin{aligned}
&rest(cons(y,x),y)\\
&= \textbf{if } y = hd(cons(y,x)) \textbf{ then } tl(cons(y,x)) \qquad = \textbf{if } y = y \textbf{ then } x \qquad = x\\
&\quad \textbf{else } cons(hd(cons(y,x)), rest(tl(cons(y,x)),y)))) \qquad \textbf{else } cons(y, rest(x,y))
\end{aligned}
$$
$$(7.4)$$

$$
\begin{aligned}
&rest(cons(y,x),s)\\
&= \textbf{if } s = hd(cons(y,x)) \textbf{ then } tl(cons(y,x)) \qquad = \textbf{if } s = y \textbf{ then } x\\
&\quad \textbf{else } cons(hd(cons(y,x)), rest(tl(cons(y,x)),s)))) \qquad \textbf{else } cons(y, rest(x,s))
\end{aligned}
$$
$$(7.5)$$

and expand (7.4) and (7.5) into (7.3) and simplify:

$$
\begin{aligned}
&(7.3)\\
&= \textbf{if } null(x) \textbf{ then } cons(y, sort(x)) \qquad\qquad = \textbf{if } null(x) \textbf{ then } cons(y, sort(x))\\
&\quad \textbf{else let } s := least(x) \textbf{ in} \qquad\qquad\qquad \textbf{else let } s := least(x) \textbf{ in}\\
&\quad\quad \textbf{if } y < s \textbf{ then } cons(y, sort(x)) \qquad\qquad \textbf{if } y \leq s \textbf{ then } cons(y, sort(x))\\
&\quad\quad \textbf{else } cons(s, sort(\textbf{if } s = y \textbf{ then } x \qquad\qquad \textbf{else } cons(s, sort(cons(y, rest(x,s)))))\\
&\quad\quad\quad\quad\quad \textbf{else } cons(y, rest(x,s))))
\end{aligned}
$$
$$(7.6)$$

Next, we perform equality reasoning and auxiliary specialization and replace sub-computations in (7.6) with retrievals from r. First, $sort(x)$ in (7.6) is replaced with r. Also, $null(x) = null(r)$ because, using auxiliary specialization twice, we have that $null(x)$ is true if and only if $null(sort(x))$ is true, so $null(x)$ in (7.6) is replaced with $null(r)$. Furthermore, when $null(x)$ is false, $sort(x)$ is specialized to $\textbf{let } k := least(x) \textbf{ in } cons(k, sort(rest(x,k)))$ by definition, which gives $least(x) = hd(r)$ and $sort(rest(x, least(x))) = tl(r)$. Thus $least(x)$ in (7.6) is replaced with $hd(r)$. Finally, recursive call $sort(cons(y, rest(x,s)))$ is replaced with $sort'(y, rest(x,s), sort(rest(x,s)))$, where $sort(rest(x,s))$ in the latter is replaced with $tl(r)$. We obtain the following, where the underlines indicate replacements:

$$
\begin{aligned}
\textbf{def } sort'(y,x,r) : \ &\textbf{if } null(\underline{r}) \textbf{ then } cons(y, \underline{r})\\
&\textbf{else let } s := \underline{hd(r)} \textbf{ in}\\
&\quad \textbf{if } y \leq s \textbf{ then } cons(y, \underline{r})\\
&\quad \textbf{else } cons(s, \underline{sort'(y, rest(x,s), tl(r))})
\end{aligned}
$$

Eliminating dead parameter x and dead code in the corresponding argument, we obtain

$$
\boxed{
\begin{aligned}
\textbf{def } sort'(y,r) : \ &\textbf{if } null(r) \textbf{ then } cons(y, r)\\
&\textbf{else let } s := hd(r) \textbf{ in}\\
&\quad \textbf{if } y \leq s \textbf{ then } cons(y, r)\\
&\quad \textbf{else } cons(s, sort'(y, tl(r)))
\end{aligned}
}
$$

which is exactly an insertion program.

Merge sort

Merge sort takes a list, separates it into two sublists of roughly equal lengths, recursively sorts both, and then merges the two sorted sublists. Consider its definition below and, again, a change operation that adds an element y to the input list.

def $sort(x)$	: **if** $null(x)$ **then** nil **else if** $null(tl(x))$ **then** x **else** $merge(sort(odd(x)), sort(even(x)))$
def $odd(x)$	: **if** $null(x)$ **then** nil **else** $cons(hd(x), even(tl(x)))$
def $even(x)$	: **if** $null(x)$ **then** nil **else** $odd(tl(x))$
def $merge(x, y)$	: **if** $null(x)$ **then** y **else if** $null(y)$ **then** x **else if** $hd(x) \leq hd(y)$ **then** $\quad cons(hd(x), merge(tl(x), y))$ **else** $cons(hd(y), merge(x, tl(y)))$

$$x \oplus y \ = \ cons(y, x)$$

If we are given that $sort(cons(y, x))$ equals merging a single-element list of y with the previously sorted list of x, then we can straightforwardly obtain an incremental version, which is essentially an insertion with a constant-factor overhead.

> **def** $sort'(y, r)$: $merge(cons(y, nil), r)$

However, this equality is nontrivial to derive. Even proving it requires a nontrivial induction. If no additional equality is given, can we compute merge sort of the new list more efficiently than computing from scratch? The answer is yes, simply using cache-and-prune.

The derivation is straightforward. We illustrate the idea with the following picture, rather than code as for selection sort. The top thicker line denotes list x; the thinner line below denotes $sort(x)$; the two thicker lines below denote $odd(x)$ and $even(x)$, respectively; and the two thinner lines below denote $sort(odd(x))$ and $sort(even(x))$, respectively. This goes down until each list has a single element.

First, cache all the intermediate results of sorted sublists, as depicted above. Then, incrementalize after a new element y is added to the top thicker line. Clearly, y belongs to one of the two thicker lines immediately below, which means that the intermediate result for the other thicker line can be reused. This goes down until a single element is left, and comes back up to perform a merge at each level. The depth is $\log n$, and the amount of work for each level, from bottom to top, is 1 unit, 2 units, 4 units, ... $n/2$ units, summing up to a total of $O(n)$ time. Finally, prune out intermediate results such as $odd(x)$ and $even(x)$. The resulting incremental merge sort is as follows:

$$
\begin{array}{ll}
\textbf{def } \widehat{sort}{}'(y, \hat{r}) : & \textbf{if } null(\mathit{lst}(\hat{r})) \textbf{ then } [\, cons(y, nil)\,] \\
& \textbf{else if } null(tl(\mathit{lst}(\hat{r}))) \textbf{ then} \\
& \quad [\, merge(cons(y,nil), \mathit{lst}(\hat{r})), [\, cons(y,nil)\,], [\, \mathit{lst}(\hat{r})\,]\,] \\
& \textbf{else let } u_1 := \widehat{sort}{}'(y, 3rd(\hat{r})) \textbf{ in} \\
& \textbf{let } u_2 := 2nd(\hat{r}) \textbf{ in} \\
& \quad [\, merge(\mathit{lst}(u_1), \mathit{lst}(u_2)), u_1, u_2\,]
\end{array}
$$

where function $merge$ is as in the given program. Note that this incremental merge sort takes $O(n \log n)$ space rather than $O(n)$ space. However, no additional equality is needed for this derivation. The resulting program $\widehat{sort}{}'(y, \hat{r})$ takes $O(n)$ time while sorting from scratch using $sort(cons(y, x))$ takes $O(n \log n)$ time. To our knowledge, this algorithm was not known previously, probably due to its $\log n$ factor of additional space, but it reduces the running time by a $\log n$ factor without additional knowledge about the problem.

7.3 Building up and breaking through abstractions

For real-world applications, software needs to be developed fast, to run correctly and efficiently, and to be easily maintainable, all at low costs. Even though the ideal way to achieve this is through development of complete high-level specifications and automatic generation of optimized code, in reality, there is little work on either, not only because both are hard, but also because there is no incentive to invest into either when there is no good method for the other. While developing high-level specifications corresponds to building up abstractions, generating optimized code requires breaking through abstractions, even though this may sound surprising. To make progress, methods for both must be studied together.

The need for building up abstraction is easy to see, but the need for breaking through abstraction is less so. It is well known that higher-level specifications are clearer and easier to read and write, and thus support faster development, higher assurance of correctness, and easier maintenance, all at lower costs, whereas breaking through abstractions seems to be the opposite. Note, however, that breaking *through* abstraction does not mean breaking abstraction; it means that optimizations need to go inside components or pieces that are encapsulated by abstraction, to make changes to improve efficiency, but can preserve the same interfaces to users of the components or pieces. For example, when objects are used for module abstraction in Chapter 6, incrementalization needs to change the inside of classes and methods but preserves the given interfaces. When sets, recursion, and rules are used for data and control abstractions in Chapters 3 to 5, incrementalization needs to change how the queries and updates are done but preserves what they compute.

The study of systematic incrementalization has led to the development of principles and methods for both building up and breaking through high-level abstractions, which are essential for cost-saving development of software for real-world systems. Building up abstractions supports correctness and composability, vital for scaled-up applications, and breaking through abstractions is essential for efficiency and adaptability in the presence of dynamic changes. We argue that development along these lines will lead to a powerful method for constructing complete and fully composable specifications and for generating efficient and optimally adaptable implementations.

Building up abstractions

Building up abstractions, by expressing both data and control at a high level, needs guiding principles that can be easily followed and checked, and that can let us achieve ambitious goals: complete, high-level, and fully composable specifications. While completeness and high-level-ness can be achieved with abstractions for both data and control, full composability requires something more drastic.

The study of incrementalization has led us to advocate the following key principles, which strive for clarity and simplicity and lead naturally to modularity and composability.

- The central principle is that only basic data should be updated in specifications, where *basic data* refers to data given and modified by external sources, in contrast to *derived data*, which refers to data that can be computed from basic data. Maintenance and update of derived data should be automatically derived based on how they depend on basic data and how basic data are updated.

- The additional principles are to specify basic data explicitly and to define derived data declaratively. Definition of each kind of derived data can be completely clear and modular by itself without worrying about updating any data. This leads to full composability as well as ease of understanding and verification.

It is easy to see that these principles best support the use of high-level abstractions and vice versa: sets, relations, and other high-level data abstraction for ease of writing updates and ease of use by queries; functions, comprehensions, and other high-level control abstraction for ease of writing queries declaratively; and objects and classes as module abstraction for ease of organizing the queries and updates.

In fact, we have already seen that these principles are applied to specifications that use query and update methods on objects and sets. In the protocol example in Chapter 6, each component has a set of basic data and query and update operations, and only the basic data is updated. In the RBAC example in Chapter 3, the queries and updates are simplified from many more updates to derived data in

the original ANSI standard for RBAC. Specifically, core RBAC, which contains
about half of the functionalities in the 47-page standard, can be specified clearly
using sets and set queries and updates in 122 lines of Python; it still contains a few
updates to derived data for maintaining integrity constraints. Specification of such
uses of constraints when input can change is one of the open problems discussed
in Section 7.5.

Breaking through abstractions

Breaking through abstractions, to generate efficient implementations from high-
level specifications, needs a powerful automated method that gives analytical performance guarantees, so that optimality and adaptability can be precisely defined
and achieved. Such a powerful method needs to explore two tightly correlated
fronts:

1. Because abstractions encapsulate definitions of derived data and separate
   them from updates to basic data, and possibly encapsulate both in components, the method needs to delve into the encapsulated components and definitions, to store derived data appropriately and maintain them incrementally
   as basic data are updated. Such principled optimizations are key to automatically generating efficient implementations.

2. The method needs to calculate the total cost of computing and maintaining
   derived data, accounting for all best ways of doing this, and using not only
   the costs of individual operations but also their frequencies, which may vary
   over time, as parameters. Such parameterized calculations are essential for
   achieving optimality and adaptability.

It is easy to see that incrementalization-based transformations on high-level specifications provide such a method.

A crucial issue in generating optimally adaptable implementations is to precisely and declaratively capture all possible transformations together with parameterized cost calculations, so that optimality and adaptability can be precisely defined. Incrementalization rules in Chapter 6 provide a means for starting to address this issue, because they precisely and declaratively express definitions and
maintenance of derived data together with costs, and frequencies are considered
in applying the rules.

For example, for core RBAC, the transformations use 9 incrementalization rules,
and modify 16 query functions and 12 update functions to store and update derived
data for efficiently answering the queries. We have not formally studied optimality
or adaptability, but we generated three versions, each for a different combination
of frequencies of the operations, and each with different guaranteed complexities for the queries and updates. A precise method for automatically achieving

optimality and adaptability is one of the subjects for further study discussed in Section 7.5.

7.4 Implementations and experiments

We discuss issues with implementations and experiments for the method. Clearly, the implementations must support not only various transformations but also powerful analyses. A critical issue is how the method can be fully automated. The experiments should be designed to evaluate not only running times, but also a range of other related measures. The discussions here are based on our experience implementing prototypes and conducting experiments for all of the transformations described in this book along with the needed analyses.

Analyses and transformations

The transformations can use standard techniques for pattern matching, variable substitution, and introduction of fresh variables. The analyses may use a combination of techniques to help determine expensive query computations and updates to values of query parameters, reason about equality for reuse, calculate costs, and identify dead code at the end. We summarize below additional analyses and transformations used for programs that use different data and control abstractions.

For loops and arrays, expensive computations are certain primitive operations and aggregate array computations. For incrementalization of primitive operations, algebraic laws, especially distributivity laws, are needed to separate computations on the increment from previous computations. For aggregate array computations, transformations are to form aggregates and incrementalize the aggregates. For both, analyses need to find simplified forms of primitive operations, including in particular integer arithmetic operations on array indices and loop variables.

For set expressions, transformations need to apply incrementalization rules for expensive set expressions, analyze types based on accesses to sets to determine the bases of based representations and to generate data structures. When fixed-point specifications are used, analyses of high-level properties such as monotonicity are needed to apply fixed-point theorems. When incrementalization rules are not available, transformations are also needed for deriving incrementalization rules, and derivations require analysis of possible bindings of variables.

For recursive functions, transformations need to introduce incremental functions, expand function calls using function definitions, simplify primitive functions and data constructions, replace expressions with retrievals from previous results, replace recursive function calls with recursive calls to incremental functions, and form iterative or recursive optimized programs. Analyses need to determine minimum input increments, reason about equality between expressions and results of previous computations, and analyze dependencies on recursive data.

For Datalog rules, analyses and transformations need to identify wild card, equal card, and shared versus unshared variables in single rules; analyze the domains of variables using their occurrences in the arguments of predicates; decompose rules that have more than two hypotheses; and generate incremental computation code, low-level data structure manipulation code, and complexity formulas. Implementations with optimal time complexities can be generated fully automatically.

For objects and classes, the analyses and transformations mentioned above are needed when the corresponding data and control abstractions are used. Additionally, analysis of aliases among object references is critical for determining updates to values of query parameters, and analysis of types helps increase the precision of alias analysis. The analysis results are also used to determine control flow; determining control flow includes method resolution, that is, determining which method is called on an object.

We do not discuss the details of these analyses here, but we should point out that, in general, these analyses are much easier, or are non-problems, for higher-level language constructs. For example, analysis of array indices and loop variables becomes extremely easy, or trivial, when aggregate expressions are used instead of loops. For another example, analysis of monotonicity is not needed when Datalog rules are used instead of fixed-point specifications.

Automation

The overall method combines many existing analyses and transformations, and puts them together in an overall step-wise procedure. Thus it is systematic. However, after all, can the method be fully automated? The answer depends on whether the analyses needed for the transformations can be fully automated, which in turn depends on the power needed from the analyses. There are mainly three kinds of analyses in question: simplifications for equality reasoning; program analyses for dependencies, aliases, types, and costs; and determining minimum increments.

Whether simplifications and equality reasoning using algebraic laws can succeed is in general undecidable, but is decidable, and thus fully automatable, for large classes of expressions involving integer arithmetics and Boolean operations. Simplifications and equality reasoning for constructed data and control structures can explore algebraic laws for them in an exhaustive way, for example, $c.i(c(x_1, \ldots, x_k)) = x_i$, that is, applying the selector for the i-th component of a constructed data of k components retrieves the i-th component, for $1 \leq i \leq k$.

Precise program analyses for dependencies, aliasing, types, and costs are also undecidable problems because they depend on program input, but many efficient algorithms have been developed for conservative analyses of dependencies, aliases, and types, as well as costs. Note that efficient analyses of dependencies, aliases, and types, as opposed to merely decidable analyses, are important because they are applied to an entire program. This contrasts simplifications and equality reasoning, as well as cost analysis, which are applied to a program region, such as a single function or a single query.

The method used for determining minimum increments needs to select minimum changes in arguments of recursive calls and take the opposite of each of them. Symbolically selecting minimums among arbitrary expressions and taking the inverse for an arbitrary operation are once again undecidable problems in general. However, selecting minimums for linear integer arithmetic expressions is decidable, and taking the opposite of subtractions is easy; using as a minimum increment the operation that adds a single element for constructed list or tree data is also easy.

In general, we do not yet know how to derive all incrementalization rules automatically, such as the rule for efficiently computing the minimum of a set by maintaining a heap. However, there has been a much smaller number of data structures for such rules, compared to the number of rules we know how to derive automatically. These rules can be written manually and put in a library so they can be reused afterward.

To summarize, the method is fully automatable if the three kinds of analyses described are automatic and a small number of incrementalization rules are given. By using restricted or conservative methods for the analyses and putting these small number of incrementalization rules in libraries, the method is fully automatic, and is powerful enough to generate efficient implementations for all the example problems we described and many many more. Last but not least, the method can certainly be used manually in algorithm design, and used semiautomatically with the analyses and transformations increasingly automated and rule libraries increasingly built.

Experiments

While it is obvious that experiments should measure and compare running times, much more needs to be considered.

First of all, the systematic design method is aimed at reducing development and maintenance costs by allowing straightforward but inefficient implementations to be transformed into would-be manually developed sophisticated implementations to achieve the desired efficiency. Evaluating this reduction requires tracking and comparing development and maintenance costs for the two kinds of implementations. It can be a significant undertaking. Related measures include the ease of developing and understanding the two kinds of implementations and the sizes of the implementations.

Another important goal of the systematic design method is to increase the level of correctness assurance through straightforward implementations and correctness-preserving transformations. Evaluating this requires tracking efforts on and results from verification, testing, and bug finding and fixing, for the two kinds of implementations and the transformations themselves. Testing, as well as efficiency evaluation discussed next, need the ability to generate appropriate random data.

When it comes to efficiency, the first measure to use is indeed running times of the implementations, which is the primary consideration in our cost model. This requires measuring and comparing the running times of straightforward but inefficient implementations and incrementalized and efficient implementations. Note that the main goal is to confirm improvements of asymptotic complexities, which may involve multiple parameters, so the experiments need to use data that vary the values of a single parameter at a time in each experiment.

Several other kinds of quantities should be measured to evaluate efficiency. The time taken to generate efficient implementations from straightforward implementations should be measured, together with sizes of the implementations. Frequencies of queries and updates should be measured too because they help understand the total running time. Space usage should be measured as well, because there are time and space trade-offs, and when too much space is used, running time might also increase. Another aspect of space usage is data locality, that is, how closely located are data that are frequently accessed closely in time, because it may affect running time considerably.

Finally, when the same problem may be specified in multiple ways using different abstractions for data and control, all the above should be measured for each of the ways, and the trade-offs should be compared.

7.5 Limitations and future work

Despite its power, there are still many limitations with the method and many research problems that need further study. These include characterizations of the method to help with understanding and improvements, extensions of the method to handle other aspects of applications, relationships with methods in continuous domains in mathematics and physics, and experiments with large-scale applications.

Characterizations

Given the unusual power and generality of the method, it is natural for us to be extremely curious about a precise characterization of the method. Such a characterization should shed light on the degree of automation and on possible improvements, and perhaps ultimately help us understand the complexity of computational problems. Unfortunately, such a precise characterization has so far been an open issue with the method.

There are in fact many ways even to ask questions about this issue.

- The most obvious way is: for what problems, or, better, what kinds of problems, can the method derive efficient implementations? This is also the least amenable way because it is not even clear how the problems, or kinds of problems, should be specified.

- A more approachable way is perhaps: for problems specified in what languages, or more specifically, for what combinations of language constructs, can the method derive efficient implementations? This is still not amenable to any direct answer, because it is not clear what efficient implementations mean.

- A more theoretical way is indeed to ask: for what complexity class of problems can the method derive efficient implementations? This uses the intrinsic efficiency, the complexity, to describe problems.

- For each of the ways above, one may also ask the negative questions: under what situations can the method not derive efficient implementations? This is useful because answers to the positive question might not be complete.

Problem specification deserves much study by itself. We only said we want to allow straightforward ways of computations to be specified easily and clearly in high-level programming languages, beyond loops and arrays, to include set expressions, recursion functions, and logic rules. For example, we did not study how problems should be specified recursively using recursive functions or rules, such as for divide and conquer, but, by helping with generating efficient implementations from recursive functions and rules, we encourage one to try all forms of recursion.

In general, efficient implementations may mean polynomial time versus exponential time, as is used in algorithms and complexity theory; linear time or close to linear time, as needed for processing massive data in practice; or anything in between or beyond. There are many practical problems, including some of the ones that our method applies to, whose efficient solutions are exponential in some parameters of the inputs but not other parameters. So, the notion of efficient implementation in practice depends on the cost models of the applications.

For the positive questions listed, we can give conservative characterizations based on the method, as described in each chapter, but formal and complete characterizations await future work. For example, for any aggregate array computation where the operator is associative and commutative and the update is addition of elements, the aggregate computation can be made more efficient. For another example, from any Datalog program, efficient implementations with time and space guarantees can be generated, and the time complexity is optimal. However, for recursive functions, we do not know how powerful the simple heuristic of finding a minimum increment is, even though it led to success for all the problems we have encountered. Note that the method depends crucially on the increments being small, which we believe is true for most problems most times. Furthermore, even when drastic changes cannot be handled efficiently, if we are better at handling small changes, we are better positioned to handle larger changes, at the very least by reducing any large change to a sequence of small changes.

For the negative questions, we can summarize our experience with using the method, but again, precise characterizations await future research. For example, the method has not been able to discover dynamic data structures such as heap, nor has it been able to find greedy properties used in greedy algorithms. Although the method has been applied to many examples, there are many more that it has not been tried on. Among all the problems it has been tested on, one particular problem has proven to be an exception to success stories: computing strongly connected components, that is, groups of vertices in a graph such that all vertices in a group reach each other following edges in the graph. While a quadratic algorithm can be derived from a simple specification using sets and fixed points, a linear-time algorithm cannot yet be derived systematically.

Extensions

Many extensions to the method described are needed, along several important dimensions including (1) handling of additional problems in the languages used and additional features in these language paradigms, (2) designing for concurrent and distributed systems, (3) designing for fault-tolerant and secure systems, (4) performing additional optimizations, and (5) designing more powerful languages.

Certainly, the method needs to be extended to handle more problems specified using the languages described, such as the strongly connected components problem. There are also many additional features in the language paradigms discussed. For example, for set-based languages, the method may be extended to systematically handle ordered sets. For recursive functions, the method could be extended to handle higher-order functions. For logic rules, the method needs to be extended to handle negation in general and to allow dynamically constructed structures that use function symbols, also called functors; some progress has been made on these, but much more needs to be done. Last but not least, the method should be extended to generate efficient implementation from a more declarative form of specification—constraints as in constraint programming; in particular, when used in systems where input can change, how to declaratively specify different ways of using the constraints for change propagation is open for study.

The method described handles only sequential and centralized programs, that is, programs with a single thread of control accessing data at a single site. Concurrent and distributed applications involve multiple threads of control and multiple sites for data and code. While the method described can handle concurrency correctly by requiring updates to be run atomically with the corresponding maintenance, and can handle distributed data and code by requiring communication with appropriate sites at each access, much more powerful optimizations are needed to make all the operations efficient. Such optimizations naturally extend the method described to be a method for designing concurrent and distributed systems. Yet another dimension to be addressed is optimization for mobility, as computers are increasingly mobile, like hand-held devices are.

Study is also needed for making systems fault-tolerant and secure. In fact, if we view faults as changes to behavior, we could view fault analysis and isolation, checkpointing and message logging, and redundancy as corresponding to exploiting the previous result, intermediate results, and auxiliary values, respectively. Of course, precise study of such a systematic method requires significant future work. We have seen that the method described can derive efficient implementations for access control and trust management; it can also derive efficient implementations for other security analysis and enforcement problems, such as information flow analysis. How to best support security frameworks and build solutions to these problems into a complete computer system requires much future study.

Many additional optimizations are needed, but two of them stand out. First, the method needs to be extended to achieve time optimality with respect to a library of incrementalization rules. When the library of rules contains multiple matches in transforming a program, how to achieve optimality of the transformed program based on the frequencies of queries and updates in the program is an open problem. Further, when frequencies of queries and updates can change dynamically, optimality also requires adaptability. Second, systematic space-driving optimizations need further study. The method described aims to minimize running time first, by storing any data that may be useful. It does save space by storing only possibly needed data, but the space used may exceed any particular given bound. Space-driven optimizations aim to design programs that run as fast as possible without exceeding a given space bound; for these, stream processing, for processing large streams of data sequentially with limited space, is a particularly important class of applications. A related and important open problem when trade-offs must be considered is automatic simplifications of complexity formulas.

Currently, there does not exist a powerful programming language that supports all of the constructs described or the programming paradigms discussed, let alone extensions that support concurrency, security, and so on at a high level. However, with the view that all programs are best organized into modules that encapsulate certain data and certain queries and updates of those data, one may have a language that supports queries and updates of data specified using all of loops, set expressions, recursive functions, and logic rules, and modularized using objects and classes. One may also specify separate aspects about concurrent query and update operations, data distribution, faults, and security. Design of such a powerful language is a subject for future study.

Relationships

We have seen that the method corresponds to differentiation and integration in calculus, except that everything is in discrete domains as opposed to continuous domains. In fact, this correspondence to differentiation and integration was found in many places in the method during the development of the method. A formal and precise correspondence is a subject for further study. This correspondence may help characterize and improve the method, since continuous domains have been studied tremendously in the long history of mathematics and physics and used substantially in engineering system design.

More specifically, the method aims to arrive at reduced-cost solutions in a given problem space by repeated incremental maintenance of appropriate invariants. This is similar to optimal engineering system design using invariance in control and physics, which also underlies the study of hybrid systems as pioneered by Anil Nerode and Wolf Kohn, combining discrete domains for digital systems and continuous domains for analog systems.

In fact, Nerode has pointed out that program invariants are the discrete analogue of conserved quantities in conservation laws in physics, and that conserved quantities are the hidden variables underlying the study of hybrid system design, parameterized complexity, and incrementalization. Indeed, the hidden variables correspond to additional values maintained for incrementalization. The most important future direction is, as Nerode stated, "We want to build a common framework for reduction of complexity in modeling and computation in digital programs, continuous physical systems, digital or analog controllers for physical systems, and many problems in physics and chemistry."

The idea underlying the method we studied applies equally well to everyday problem solving. Life involves mostly small changes from day to day, not like a war today and an earthquake tomorrow. So we save the work from the previous day for reuse the next day. Exploiting data structures in reuse is like reusing parts of work when the whole thing cannot be reused, and exploiting control structures in reuse is like reusing under certain conditions if reuse cannot be done unconditionally. Of course we also save and reuse appropriate intermediate work results and other additional results that we can determine.

Experiments

Finally, the method and future developments need to be validated through substantial effort applying them to more problems in the real world. Only by validation of such methods through real-world experiments can computer science become a science like physics and chemistry.

Bibliographical notes

The approach for deriving incremental programs using semantics-based transformations was developed in Liu's dissertation work [216] at Cornell University. The overview presented in this chapter is based on Liu [188]. There are also separate publications describing the details for exploiting previous results [213], intermediate results [212, 210], and auxiliary values [209, 211]. Contrasting with the use of cache-and-prune [212, 210] discussed in this chapter for maintaining additional values, selective caching [196, 204] can be used, as discussed in Chapter 4.

Much effort has also been spent on developing prototypes of program transformation systems in general and conducting experiments [248, 307]. Some are more extensively studied than others in terms of deriving efficient algorithms and programs from straightforward specifications or programs. Examples are CIP [38, 21, 249], KIDS [287, 288], APTS [46, 241], Cachet [185, 332], and InvTS [105, 190]. These systems need very powerful analyses. For example, APTS needs a powerful type analysis for data structure design [42]. Cachet needs powerful dependency analysis for recursive data [187, 198] and used powerful tools, Omega [259] and MONA [170], for algebraic simplification of arithmetic and Boolean expressions. InvTS needs powerful data type, control flow, and alias analyses [104] for detecting updates in the presence of object references and applying invariant rules. Prototypes and experiments for different parts of the III method are discussed in the references given for the method in each chapter.

Even in areas of characterizations and extensions for future work, there has already been much research. For example, descriptive complexity characterizes complexity classes by the kind of logic needed to express the formal languages in these classes [149], and finite model theory studies the expressive power of logics on finite models [79, 114]. Many powerful languages for programming and specification have been studied, for example, languages for constraint programming [275] and for specifying distributed algorithms [175]. Some newer languages well support the use of all of loops, sets, functions, and objects, especially advanced features such as true iterators, set comprehension, and higher-order functions. Python is a good example. Logic languages with advanced features include F-logic [167] that provides encapsulation through objects, transaction logic [36] that can specify state changes, and HiLog [52] for higher-order logic programming. The author's research group has started pursuing some of the extensions, for example, developing optimizations for general quantifications and distributed algorithms [208, 207] and for logic rules with general negation.

Nerode [229] reveals that hidden variables underlie hybrid system design, parameterized complexity, and incrementalization, and correspond to conserved quantities in conservation laws. Nerode and his coauthors have done much pioneering hybrid systems research that relates deeply with mathematics and physics. For example, Kohn, Brayman, and Nerode [172] describe control synthesis for hybrid systems based on Finsler geometry, where a key step in their synthesis procedure is a new method to solve a dynamic programming problem. Another branch of related work to incrementalization is automatic differentiation, sometimes also called algorithmic differentiation, in mathematics and computer algebra [263, 121]. It is a method to numerically evaluate the derivative of a function specified by a computer program through slight program modification and exploitation of the chain rule. In the area of concurrent systems, Sintzoff et al. study the theory of synthesizing optimal control systems and games [286, 100], among a large literature of work in related areas.

References

[1] Martin Abadi, Butler Lampson, and Jean-Jacques Lévy. Analysis and caching of dependencies. In *Proceedings of the 1996 ACM SIGPLAN International Conference on Functional Programming*, pages 83–91. ACM Press, 1996.

[2] Serge Abiteboul. Querying semi-structured data. In *Proceedings of the International Conference on Database Theory*, pages 1–18. Springer, 1997.

[3] Serge Abiteboul, Richard Hull, and Victor Vianu. *Foundations of Databases*. Addison-Wesley, 1995.

[4] Jean-Raymond Abrial. *The B-Book: Assigning Programs to Meanings*. Cambridge University Press, 1996.

[5] Umut A. Acar, Guy E. Blelloch, and Robert Harper. Selective memoization. In *Proceedings of the 30th ACM SIGPLAN-SIGACT Symposium on Principles of Programming Languages*, pages 14–25. ACM Press, 2003.

[6] Alfred V. Aho, John E. Hopcroft, and Jeffrey D. Ullman. *Data Structures and Algorithms*. Addison-Wesley, 1983.

[7] J. H. Ahrens and G. Finke. Merging and sorting applied to the 0-1 knapsack problem. *Operations Research*, 23(6):1099–1109, 1975.

[8] Alex Aiken. Introduction to set constraint-based program analysis. *Science of Computer Programming*, 35(2–3):79–111, 1999.

[9] Frances E. Allen. Program optimization. In *Annual Review of Automatic Programming*, volume 5, pages 239–307. Pergamon Press, 1969.

[10] Frances E. Allen, John Cocke, and Ken Kennedy. Reduction of operator strength. In Steven S. Muchnick and Neil D. Jones, editors, *Program Flow Analysis*, pages 79–101. Prentice-Hall, 1981.

[11] C. Scott Ananian and Martin Rinard. Data size optimizations for Java programs. In *Proceedings of the 2003 ACM SIGPLAN Conference on Language, Compiler, and Tool for Embedded Systems*, pages 59–68. ACM Press, 2003.

[12] Lars Ole Andersen. *Program Analysis and Specialization for the C Programming Language*. PhD thesis, DIKU, University of Copenhagen, 1994.

[13] ANSI INCITS. Role-Based Access Control. ANSI INCITS 359-2004, American National Standards Institute, International Committee for Information Technology Standards, 2004.

[14] Jacques J. Arsac and Yves Kodratoff. Some techniques for recursion removal from recursive functions. *ACM Transactions on Programming Languages and Systems*, 4(2):295–322, 1982.

[15] John Backus. Can programming be liberated from the von Neumann style? A functional style and its algebra of programs. *Communications of the ACM*, 21(8):613–641, 1978.

[16] John Backus. From function level semantics to program transformation and optimization. In *Proceedings of the International Joint Conference on Theory and Practice of Software Development*, pages 60–91. Springer, 1985.

[17] David F. Bacon and Peter F. Sweeney. Fast static analysis of C++ virtual function calls. In *Proceedings of the 11th ACM SIGPLAN Conference on Object-Oriented Programming, Systems, Languages, and Applications*, pages 324–341. ACM Press, 1996.

[18] Francois Bancilhon, David Maier, Yehoshua Sagiv, and Jeffrey D. Ullman. Magic sets and other strange ways to implement logic programs. In *Proceedings of the 5th ACM SIGACT-SIGMOD Symposium on Principles of Database Systems*, pages 1–16. ACM Press, 1986.

[19] F. L. Bauer, R. Berghammer, M. Broy, W. Dosch, F. Geiselbrechtinger, R. Gnatz, E. Hangel, W. Hesse, B. Krieg-Brückner, A. Laut, T. Matzner, B. Möller, F. Nickl, H. Partsch, P. Pepper, K. Samelson, M. Wirsing, and H. Wössner. *The Munich Project CIP. Volume I: The Wide Spectrum Language CIP-L*, volume 183 of *Lecture Notes in Computer Science*. Springer, 1985.

[20] Friedrich L. Bauer and Hans Wössner. *Algorithmic Language and Program Development*. Springer, 1982.

[21] Friedrich Ludwig Bauer, Bernhard Möller, Helmut Partsch, and Peter Pepper. Formal program construction by transformations—Computer-aided, intuition-guided programming. *IEEE Transactions on Software Engineering*, 15(2):165–180, 1989.

[22] Moritz Y. Becker. Cassandra: Flexible trust management and its application to electronic health records. PhD dissertation, Technical Report UCAM-CL-TR-648, Computer Laboratory, University of Cambridge, 2005.

[23] Moritz Y. Becker. A formal security policy for an NHS electronic health record service. Technical Report UCAM-CL-TR-628, Computer Laboratory, University of Cambridge, 2005.

[24] Moritz Y. Becker and Peter Sewell. Cassandra: Flexible trust management, applied to electronic health records. In *Proceedings of the 17th IEEE Computer Security Foundations Workshop*, pages 139–154. IEEE CS Press, 2004.

[25] Catriel Beeri and Philip A. Bernstein. Computational problems related to the design of normal form relational schemas. *ACM Transactions on Database Systems*, 4(1):30–59, 1979.

[26] Catriel Beeri and Raghu Ramakrishnan. On the power of magic. *Journal of Logic Programming*, 10(3–4):255–299, 1991.

[27] Richard Ernest Bellman. *Dynamic Programming*. Princeton University Press, 1957.

[28] Richard Bird and Oege de Moor. *Algebra of Programming*. Prentice-Hall, 1996.

[29] Richard S. Bird. Tabulation techniques for recursive programs. *ACM Computing Surveys*, 12(4):403–417, 1980.

[30] Richard S. Bird. The promotion and accumulation strategies in transformational programming. *ACM Transactions on Programming Languages and Systems*, 6(4):487–504, 1984.

[31] Richard S. Bird. Addendum: The promotion and accumulation strategies in transformational programming. *ACM Transactions on Programming Languages and Systems*, 7(3):490–492, 1985.

[32] Lee Blaine and Allen Goldberg. DTRE—A semi-automatic transformation system. In B. Möller, editor, *Constructing Programs from Specifications*, pages 165–203. North-Holland, 1991.

[33] Bard Bloom and Robert Paige. Transformational design and implementation of a new efficient solution to the ready simulation problem. *Science of Computer Programming*, 24(3):189–220, 1995.

[34] Eerke A. Boiten. Improving recursive functions by inverting the order of evaluation. *Science of Computer Programming*, 18(2):139–179, 1992.

[35] Piero A. Bonatti and Pierangela Samarati. Logics for authorization and security. In Jan Chomicki, van der Meyden, and Gunter Saake, editors, *Logics for Emerging Applications of Databases*, pages 277–323. Springer, 2003.

[36] Anthony J. Bonner and Michael Kifer. An overview of transaction logic. *Theoretical Computer Science*, 133(2):205–265, 1994.

[37] Robert S. Boyer and J. Strother Moore. *A Computational Logic*. Academic Press, 1979.

[38] Manfred Broy. Algebraic methods for program construction: The project CIP. In Peter. Pepper, editor, *Program Transformation and Programming Environments*, pages 199–222. Springer, 1984.

[39] R. M. Burstall and John Darlington. A transformation system for developing recursive programs. *Journal of the ACM*, 24(1):44–67, 1977.

[40] Jiazhen Cai. *Fixed Point Computation and Transformational Programming*. PhD thesis, Department of Computer Science, Rutgers, The State University of New Jersey, 1987.

[41] Jiazhen Cai. A language for semantic analysis. Technical Report 635, Department of Computer Science, Courant Institute of Mathematical Science, New York University, 1993.

[42] Jiazhen Cai, Philippe Facon, Fritz Henglein, Robert Paige, and Edmond Schonberg. Type analysis and data structure selection. In Möller [225], pages 126–164.

[43] Jiazhen Cai and Robert Paige. Binding performance at language design time. In *Conference Record of the 14th Annual ACM Symposium on Principles of Programming Languages*, pages 85–97. ACM Press, 1987.

[44] Jiazhen Cai and Robert Paige. Program derivation by fixed point computation. *Science of Computer Programming*, 11:197–261, 1988.

[45] Jiazhen Cai and Robert Paige. Languages polynomial in the input plus output. In *Proceedings of the 2nd International Conference on Algebraic Methodology and Software Technology*, pages 287–300. Springer, 1991.

[46] Jiazhen Cai and Robert Paige. Towards increased productivity of algorithm implementation. In *Proceedings of the ACM SIGSOFT'93 Symposium on Foundations of Software Engineering*, pages 71–78. ACM Press, 1993.

[47] Jiazhen Cai and Robert Paige. Using multiset discrimination to solve language processing problems without hashing. *Theoretical Computer Science*, 145(1–2):189–228, 1995.

[48] Jiazhen Cai, Robert Paige, and Robert Tarjan. More efficient bottom-up multi-pattern matching in trees. *Theoretical Computer Science*, 106(1):21–60, 1992.

[49] Stefano Ceri, Georg Gottlob, and Letizia Tanca. *Logic Programming and Databases*. Springer, 1990.

[50] Stefano Ceri and Jennifer Widom. Deriving production rules for incremental view maintenance. In *Proceedings of the 17th International Conference on Very Large Data Bases*, pages 577–589. Morgan Kaufman, 1991.

[51] Chia-Hsiang Chang and Robert Paige. From regular expressions to DFA's using compressed NFA's. *Theoretical Computer Science*, 178(1–2):1–36, 1997.

[52] Weidong Chen, Michael Kifer, and David S. Warren. HiLog: A foundation for higher-order logic programming. *Journal of Logic Programming*, 15(3):187–230, 1993.

[53] Weidong Chen and David S. Warren. Tabled evaluation with delaying for general logic programs. *Journal of the ACM*, 43(1):20–74, 1996.

[54] Wei-Ngan Chin. Safe fusion of functional expressions. In *Proceedings of the 1992 ACM Conference on LISP and Functional Programming*, pages 11–20. ACM Press, 1992.

[55] Wei-Ngan Chin. Towards an automated tupling strategy. In *Proceedings of the ACM SIGPLAN Symposium on Partial Evaluation and Semantics-Based Program Manipulation*, pages 119–132. ACM Press, 1993.

[56] Wei-Ngan Chin and Masami Hagiya. A bounds inference method for vector-based memoization. In ICFP 1997 [148], pages 176–187.

[57] Wei-Ngan Chin and Siau-Cheng Khoo. Tupling functions with multiple recursion parameters. In *Proceedings of the 3rd International Workshop on Static Analysis*, pages 124–140. Springer, 1993.

[58] Wei-Ngan Chin, Siau-Cheng Khoo, and Neil Jones. Redundant call elimination via tupling. *Fundamenta Informaticae*, 69(1–2):1–37, 2006.

[59] Dwaine E. Clarke, Jean-Emile Elien, Carl M. Ellison, Matt Fredette, Alexander Morcos, and Ronald L. Rivest. Certificate chain discovery in SPKI/SDSI. *Journal of Computer Security*, 9(4):285–322, 2001.

[60] Edmund M. Clarke, Jr., Orna Grumberg, and Doron A. Peled. *Model Checking*. MIT Press, 1999.

[61] John Cocke and Ken Kennedy. An algorithm for reduction of operator strength. *Communications of the ACM*, 20(11):850–856, 1977.

[62] John Cocke and John T. Schwartz. *Programming Languages and Their Compilers: Preliminary Notes*. Courant Institute of Mathematical Sciences, New York University, 1970.

[63] Norman H. Cohen. Eliminating redundant recursive calls. *ACM Transactions on Programming Languages and Systems*, 5(3):265–299, 1983.

[64] Robert L. Constable et al. *Implementing Mathematics with the Nuprl Proof Development System*. Prentice-Hall, 1986.

[65] Thomas H. Cormen, Charles E. Leiserson, and Ronald L. Rivest. *Introduction to Algorithms*. MIT Press and McGraw-Hill, 1990.

[66] Vítor Santos Costa, Luís Damas, Rogério Reis, and Rúben Azevedo. *YAP User's Manual, Version 6.2.0*. CRACS and LIACC/Universidade do Porto, 2010. http://www.dcc.fc.up.pt/~vsc/Yap.

[67] Patrick Cousot and Radhia Cousot. Abstract interpretation: A unified lattice model for static analysis of programs by construction or approximation of fixpoints. In POPL 1977 [255], pages 238–252.

[68] Evgeny Dantsin, Thomas Eiter, Georg Gottlob, and Andrei Voronkov. Complexity and expressive power of logic programming. *ACM Computing Surveys*, 33(3):374–425, 2001.

[69] John Darlington and R. M. Burstall. A system which automatically improves programs. *Acta Informatica*, 6(1):41–60, 1976.

[70] Oege de Moor, David Lacey, and Eric Van Wyk. Universal regular path queries. *Higher-Order and Symbolic Computation*, 16(1–2):15–35, 2003.

[71] Jeffrey Dean, Greg DeFouw, David Grove, Vassily Litvinov, and Craig Chambers. Vortex: An optimizing compiler for object-oriented languages. In *Proceedings of the 11th ACM SIGPLAN Conference on Object-Oriented Programming, Systems, Languages, and Applications*, pages 83–100. ACM Press, 1996.

[72] Jan Van der Spiegel, James F. Tau, Titiimaea F. Ala'ilima, and Lin Ping Ang. The ENIAC: History, operation, and reconstruction in VLSI. In *The First Computers: History and Architectures*, pages 121–178. MIT Press, 2000.

[73] Nachum Dershowitz. *The Evolution of Programs*. Birkhäuser, 1983.

[74] John DeTreville. Binder, a logic-based security language. In *Proceedings of the 2002 IEEE Symposium on Security and Privacy*, pages 105–113. IEEE CS Press, 2002.

[75] Edsger W. Dijkstra. The humble programmer. *Communications of the ACM*, 15(10):859–866, 1972.

[76] Edsger Wybe Dijkstra. *A Discipline of Programming*. Prentice-Hall, 1976.

[77] Amer Diwan, Kathryn S. McKinley, and J. Eliot B. Moss. Using types to analyze and optimize object-oriented programs. *ACM Transactions on Programming Languages and Systems*, 23(1):30–72, 2001.

[78] Jay Earley. High level iterators and a method for automatically designing data structure representation. *Journal of Computer Languages*, 1:321–342, 1976.

[79] Heinz-Dieter Ebbinghaus and Jörg Flum. *Finite Model Theory*. Springer, 2nd edition, 1999.

[80] C. Ellison, B. Frantz, B. Lampson, R. L. Rivest, B. Thomas, and T. Ylonen. RFC 2693: SPKI Certificate Theory, 1999. http://www.ietf.org/rfc/rfc2693.txt.

[81] Dawson Engler, David Y. Chen, Seth Hallem, Andy Chou, and Benjamin Chelf. Bugs as deviant behavior: A general approach to inferring errors in systems code. *ACM SIGOPS Operating Systems Review*, 35(5):57–72, 2001.

[82] Javier Esparza, David Hansel, Peter Rossmanith, and Stefan Schwoon. Efficient algorithms for model checking pushdown systems. In *Proceedings of the 12th International Conference on Computer-Aided Verification*, pages 232–247. Springer, 2000.

[83] Martin S. Feather. A survey and classification of some program transformation approaches and techniques. In L. G. L. T. Meertens, editor, *Program Specification and Transformation*, pages 165–195. North-Holland, 1987.

[84] John Henry Field. *Incremental Reduction in the Lambda Calculus and Related Reduction Systems*. PhD thesis, Department of Computer Science, Cornell University, 1991.

[85] Andrzej Filinski. Recursion from iteration. *LISP and Symbolic Computation*, 7(1):11–38, 1994.

[86] Amelia C. Fong. Generalized common subexpressions in very high level languages. In POPL 1977 [255], pages 48–57.

[87] Amelia C. Fong. Inductively computable constructs in very high level languages. In *Conference Record of the 6th Annual ACM Symposium on Principles of Programming Languages*, pages 21–28. ACM Press, 1979.

[88] Amelia C. Fong and Jeffrey D. Ullman. Inductive variables in very high level languages. In *Conference Record of the 3rd Annual ACM Symposium on Principles of Programming Languages*, pages 104–112. ACM Press, 1976.

[89] Charles L. Forgy. Rete: A fast algorithm for the many pattern/many object pattern match problem. *Artificial Intelligence*, 19(1):17–37, 1982.

[90] Jeffrey S. Foster, Manuel Fahndrich, and Alex Aiken. Polymorphic versus monomorphic flow-insensitive points-to analysis for C. In *Proceedings of the 7th International Static Analysis Symposium*, pages 175–198. Springer, 2000.

[91] Ole Immanuel Franksen. *Mr. Babbage's Secret : The Tale of a Cypher and APL*. Prentice-Hall, 1985.

[92] Daniel P. Friedman, Mitchell Wand, and Christopher T. Haynes. *Essentials of Programming Languages*. MIT Press and McGraw-Hill, 1992.

[93] Daniel P. Friedman, David S. Wise, and Mitchell Wand. Recursive programming through table look-up. In *Proceedings of the 1976 ACM Symposium on Symbolic and Algebraic Computation*, pages 85–89. ACM Press, 1976.

[94] Erich Gamma, Richard Helm, Ralph Johnson, and John Vlissides. *Design Patterns: Elements of Reusable Object-Oriented Software*. Addison-Wesley, 1995.

[95] Harald Ganzinger and David A. McAllester. A new meta-complexity theorem for bottom-up logic programs. In *Proceedings of the 1st International Joint Conference on Automated Reasoning*, pages 514–528. Springer, 2001.

[96] Harald Ganzinger and David A. McAllester. Logical algorithms. In *Proceedings of the 18th International Conference on Logic Programming*, pages 209–223. Springer, 2002.

[97] Stephen J. Garland and David C. Luckham. Program schemes, recursion schemes, and formal languages. *Journal of Computer and System Sciences*, 7:119–160, 1973.

[98] Gautam and S. Rajopadhye. Simplifying reductions. In *Conference Record of the 33rd ACM SIGPLAN-SIGACT Symposium on Principles of Programming Languages*, pages 30–41. ACM Press, 2006.

[99] James Glanz. Mathematical logic flushes out the bugs in chip designs. *Science*, 267:332–333, 1995.

[100] Roland Glück, Bernhard Möller, and Michel Sintzoff. Model refinement using bisimulation quotients. In *Proceedings of the 10th International Conference on Mathematics of Program Construction*, pages 76–91. Springer, 2010.

[101] Allen Goldberg and Robert Paige. Stream processing. In LFP 1984 [179], pages 53–62.

[102] Herman H. Goldstine. Charles Babbage and his Analytical Engine. In *The Computer from Pascal to von Neumann*, pages 10–26. Princeton University Press, 1972.

[103] Michael Gorbovitski, Yanhong A. Liu, Scott D. Stoller, and Tom Rothamel. Composing transformations for instrumentation and optimization. In *Proceedings of the ACM SIGPLAN 2012 Workshop on Partial Evaluation and Program Manipulation*, pages 53–62. ACM Press, 2012.

[104] Michael Gorbovitski, Yanhong A. Liu, Scott D. Stoller, Tom Rothamel, and Tuncay Tekle. Alias analysis for optimization of dynamic languages. In *Proceedings of the 6th Symposium on Dynamic Languages*, pages 27–42. ACM Press, 2010.

[105] Michael Gorbovitski, Tom Rothamel, Yanhong A. Liu, and Scott D. Stoller. Implementing incrementalization across object abstraction. In *Conference Companion of the 20th ACM Conference on Object-Oriented Programming, Systems, Languages, and Applications*, pages 116–117. ACM Press, 2005.

[106] Michael Gorbovitski, Tom Rothamel, Yanhong A. Liu, and Scott D. Stoller. Efficient runtime invariant checking: A framework and case study. In *Proceedings of the 6th International Workshop on Dynamic Analysis*, pages 43–49. ACM Press, 2008.

[107] Michael Gorbovitski, K. Tuncay Tekle, Tom Rothamel, Scott D. Stoller, and Yanhong A. Liu. Analysis and transformations for efficient query-based debugging. In *Proceedings of the 8th IEEE International Working Conference on Source Code Analysis and Manipulation*, pages 174–183. IEEE CS Press, 2008.

[108] Georg Gottlob, Christoph Koch, and Klaus U. Schulz. Conjunctive queries over trees. *Journal of the ACM*, 53(2):238–272, 2006.

[109] Georg Gottlob and Christos Papadimitriou. On the complexity of single-rule Datalog queries. *Information and Computation*, 183(1):104–122, 2003.

[110] Deepak Goyal. *A Language Theoretic Approach to Algorithms*. PhD thesis, Department of Computer Science, New York University, 2000.

[111] Deepak Goyal. Transformational derivation of an improved alias analysis algorithm. *Higher-Order and Symbolic Computation*, 18(1–2):15–49, 2005.

[112] Deepak Goyal and Robert Paige. The formal reconstruction and improvement of the linear time fragment of Willard's relational calculus subset. In *Algorithmic Languages and Calculi*, pages 382–414. Chapman & Hall, 1997.

[113] Deepak Goyal and Robert Paige. A new solution to the hidden copy problem. In *Proceedings of the 5th International Symposium on Static Analysis*, pages 327–348. Springer, 1998.

[114] Erich Grädel, Phokion G. Kolaitis, Leonid Libkin, Maarten Marx, Joel Spencer, Moshe Y. Vardi, Yde Venema, and Scott Weinstein. *Finite Model Theory and Its Applications.* Springer, 2007.

[115] Tyrone Grandison and Morris Sloman. A survey of trust in Internet applications. *IEEE Communications Surveys and Tutorials,* 3(4):2–16, 2000.

[116] A. A. Grau, U. Hill, and H. Langmaac. *Translation of ALGOL 60,* volume 1 of *Handbook for Automatic Computation.* Springer, 1967.

[117] Sheila A. Greibach. *Theory of Program Structures: Schemes, Semantics, Verification,* volume 36 of *Lecture Notes in Computer Science.* Springer, 1975.

[118] David Gries. *Compiler Construction for Digital Computers.* Wiley, 1971.

[119] David Gries. *The Science of Programming.* Springer, 1981.

[120] David Gries. A note on a standard strategy for developing loop invariants and loops. *Science of Computer Programming,* 2:207–214, 1984.

[121] Andreas Griewank. *Evaluating Derivatives: Principles and Techniques of Algorithmic Differentiation,* volume 19 of *Frontiers in Applied Mathematics.* Society for Industrial and Applied Mathematics, 2000.

[122] Leo J. Guibas and Douglas K. Wyatt. Compilation and delayed evaluation in APL. In *Conference Record of the 5th Annual ACM Symposium on Principles of Programming Languages,* pages 1–8. ACM Press, 1978.

[123] Ashish Gupta and Inderpal Singh Mumick. Maintenance of materialized views: Problems, techniques, and applications. In *Materialized Views: Techniques, Implementations, and Applications,* pages 145–157. MIT Press, 1999.

[124] Ashish Gupta, Inderpal Singh Mumick, and V. S. Subrahmanian. Maintaining views incrementally. In *Proceedings of the 1993 ACM SIGMOD International Conference on Management of Data,* pages 157–166. ACM Press, 1993.

[125] Elnar Hajiyev, Mathieu Verbaere, and Oege De Moor. CodeQuest: Scalable source code queries with Datalog. In *Proceedings of the 20th European Conference on Object-Oriented Programming,* pages 2–27. Springer, 2006.

[126] Marsha Jo Hannah. *Computer Matching of Areas in Stereo Images.* PhD thesis, Department of Computer Science, Stanford University, 1974.

[127] Peter G. Harrison. Linearisation: An optimization for nonlinear functional programs. *Science of Computer Programming,* 10:281–318, 1988.

[128] Peter G. Harrison and Hessam Khoshnevisan. A new approach to recursion removal. *Theoretical Computer Science,* 93(1):91–113, 1992.

[129] Williams Ludwell Harrison, III. The interprocedural analysis and automatic parallelization of scheme programs. *LISP and Symbolic Computation,* 2(3/4):179–396, 1989.

[130] Ken Hartness. Robocode: Using games to teach artificial intelligence. *Journal of Computing Sciences in Colleges,* 19(4):287–291, 2004.

[131] Nevin Heintze and Joxan Jaffar. Set constraints and set-based analysis. In *Proceedings of the 2nd International Workshop on Principles and Practice of Constraint Programming,* pages 281–298. Springer, 1994.

[132] Nevin Heintze and Olivier Tardieu. Demand-driven pointer analysis. In *Proceedings of the ACM SIGPLAN 2001 Conference on Programming Language Design and Implementation,* pages 24–34. ACM Press, 2001.

[133] Nevin Heintze and Olivier Tardieu. Ultra-fast aliasing analysis using CLA: A million lines of C code in a second. In *Proceedings of the ACM SIGPLAN 2001 Conference on Programming Language Design and Implementation*, pages 254–263. ACM Press, 2001.

[134] C. A. R. Hoare. Proof of correctness of data representation. *Acta Informatica*, 1:271–281, 1972.

[135] Christian Holzbaur, Maria Garcia De La Banda, Peter J. Stuckey, and Gregory J. Duck. Optimizing compilation of constraint handling rules in HAL. *Theory and Practice of Logic Programming*, 5(4–5):503–531, 2005.

[136] Roger Scott Hoover. *Incremental Graph Evaluation*. PhD thesis, Department of Computer Science, Cornell University, 1987.

[137] John Hopcroft and Robert Tarjan. Algorithm 447: Efficient algorithms for graph manipulation. *Communications of the ACM*, 16(6):372–378, 1973.

[138] John E. Hopcroft and Jeffrey D. Ullman. *Introduction to Automata Theory, Languages, and Computation*. Addison-Wesley, 1979.

[139] Susan Horwitz and Tim Teitelbaum. Generating editing environments based on relations and attributes. *ACM Transactions on Programming Languages and Systems*, 8(4):577–608, 1986.

[140] Susan Beth Horwitz. *Generating Language-Based Editors: A Relationally-Attributed Approach*. PhD thesis, Department of Computer Science, Cornell University, 1985.

[141] David Hovemeyer and William Pugh. Finding bugs is easy. *ACM SIGPLAN Notices*, 39(12):92–106, 2004.

[142] Katia Hristova and Yanhong A. Liu. Improved algorithm complexities for linear temporal logic model checking of push down systems. In *Proceedings of the 7th International Conference on Verification, Model Checking and Abstract Interpretation*, pages 190–206. Springer, 2006.

[143] Katia Hristova, Tom Rothamel, Yanhong A. Liu, and Scott D. Stoller. Efficient type inference for secure information flow. In *Proceedings of the ACM SIGPLAN Workshop on Programming Languages and Analysis for Security*, pages 85–94. ACM Press, 2006.

[144] Katia Hristova, K. Tuncay Tekle, and Yanhong A. Liu. Efficient trust management policy analysis from rules. In *Proceedings of the 9th ACM SIGPLAN International Conference on Principles and Practice of Declarative Programming*, pages 211–220. ACM Press, 2007.

[145] Zhenjiang Hu, Hideya Iwasaki, and Masato Takeichi. Deriving structural hylomorphisms from recursive definitions. In *Proceedings of the 1996 ACM SIGPLAN International Conference on Functional Programming*, pages 73–82. ACM Press, 1996.

[146] Zhenjiang Hu, Hideya Iwasaki, Masato Takeichi, and Akihiko Takano. Tupling calculation eliminates multiple data traversals. In ICFP 1997 [148], pages 164–175.

[147] John Hughes. Lazy memo-functions. In *Proceedings of the 2nd Conference on Functional Programming Languages and Computer Architecture*, pages 129–146. Springer, 1985.

[148] *Proceedings of the 1997 ACM SIGPLAN International Conference on Functional Programming*. ACM Press, 1997.

[149] Neil Immerman. *Descriptive Complexity*. Springer, 1999.

[150] ISO. Z formal specification notation—Syntax, type system and semantics. ISO/IEC 13568, International Organization for Standardization, 2002.

[151] Daniel Jackson. *Software Abstractions: Logic, Language, and Analysis.* MIT Press, 2006.

[152] Sushil Jajodia, Pierangela Samarati, and V. S. Subrahmanian. A logical language for expressing authorizations. In *Proceedings of the 1997 IEEE Symposium on Security and Privacy*, pages 31–42. IEEE CS Press, 1997.

[153] Somesh Jha and Thomas W. Reps. Model checking SPKI/SDSI. *Journal of Computer Security*, 12(3–4):317–353, 2004.

[154] Trevor Jim. SD3: A trust management system with certified evaluation. In *Proceedings of the 2001 IEEE Symposium on Security and Privacy*, pages 106–115. IEEE CS Press, 2001.

[155] Steve D. Johnson, Yanhong A. Liu, and Yuchen Zhang. A systematic incrementalization technique and its application to hardware design. *International Journal on Software Tools for Technology Transfer*, 4(2):211–223, 2003.

[156] Neil D. Jones, Carsten K. Gomard, and Peter Sestoft. *Partial Evaluation and Automatic Program Generation.* Prentice-Hall, 1993.

[157] C. Jung, S. Rus, B. P. Railing, N. Clark, and S. Pande. Brainy: Effective selection of data structures. In *Proceedings of the 32nd ACM SIGPLAN Conference on Programming Language Design and Implementation*, pages 86–97. ACM Press, 2011.

[158] Jeong A. Kang and Albert Mo Kim Cheng. Shortening matching time in OPS5 production systems. *IEEE Transactions on Software Engineering*, 30(7):448–457, 2004.

[159] Shmuel Katz. Program optimization using invariants. *IEEE Transactions on Software Engineering*, SE-4(5):378–389, 1978.

[160] J. P. Keller and Robert Paige. Program derivation with verified transformations—A case study. *Communications on Pure and Applied Mathematics*, 48(9–10):1053–1113, 1995.

[161] Robert M. Keller and M. Ronan Sleep. Applicative caching. *ACM Transactions on Programming Languages and Systems*, 8(1):88–108, 1986.

[162] Assaf J. Kfoury. Recursion versus iteration at higher-orders. In *Foundations of Software Technology and Theoretical Computer Science*, volume 1346 of *Lecture Notes in Computer Science*, pages 57–73. Springer, 1997.

[163] Hessam Khoshnevisan. Efficient memo-table management strategies. *Acta Informatica*, 28(1):43–81, 1990.

[164] Gregor Kiczales, John Lamping, Anurag Mendhekar, Chris Maeda, Cristina Lopes, Jean-Marc Loingtier, and John Irwin. Aspect-oriented programming. In *Proceedings of the 11th European Conference on Object-Oriented Programming*, pages 220–242. Springer, 1997.

[165] Richard B. Kieburtz and Jonathan Shultis. Transformations of FP program schemes. In *Proceedings of the ACM Conference on Functional Programming Languages and Computer Architecture*, pages 41–48. ACM Press, 1981.

[166] Michael Kifer, Arthur Bernstein, and Philip M. Lewis. *Database Systems: An Application Oriented Approach, Complete Version.* Addison-Wesley, 2nd edition, 2006.

[167] Michael Kifer, Georg Lausen, and James Wu. Logical foundations of object-oriented and frame-based languages. *Journal of the ACM*, 42(4):741–843, 1995.

[168] Michael Kifer and Eliezer L. Lozinskii. A framework for an efficient implementation of deductive databases. In *Proceedings of the 6th Advanced Database Symposium*, pages 109–116. IPS Japan, 1986.

[169] Michael Kifer and Eliezer L. Lozinskii. On compile-time query optimization in deductive databases by means of static filtering. *ACM Transactions on Database Systems*, 15(3):385–426, 1990.

[170] Nils Klarlund and Anders Møller. *MONA Version 1.4 User Manual*. BRICS, Department of Computer Science, Aarhus University, 2001. http://www.brics.dk/mona/.

[171] Jon Kleinberg and Eva Tardos. *Algorithm Design*. Addison-Wesley, 2006.

[172] Wolf Kohn, Vladimir Brayman, and Anil Nerode. Control synthesis in hybrid systems with Finsler dynamics. *Houston Journal of Mathematics*, 28(2):353–375, 2002.

[173] Phokion G. Kolaitis and Moshe Y. Vardi. On the expressive power of Datalog: Tools and a case study. *Journal of Computer and System Sciences*, 51(1):110–134, 1995.

[174] Monica S. Lam, John Whaley, V. Benjamin Livshits, Michael C. Martin, Dzintars Avots, Michael Carbin, and Christopher Unkel. Context-sensitive program analysis as database queries. In *Proceedings of the 24th ACM SIGMOD-SIGACT-SIGART Symposium on Principles of Database Systems*, pages 1–12. ACM Press, 2005.

[175] Leslie Lamport. The PlusCal algorithm language. In *Proceedings of the 6th International Colloquium on Theoretical Aspects of Computing*, pages 36–60. Springer, 2009.

[176] Daniel Le Métayer. ACE: An automatic complexity evaluator. *ACM Transactions on Programming Languages and Systems*, 10(2):248–266, 1988.

[177] Ho Soo Lee and Marshall I. Schor. Match algorithms for generalized Rete networks. *Artificial Intelligence*, 54(3):249–274, 1992.

[178] Michael Leuschel. Logic program specialisation. In John Hatcliff, Torben Æ. Mogensen, and Peter Thiemann, editors, *Partial Evaluation*, pages 155–188. Springer, 1998.

[179] *Conference Record of the 1984 ACM Symposium on LISP and Functional Programming*. ACM Press, 1984.

[180] Ninghui Li and John C. Mitchell. Datalog with constraints: A foundation for trust management languages. In *Proceedings of the 5th International Symposium on Practical Aspects of Declarative Languages*, pages 58–73. Springer, 2003.

[181] Ninghui Li and John C. Mitchell. Understanding SPKI/SDSI using first-order logic. *International Journal of Information Security*, 5(1):48–64, 2006.

[182] Ninghui Li, William H. Winsborough, and John C. Mitchell. Distributed credential chain discovery in trust management. *Journal of Computer Security*, 11(1):35–86, 2003.

[183] Senlin Liang, Paul Fodor, Hui Wan, and Michael Kifer. OpenRuleBench: An analysis of the performance of rule engines. In *Proceedings of the 18th*

International Conference on World Wide Web, pages 601–610. ACM Press, 2009.

[184] Barbara Liskov and Stephen Zilles. Programming with abstract data types. In *Proceedings of the ACM SIGPLAN Symposium on Very High Level Languages*, pages 50–59. ACM Press, 1974.

[185] Yanhong A. Liu. CACHET: An interactive, incremental-attribution-based program transformation system for deriving incremental programs. In *Proceedings of the 10th IEEE Knowledge-Based Software Engineering Conference*, pages 19–26. IEEE CS Press, 1995.

[186] Yanhong A. Liu. Principled strength reduction. In Richard Bird and Lambert Meertens, editors, *Algorithmic Languages and Calculi*, pages 357–381. Chapman & Hall, 1997.

[187] Yanhong A. Liu. Dependence analysis for recursive data. In *Proceedings of the IEEE 1998 International Conference on Computer Languages*, pages 206–215. IEEE CS Press, 1998.

[188] Yanhong A. Liu. Efficiency by incrementalization: An introduction. *Higher-Order and Symbolic Computation*, 13(4):289–313, 2000.

[189] Yanhong A. Liu and Gustavo Gómez. Automatic accurate cost-bound analysis for high-level languages. *IEEE Transactions on Computers*, 50(12):1295–1309, 2001.

[190] Yanhong A. Liu, Michael Gorbovitski, and Scott D. Stoller. A language and framework for invariant-driven transformations. In *Proceedings of the 8th International Conference on Generative Programming and Component Engineering*, pages 55–64. ACM Press, 2009.

[191] Yanhong A. Liu, Ning Li, and Scott D. Stoller. Solving regular tree grammar based constraints. In *Proceedings of the 8th International Static Analysis Symposium*, pages 213–233. Springer, 2001.

[192] Yanhong A. Liu, Tom Rothamel, Fuxiang Yu, Scott Stoller, and Nanjun Hu. Parametric regular path queries. In *Proceedings of the ACM SIGPLAN 2004 Conference on Programming Language Design and Implementation*, pages 219–230. ACM Press, 2004.

[193] Yanhong A. Liu and Scott D. Stoller. Loop optimization for aggregate array computations. In *Proceedings of the IEEE 1998 International Conference on Computer Languages*, pages 262–271. IEEE CS Press, 1998.

[194] Yanhong A. Liu and Scott D. Stoller. Dynamic programming via static incrementalization. In *Proceedings of the 8th European Symposium on Programming*, pages 288–305. Springer, 1999.

[195] Yanhong A. Liu and Scott D. Stoller. From recursion to iteration: What are the optimizations? In *Proceedings of the ACM SIGPLAN 2000 Workshop on Partial Evaluation and Semantics-Based Program Manipulation*, pages 73–82. ACM Press, 2000.

[196] Yanhong A. Liu and Scott D. Stoller. Program optimization using indexed and recursive data structures. In *Proceedings of the ACM SIGPLAN 2002 Workshop on Partial Evaluation and Semantics-Based Program Manipulation*, pages 108–118. ACM Press, 2002.

[197] Yanhong A. Liu and Scott D. Stoller. Dynamic programming via static incrementalization. *Higher-Order and Symbolic Computation*, 16(1–2):37–62, 2003.

[198] Yanhong A. Liu and Scott D. Stoller. Eliminating dead code on recursive data. *Science of Computer Programming*, 47(2–3):221–242, 2003.

[199] Yanhong A. Liu and Scott D. Stoller. From Datalog rules to efficient programs with time and space guarantees. In *Proceedings of the 5th ACM SIG-PLAN International Conference on Principles and Practice of Declarative Programming*, pages 172–183. ACM Press, 2003.

[200] Yanhong A. Liu and Scott D. Stoller. Optimizing Ackermann's function by incrementalization. In *Proceedings of the ACM SIGPLAN 2003 Workshop on Partial Evaluation and Semantics-Based Program Manipulation*, pages 85–91. ACM Press, 2003.

[201] Yanhong A. Liu and Scott D. Stoller. Querying complex graphs. In *Proceedings of the 8th International Symposium on Practical Aspects of Declarative Languages*, pages 199–214. Springer, 2006.

[202] Yanhong A. Liu and Scott D. Stoller. Role-based access control: A corrected and simplified specification. In *Department of Defense Sponsored Information Security Research: New Methods for Protecting Against Cyber Threats*, pages 425–439. Wiley, 2007.

[203] Yanhong A. Liu and Scott D. Stoller. From Datalog rules to efficient programs with time and space guarantees. *ACM Transactions on Programming Languages and Systems*, 31(6):1–38, 2009.

[204] Yanhong A. Liu and Scott D. Stoller. Program optimization using indexed and recursive data structures. Technical Report DAR 09-45, Computer Science Department, Stony Brook University, 2009.

[205] Yanhong A. Liu, Scott D. Stoller, Michael Gorbovitski, Tom Rothamel, and Yanni E. Liu. Incrementalization across object abstraction. In *Proceedings of the 20th ACM Conference on Object-Oriented Programming, Systems, Languages, and Applications*, pages 473–486. ACM Press, 2005.

[206] Yanhong A. Liu, Scott D. Stoller, Ning Li, and Tom Rothamel. Optimizing aggregate array computations in loops. *ACM Transactions on Programming Languages and Systems*, 27(1):91–125, 2005.

[207] Yanhong A. Liu, Scott D. Stoller, and Bo Lin. High-level executable specifications of distributed algorithms. In *Proceedings of the 14th International Symposium on Stabilization, Safety, and Security of Distributed Systems*, pages 95–110. Springer, 2012.

[208] Yanhong A. Liu, Scott D. Stoller, Bo Lin, and Michael Gorbovitski. From clarity to efficiency for distributed algorithms. In *Proceedings of the 27th ACM SIGPLAN Conference on Object-Oriented Programming, Systems, Languages and Applications*, pages 395–410. ACM Press, 2012.

[209] Yanhong A. Liu, Scott D. Stoller, and Tim Teitelbaum. Discovering auxiliary information for incremental computation. In *Conference Record of the 23rd Annual ACM Symposium on Principles of Programming Languages*, pages 157–170. ACM Press, 1996.

[210] Yanhong A. Liu, Scott D. Stoller, and Tim Teitelbaum. Static caching for incremental computation. *ACM Transactions on Programming Languages and Systems*, 20(3):546–585, 1998.

[211] Yanhong A. Liu, Scott D. Stoller, and Tim Teitelbaum. Strengthening invariants for efficient computation. *Science of Computer Programming*, 41(2):139–172, 2001.

[212] Yanhong A. Liu and Tim Teitelbaum. Caching intermediate results for program improvement. In *Proceedings of the ACM SIGPLAN Symposium on Partial Evaluation and Semantics-Based Program Manipulation*, pages 190–201. ACM Press, 1995.

[213] Yanhong A. Liu and Tim Teitelbaum. Systematic derivation of incremental programs. *Science of Computer Programming*, 24(1):1–39, 1995.

[214] Yanhong A. Liu, Chen Wang, Michael Gorbovitski, Tom Rothamel, Yongxi Cheng, Yingchao Zhao, and Jing Zhang. Core role-based access control: Efficient implementations by transformations. In *Proceedings of the ACM SIGPLAN 2006 Workshop on Partial Evaluation and Semantics-Based Program Manipulation*, pages 112–120. ACM Press, 2006.

[215] Yanhong A. Liu and Fuxiang Yu. Solving regular path queries. In *Proceedings of the 6th International Conference on Mathematics of Program Construction*, pages 195–208. Springer, 2002.

[216] Yanhong Annie Liu. *Incremental Computation: A Semantics-Based Systematic Transformational Approach*. PhD thesis, Department of Computer Science, Cornell University, 1996.

[217] John W. Lloyd and John C. Shepherdson. Partial evaluation in logic programming. *Journal of Logic Programming*, 11(3–4):217–242, 1991.

[218] Boon Thau Loo, Tyson Condie, Minos Garofalakis, David E. Gay, Joseph M. Hellerstein, Petros Maniatis, Raghu Ramakrishnan, Timothy Roscoe, and Ion Stoica. Declarative networking. *Communications of the ACM*, 52:87–95, 2009.

[219] Beatrice Luca, Stefan Andrei, Hugh Anderson, and Siau-Cheng Khoo. Program transformation by solving recurrences. In *Proceedings of the 2006 ACM SIGPLAN Symposium on Partial Evaluation and Semantics-Based Program Manipulation*, pages 121–129. ACM Press, 2006.

[220] Zohar Manna and Richard Waldinger. A deductive approach to program synthesis. *ACM Transactions on Programming Languages and Systems*, 2(1):90–121, 1980.

[221] Zohar Manna and Richard Waldinger. *The Deductive Foundations of Computer Programming*. Addison-Wesley, 1993.

[222] David A. McAllester. On the complexity analysis of static analyses. In *Proceedings of the 6th International Static Analysis Symposium*, pages 312–329. Springer, 1999.

[223] Donald Michie. "Memo" functions and machine learning. *Nature*, 218:19–22, 1968.

[224] Daniel P. Miranker and Bernie J. Lofaso. The organization and performance of a TREAT-based production system compiler. *IEEE Transactions on Knowledge and Data Engineering*, 3(1):3–10, 1991.

[225] Bernhard Möller, editor. *Constructing Programs from Specifications*. North-Holland, 1991.

[226] D. Jack Mostow and Donald Cohen. Automating program speedup by deciding what to cache. In *Proceedings of the 9th International Joint Conference on Artificial Intelligence*, pages 165–172. Morgan Kaufman, 1985.

[227] Hiroaki Nakamura. Incremental computation of complex object queries. In *Proceedings of the 16th ACM SIGPLAN Conference on Object-Oriented Programming, Systems, Languages, and Applications*, pages 156–165. ACM Press, 2001.

[228] Jeffrey F. Naughton and Raghu Ramakrishnan. Bottom-up evaluation of logic programs. In *Computational Logic: Essays in Honor of Alan Robinson*, pages 640–700. MIT Press, 1991.

[229] Anil Nerode. Computation and Control: Hidden Variables, May 2012.

[230] Flemming Nielson, Hanne Riis Nielson, and Chris Hankin. *Principles of Program Analysis*. Springer, 1999.

[231] Flemming Nielson, Hanne Riis Nielson, and Helmut Seidl. Automatic complexity analysis. In *Proceedings of the 11th European Symposium on Programming*, pages 243–261. Springer, 2002.

[232] Jackie O'Kelly and J. Paul Gibson. RoboCode & problem-based learning: A non-prescriptive approach to teaching programming. In *Proceedings of the 11th Annual Conference on Innovation and Technology in Computer Science Education*, pages 217–221. ACM Press, 2006.

[233] John O'Leary, Miriam Leeser, Jason Hickey, and Mark Aagaard. Nonrestoring integer square root: A case study in design by principled optimization. In *Proceedings of the 2nd International Conference on Theorem Provers in Circuit Design: Theory, Practice, and Experience*, pages 52–71. Springer, 1995.

[234] OMG. Object Constraint Language. OMB Available Specification OCL 2.0, Object Management Group, 2006.

[235] Bob Paige and J. T. Schwartz. Expression continuity and the formal differentiation of algorithms. In POPL 1977 [255], pages 58–71.

[236] Robert Paige. *Formal Differentiation: A Program Synthesis Technique*. UMI Research Press, 1981. Revision of PhD dissertation, New York University, 1979.

[237] Robert Paige. Applications of finite differencing to database integrity control and query/transaction optimization. In *Advances in Database Theory*, volume 2, pages 171–210. Plenum Press, 1984.

[238] Robert Paige. Programming with invariants. *IEEE Software*, 3(1):56–69, 1986.

[239] Robert Paige. Real-time simulation of a set machine on a RAM. In *Proceedings of the International Conference on Computing and Information*, pages 69–73. Canadian Scholars Press, 1989.

[240] Robert Paige. Efficient translation of external input in a dynamically typed language. In *Proceedings of IFIP Congress 94*, pages 603–608. North-Holland, 1994.

[241] Robert Paige. Viewing a program transformation system at work. In *Proceedings of Joint 6th International Conference on Programming Languages: Implementations, Logics and Programs and 4th International Conference on Algebraic and Logic Programming*, pages 5–24. Springer, 1994.

[242] Robert Paige and Fritz Henglein. Mechanical translation of set theoretic problem specifications into efficient RAM code—A case study. *Journal of Symbolic Computation*, 4(2):207–232, 1987.

[243] Robert Paige and Shaye Koenig. Finite differencing of computable expressions. *ACM Transactions on Programming Languages and Systems*, 4(3):402–454, 1982.

[244] Robert Paige and Robert Tarjan. Three partition refinement algorithms. *SIAM Journal on Computing*, 16(6):973–989, 1987.

[245] Robert Paige, Robert Tarjan, and Robert Bonic. A linear time solution to the single coarsest partition problem. *Theoretical Computer Science*, 40:67–84, 1985.

[246] Robert Paige and Zhe Yang. High level reading and data structure compilation. In *Conference Record of the 24th Annual ACM Symposium on Principles of Programming Languages*, pages 456–469. ACM Press, 1997.

[247] David L. Parnas. A technique for software module specification with examples. *Communications of the ACM*, 15(5):330–336, 1972.

[248] Helmut Partsch and Ralf Steinbrüggen. Program transformation systems. *ACM Computing Surveys*, 15(3):199–236, 1983.

[249] Helmut A. Partsch. *Specification and Transformation of Programs—A Formal Approach to Software Development*. Springer, 1990.

[250] Michael S. Paterson and Carl E. Hewitt. Comparative schematology. In *Project MAC Conference on Concurrent Systems and Parallel Computation*, pages 119–127. ACM Press, 1970.

[251] Dusko Pavlovic and Douglas R. Smith. Software development by refinement. In *UNU/IIST 10th Anniversary Colloquium, Formal Methods at the Crossroads: From Panaea to Foundational Support*, pages 267–286. Springer, 2003.

[252] Alberto Pettorossi. A powerful strategy for deriving efficient programs by transformation. In LFP 1984 [179], pages 273–281.

[253] Alberto Pettorossi and M. Proietti. Rules and strategies for transforming functional and logic programs. *ACM Computing Surveys*, 28(2):360–414, 1996.

[254] Alberto Pettorossi and Maurizio Proietti. Program derivation via list introduction. In *Algorithmic Languages and Calculi*, pages 296–323. Chapman & Hall, 1997.

[255] *Conference Record of the 4th Annual ACM Symposium on Principles of Programming Languages*. ACM Press, 1977.

[256] Gayathri Priyalakshmi. Generating efficient programs for solving relational database queries. Master's thesis, Computer Science Department, Stony Brook University, 2004.

[257] William Pugh. An improved cache replacement strategy for function caching. In *Proceedings of the 1988 ACM Conference on LISP and Functional Programming*, pages 269–276. ACM Press, 1988.

[258] William Pugh. Skip lists: A probabilistic alternative to balanced trees. *Communications of the ACM*, 33(6):668–676, 1990.

[259] William Pugh. The Omega Test: A fast and practical integer programming algorithm for dependence analysis. *Communications of the ACM*, 31(8):102–114, 1992.

[260] William Pugh and Tim Teitelbaum. Incremental computation via function caching. In *Conference Record of the 16th Annual ACM Symposium on Principles of Programming Languages*, pages 315–328. ACM Press, 1989.

[261] William Worthington Pugh, Jr. *Incremental Computation and the Incremental Evaluation of Functional Programs*. PhD thesis, Department of Computer Science, Cornell University, 1988.

[262] Paul Walton Purdom and Cynthia A. Brown. *The Analysis of Algorithms*. Holt, Rinehart and Winston, 1985.

[263] Louis B Rall. *Automatic Differentiation: Techniques and Applications*, volume 120 of *Lecture Notes in Computer Science*. Springer, 1981.

[264] I. V. Ramakrishnan, R. C. Sekar, and Andrei Voronkov. Term indexing. In John Alan Robinson and Andrei Voronkov, editors, *Handbook of Automated Reasoning*, pages 1853–1964. Elsevier and MIT Press, 2001.

[265] G. Ramalingam and Thomas Reps. A categorized bibliography on incremental computation. In *Conference Record of the 20th Annual ACM Symposium on Principles of Programming Languages*, pages 502–510. ACM Press, 1993.

[266] Thomas Reps. Optimal-time incremental semantic analysis for syntax-directed editors. In *Conference Record of the 9th Annual ACM Symposium on Principles of Programming Languages*, pages 169–176. ACM Press, 1982.

[267] Thomas Reps. Program analysis via graph reachability. *Information and Software Technology*, 40(11–12):701–726, 1998.

[268] Thomas Reps and Tim Teitelbaum. *The Synthesizer Generator: A System for Constructing Language-Based Editors*. Springer, 1988.

[269] Thomas William Reps. *Generating Language-Based Environments*. PhD thesis, Computer Science Department, Cornell University, 1982. ACM Doctoral Dissertation Award, MIT Press, 1984.

[270] John C. Reynolds. *The Craft of Programming*. Prentice-Hall, 1981.

[271] Tom Rothamel. *Automatic Incrementalization of Queries in Object-Oriented Programs*. PhD thesis, Computer Science Department, Stony Brook University, 2008.

[272] Tom Rothamel and Yanhong A. Liu. Efficient implementation of tuple pattern based retrieval. In *Proceedings of the ACM SIGPLAN 2007 Workshop on Partial Evaluation and Semantics-Based Program Manipulation*, pages 81–90. ACM Press, 2007.

[273] Tom Rothamel and Yanhong A. Liu. Generating incremental implementations of object-set queries. In *Proceedings of the 7th International Conference on Generative Programming and Component Engineering*, pages 55–66. ACM Press, 2008.

[274] Konstantinos Sagonas, Terrance Swift, and David S. Warren. XSB as an efficient deductive database engine. In *Proceedings of the 1994 ACM SIGMOD International Conference on Management of Data*, pages 442–453. ACM Press, 1994.

[275] Vijay Saraswat and Pascal Van Hentenryck, editors. *Principles and Practice of Constraint Programming*. MIT Press, 1995.

[276] William L. Scherlis. Program improvement by internal specialization. In *Conference Record of the 8th Annual ACM Symposium on Principles of Programming Languages*, pages 41–49. ACM Press, 1981.

[277] Edmond Schonberg, Jacob Schwartz, and Micha Sharir. An automatic technique for the selection of data representations in SETL programs. *ACM Transactions on Programming Languages and Systems*, 3(2):126–143, 1981.

[278] Tom Schrijvers. *Analyses, Optimizations and Extensions of Constraint Handling Rules*. PhD thesis, Department of Computer Science, Katholieke Universiteit Leuven, 2005.

[279] Ulrik P. Schultz, Julia L. Lawall, and Charles Consel. Automatic program specialization for Java. *ACM Transactions on Programming Languages and Systems*, 25(4):452–499, 2003.

[280] Jacob T. Schwartz, Robert B. K. Dewar, Ed Dubinsky, and Edmond Schonberg. *Programming with Sets: An Introduction to SETL*. Springer, 1986.

[281] Michael L. Scott. *Programming Language Pragmatics*. Morgan Kaufman, 3rd edition, 2009.

[282] A. Shankar and R. Bodík. DITTO: Automatic incrementalization of data structure invariant checks (in Java). In *Proceedings of the 2007 ACM SIGPLAN Conference on Programming Language Design and Implementation*, pages 310–319. ACM Press, 2007.

[283] Zhong Shao, John H. Reppy, and Andrew W. Appel. Unrolling lists. In *Proceedings of the 1994 ACM Conference on LISP and Functional Programming*, pages 185–195. ACM Press, 1994.

[284] Micha Sharir. Formal integration: A program transformation technique. *Journal of Computer Languages*, 6(1):35–46, 1981.

[285] Micha Sharir. Some observations concerning formal differentiation of set theoretic expressions. *ACM Transactions on Programming Languages and Systems*, 4(2):196–225, 1982.

[286] Michel Sintzoff. Iterative synthesis of control guards ensuring invariance and inevitability in discrete-decision games. In *From Object-Orientation to Formal Methods, Essays in Memory of Ole-Johan Dahl*, pages 272–301. Springer, 2004.

[287] Douglas R. Smith. KIDS: A semiautomatic program development system. *IEEE Transactions on Software Engineering*, 16(9):1024–1043, 1990.

[288] Douglas R. Smith. KIDS—A knowledge-based software development system. In Michael R. Lowry and Robert D. McCartney, editors, *Automating Software Design*, pages 483–514. AAAI Press and MIT Press, 1991.

[289] Douglas R. Smith. Structure and design of problem reduction generators. In Möller [225], pages 91–124.

[290] Douglas R. Smith. Aspects as invariants. In O. Danvy, H. Mairson, F Henglein, and A. Pettorossi, editors, *Automatic Program Development: A Tribute to Robert Paige*, pages 270–286. Springer, 2008.

[291] Douglas R. Smith and Michael R. Lowry. Algorithm theories and design tactics. *Science of Computer Programming*, 14:305–321, 1990.

[292] W. Kirk Snyder. The SETL2 Programming Language. Technical Report 490, Courant Institute of Mathematical Sciences, New York University, 1990.

[293] J. Michael Spivey. *The Z Notation: A Reference Manual*. Prentice-Hall, 2nd edition, 1992.

[294] Manu Sridharan and Stephen J. Fink. The complexity of Andersen's analysis in practice. In *Proceedings of the 16th International Static Analysis Symposium*, pages 205–221. Springer, 2009.

[295] Michael Steinbrunn, Guido Moerkotte, and Alfons Kemper. Heuristic and randomized optimization for the join ordering problem. *The VLDB Journal*, 6(3):191–208, 1997.

[296] Terrance Swift, David S. Warren, et al. *The XSB System Version 3.3*. Sourceforge.net, 2011. http://xsb.sourceforge.net/.

[297] Hisao Tamaki and Taisuke Sato. OLD resolution with tabulation. In *Proceedings of the 3rd International Conference on Logic Programming*, pages 84–98. Springer, 1986.

[298] Tim Teitelbaum and Thomas Reps. The Cornell program synthesizer: A syntax-directed programming environment. *Communications of the ACM*, 24(9):563–573, 1981.

[299] K. Tuncay Tekle, Michael Gorbovitski, and Yanhong A. Liu. Graph queries through Datalog optimizations. In *Proceedings of the 12th ACM SIGPLAN International Conference on Principles and Practice of Declarative Programming*, pages 25–34. ACM Press, 2010.

[300] K. Tuncay Tekle and Yanhong A. Liu. Precise complexity analysis for efficient Datalog queries. In *Proceedings of the 12th ACM SIGPLAN International Conference on Principles and Practice of Declarative Programming*, pages 35–44. ACM Press, 2010.

[301] K. Tuncay Tekle and Yanhong A. Liu. More efficient Datalog queries: Subsumptive tabling beats magic sets. In *Proceedings of the 2011 ACM SIGMOD International Conference on Management of Data*, pages 661–672. ACM Press, 2011.

[302] Kazim Tuncay Tekle. *Efficient Datalog Queries with Time and Space Complexity Guarantees*. PhD thesis, Computer Science Department, Stony Brook University, 2010.

[303] Leena Unnikrishnan and Scott D. Stoller. Parametric heap usage analysis for functional programs. In *Proceedings of the 2009 International Symposium on Memory Management*, pages 139–148. ACM Press, 2009.

[304] Leena Unnikrishnan, Scott D. Stoller, and Yanhong A. Liu. Optimized live heap bound analysis. In *Proceedings of the 4th International Conference on Verification, Model Checking and Abstract Interpretation*, pages 70–85. Springer, 2003.

[305] Moshe Y. Vardi. The complexity of relational query languages (Extended Abstract). In *Proceedings of the 14th Annual ACM Symposium on Theory of Computing*, pages 137–146. ACM Press, 1982.

[306] M. Verbaere, R. Ettinger, and O. de Moor. JunGL: A scripting language for refactoring. In *Proceedings of the 28th International Conference on Software Engineering*, pages 172–181. ACM Press, 2006.

[307] Eelco Visser. A survey of strategies in rule-based program transformation systems. *Journal of Symbolic Computation*, 40(1):831–873, 2005.

[308] Nic Volanschi. A portable compiler-integrated approach to permanent checking. *Automated Software Engineering*, 15(1):3–33, 2008.

[309] Philip Wadler. Deforestation: Transforming programs to eliminate trees. *Theoretical Computer Science*, 73:231–248, 1990.

[310] S. A. Walker and H. Raymond Strong. Characterizations of flowchartable recursions. *Journal of Computer and System Sciences*, 7(4):404–447, 1973.

[311] Mitchell Wand. Continuation-based program transformation strategies. *Journal of the ACM*, 27(1):164–180, 1980.

[312] Richard C. Waters. Automatic transformation of series expressions into loops. *ACM Transactions on Programming Languages and Systems*, 13(1):52–98, 1991.

[313] Jon A. Webb. Steps towards architecture-independent image processing. *IEEE Computer*, 25(2):21–31, 1992.

[314] Adam Webber. Optimization of functional programs by grammar thinning. *ACM Transactions on Programming Languages and Systems*, 17(2):293–330, 1995.

[315] Ben Wegbreit. Goal-directed program transformation. *IEEE Transactions on Software Engineering*, SE-2(2):69–80, 1976.

[316] William M. Wells, III. Efficient synthesis of Gaussian filters by cascaded uniform filters. *IEEE Transactions on Pattern Analysis and Machine Intelligence*, 8(2):234–239, 1986.

[317] John Whaley and Monica S. Lam. Cloning-based context-sensitive pointer alias analysis using binary decision diagrams. In *Proceedings of the ACM SIGPLAN 2004 Conference on Programming Language Design and Implementation*, pages 131–144. ACM Press, 2004.

[318] John Whaley and Martin Rinard. Compositional pointer and escape analysis for Java programs. In *Proceedings of the 14th ACM SIGPLAN Conference on Object-Oriented Programming, Systems, Languages, and Applications*, pages 187–206. ACM Press, 1999.

[319] Wikipedia. Design. http://en.wikipedia.org/wiki/Design, Sept. 8 2008.

[320] Dan E. Willard. *Predicate-Oriented Database Search Algorithms*. PhD thesis, Harvard University, 1978. Outstanding Dissertations in Computer Science, Garland Publishing, 1979.

[321] Dan E. Willard. Efficient processing of relational calculus expressions using range query theory. In *Proceedings of the 1984 ACM SIGMOD International Conference on Management of Data*, pages 164–175. ACM Press, 1984.

[322] Dan E. Willard. Quasilinear algorithms for processing relational calculus expressions (preliminary report). In *Proceedings of 9th ACM SIGACT-SIGMOD-SIGART Symposium on Principles of Database Systems*, pages 243–257. ACM Press, 1990.

[323] Dan E. Willard. Applications of range query theory to relational data base join and selection operations. *Journal of Computer and System Sciences*, 52(1):157–169, 1996.

[324] Dan E. Willard. An algorithm for handling many relational calculus queries efficiently. *Journal of Computer and System Sciences*, 65:295–331, 2002.

[325] Darren Willis, David J. Pearce, and James Noble. Caching and incrementalisation in the Java query language. In *Proceedings of the 23rd ACM SIGPLAN Conference on Object-Oriented Programming, Systems, Languages, and Applications*, pages 1–18. ACM Press, 2008.

[326] Guizhen Yang and Michael Kifer. FLORA: Implementing an efficient DOOD system using a tabling logic engine. In *Proceedings of the 1st International Conference on Computational Logic*, pages 1078–1093. Springer, 2000.

[327] Guizhen Yang, Michael Kifer, Hui Wan, and Chang Zhao. *Flora-2: User's Manual Version 0.95*. Sourceforge.net and Stony Brook University, 2008. http://flora.sourceforge.net/.

[328] Mihalis Yannakakis. Graph-theoretic methods in database theory. In *Proceedings of the ACM Symposium on Principles of Database Systems*, pages 230–242. ACM Press, 1990.

[329] Daniel M. Yellin and Robert E. Strom. INC: A language for incremental computations. *ACM Transactions on Programming Languages and Systems*, 13(2):211–236, 1991.

[330] Ramin Zabih. *Individuating Unknown Objects by Combining Motion and Stereo*. PhD thesis, Department of Computer Science, Stanford University, 1994.

[331] Ramin Zabih and John Woodfill. Non-parametric local transforms for computing visual correspondence. In *Proceedings of the 3rd European Conference on Computer Vision*, pages 151–158. Springer, 1994.

[332] Yuchen Zhang and Yanhong A. Liu. Automating derivation of incremental programs. In *Proceedings of the 1998 ACM SIGPLAN International Conference on Functional Programming*, page 350. ACM Press, 1998.

[333] Paul Zimmermann and Wolf Zimmermann. The automatic complexity analysis of divide-and-conquer algorithms. In *Proceedings of the 6th International Symposium on Computer and Information Sciences*, pages 395–404. Elsevier, 1991.

Index

235